ORAL TRADITION
IN LITERATURE

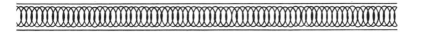

ORAL TRADITION
IN LITERATURE

Interpretation in Context

Edited by
John Miles Foley

University of Missouri Press
Columbia, 1986

Library of Congress Cataloging-in-Publication Data
Main entry under title:

Oral tradition in literature.

Bibliography: p.
Includes index.
1. Oral tradition—Addresses, essays, lectures.
2. Folk literature—History and criticism—Addresses,
essays, lectures.   3. Oral-formulaic analysis—
Addresses, essays, lectures.   I. Foley, John Miles.
GR72.069   1986   398.2   85-20680
ISBN 0-8262-0490-2 (alk. paper)

For the *glaukōpis* Lizzie,
who understands as well as anyone
the meaning of orality

ACKNOWLEDGMENTS

An editor of a volume such as this one must always be grateful primarily to the authors whose essays make it up, and so I thank first Robert P. Creed, Albert B. Lord, Gregory Nagy, Walter J. Ong, Alain Renoir, and Ruth H. Webber. All these fine scholars, leaders in their respective fields, wrote first versions of these essays for the presentation at the Missouri Oral Literature Symposium, which took place on the University of Missouri–Columbia campus on 8–11 March 1984. All contributors have substantially revised those original papers to focus even more closely on the central issue of this collection: How does the fact that a literary work has roots in oral tradition affect its reading and interpretation?

The symposium received major funding from the Missouri Committee for the Humanities, the state-based arm of the National Endowment for the Humanities, and I am very grateful to that organization for its support. Melvin D. George, former Vice-President of the University of Missouri campuses and now President of St. Olaf College, stood behind the symposium from the start and provided substantial additional funds. I must also thank the English Department, especially its Chair, Timothy Materer, and the University Lectures Series for their generous support.

A number of colleagues gave of their time, energy, and talents to assist in the organization and running of the symposium; let me remember especially Thomas D. Cooke, Ruth H. Firestone, Howard Fulweiler, and Homer Thomas. Ward Parks, now of Louisiana State University, was also of great assistance.

As the contributions were being expanded, the two readers appointed by the Press, Donald K. Fry, Jr., and Carl Lindahl, were extremely helpful in suggesting various means of improving and coordinating the contents.

Finally, I would also like to express my gratitude to my wife, Anne-Marie Foley, who has been a partner in all associated with this book and much more.

J. M. F.
Columbia, Mo.
November 1985

CONTENTS

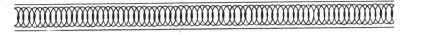

1
INTRODUCTION
John Miles Foley

How do we interpret works of literature whose roots lie in oral tradition? What difference does a work's oral aspect make to its criticism, explanation, and study? Not long ago questions of this sort would have been effectively unanswerable, and not long before that they could not have been posed, much less answered. Awareness of the vast prehistory of oral tradition as the necessary precursor of manuscript and print cultures is, ironically enough, a product of the same age in which we have learned not only to write and read and later to moveably print letters and words but also to process words with computers. Only with the advent of what many have called the "secondary orality" of mass electronic media have we managed to come to grips with the "primary orality" that was the highly structured, many-layered medium of preliterate peoples back to the Indo-Europeans of 6000 B.C. and well beyond.

For many years the very idea of "oral literature" or "oral tradi-tion" seemed to most scholars either a contradiction in terms or a less than adequate concept of what precedes true literature in pre-literate societies. Now, thanks to research that began in this coun-try during the 1920s, we are beginning to recognize that stories and histories as vital to our civilization as the biblical gospels, Old Testament Scriptures, the ancient Greek *Iliad* and *Odyssey,* and most of the early literary works of the European nations had their roots in oral tradition. As thinkers like Walter J. Ong and Eric Havelock have demonstrated, oral cultures are by no means primi-tive; we cannot anymore smile benignly and admire the simplicity of the noble savage. In the enormous era preceding the relatively recent evolution of writing, cultures stored and transmitted all available knowledge orally, and they did so with considerable sophistication. And as scholars like the Chadwicks and Ruth Finnegan have shown, often using evidence gathered from the first-hand experience of fieldwork in oral societies, this is indisputably a general phenomenon: no matter where we look in the world, we find either traces of an oral tradition that preceded (and in some cases still subsists alongside) written traditions or an ongoing oral tradition still very much alive. First to lay bare these roots, and then to understand the meaning they may have for later and contemporary modes of thought—these have been and are the scholarly tasks of studies in oral tradition.

A BRIEF HISTORY OF THE FIELD

Oral literature research has in recent times become an important new field of its own, an interdisciplinary field that promises to gain substantially in significance for a growing number of scholars and academic specialties during the next decade. Even at present this area of investigation enlists the disciplines of literary studies, linguistics, folklore, history, and anthropology; among the more than ninety national literatures already involved are English, French, Spanish, German, Greek, Russian, Serbo-Croatian, a number of American Indian traditions, Japanese, Chinese, Bulgarian, Albanian, Turkish, Eskimo, Sanskrit, Sumerian, Arabic, the languages of the Bible, a host of African language families, and the folk-preaching of the American rural South.[1] And since the field

1. As merely the briefest of selections, see Joseph J. Duggan, *The Song of Roland: Formulaic Style and Poetic Craft* (Berkeley: University of California Press, 1973); Ruth Webber, "Formulistic Diction in the Spanish Ballad," *University of California Publications in Modern Philology* 34, no. 2 (1951): 175–277; Edward R. Haymes, *Mündliches Epos in mittelhochdeutscher Zeit* (Erlangen: Palm und Ecke, 1970; rev. ed. Göppingen: A. Kümmerle, 1975); Michael N. Nagler, *Spontaneity and Tradition: A Study in the Oral Art of Homer* (Berkeley: University of California Press, 1974); Gregory Nagy, *Comparative Studies in Greek and Indic Meter* (Cambridge, Mass.: Harvard University Press, 1974); Ruth H. Finnegan, *Oral Literature in Africa* (Oxford: Clarendon Press, 1970); Ching-Hsien Wang, *The Bell and the Drum: "Shih Ching" as Formulaic Poetry in an Oral Tradition* (Berkeley: University of California Press, 1974); Michael J. Zwettler, *The Oral Tradition of Classical Arabic Poetry* (Columbus: Ohio State University Press, 1978); and Bruce A. Rosenberg, *The Art of the American Folk Preacher* (New York: Oxford University Press, 1970). An exhaustive listing of materials in ninety-nine language areas through 1982 is available in my *Oral-Formulaic Theory and Research: An Introduction and Annotated Bibliography* (New York: Garland, 1985), which contains

is still in the process of discovering its premises and methodologies, its influence and coverage can only continue to increase in importance and extent.

Scholars first began to recognize the existence and importance of oral literature—that is, literature composed without the aid of writing—as a result of the pioneering efforts of the American classicist Milman Parry.[2] In 1928 Parry published two doctoral theses on the ancient Greek *Iliad* and *Odyssey* that offered an innovative answer to the centuries-old "Homeric Question" of just who Homer was and how he composed his great poems in an age that did not yet know writing. Instead of either subjecting the poems to a historical dismemberment in order to prove multiple authorship (the German school of so-called Analysis) or arguing in an often facile way for their literary unity (an Anglo-American reaction practiced by those termed Unitarians), Parry theorized that the *Iliad* and *Odyssey* were the collective creations of many generations of bards working not individually but within a poetic tradition. This tradition, as Parry described it, developed its own diction, a specialized poetic language consisting of substitutable "formulas" that enabled a poet to make his verses extemporaneously without having to depend on rote memorization.[3] In much the same way as a mathematician manipulates algebraic formulas or a computer programmer tailors various algorithms to suit specific tasks, the ancient Greek poet was seen as employing the generalized idiomatic language to compose an individual poem (or version of a poem) on the model given him by tradition. Parry's theory accounted in a startling new way for textual problems that had remained unsolved since the time of the Alexandrians.

Soon after this first approximation, in articles published in 1930

more than eighteen hundred items. This bibliography will be updated annually in the third (October) issue of the new journal *Oral Tradition*. A selected bibliography can be found at the back of the present volume.

2. For the complete corpus of Parry's published and unpublished work, see *The Making of Homeric Verse: The Collected Papers of Milman Parry*, ed. Adam Parry (Oxford: Clarendon Press, 1971), hereafter cited as *MHV*. The introduction to this volume tracks the development of Parry's ideas from contemporary linguistic theory and ethnography; see further the introduction to my bibliography (n. 1).

3. Parry defined the *formula* as "a group of words which is regularly employed under the same metrical conditions to express a given essential idea" (*MHV*, p. 272).

and 1932,[4] Parry took another bold step: he argued that such a poetic tradition of verse-making could arise only if there were a need for Homer to make his *traditional* poetry in performance, only if, in short, the poet were unlettered and his poetry *oral*. This perception of a necessary connection between traditional and oral, which agreed in principle with Friedrich Wolf's archaeologically and historically based observation in 1795 that writing could not have existed in Homeric times, cleared the way for one of the most influential comparative investigations of this century. For Parry and his assistant Albert Lord then embarked on a fieldwork expedition to various regions in Yugoslavia, a trip during which they recorded and interviewed the illiterate singers (or *guslari*) who still performed oral traditional epic in the Balkans.[5] They sought, in other words, to prove Parry's hypothesis, itself drawn from dead-language, manuscript materials, in the living laboratory of Yugoslav oral tradition.

The results of this "literary anthropology" have been many and far-reaching. The actual recordings they made in the field now compose the core of the Milman Parry Collection of Oral Literature at Harvard University; a number of epics have been edited, translated, and published in the series *Serbo-Croatian Heroic Songs,* among them *The Wedding of Smailagić Meho,* a 13,000-line text similar in structure and equivalent in length to the Homeric *Odyssey.* Also, in 1960 Lord's monumental comparative work, *The Singer of Tales,*[6] appeared, in which the author applied the new knowledge gained by analysis of the Yugoslav

4. "Studies in the Epic Technique of Oral Verse-Making. I. Homer and Homeric Style," *Harvard Studies in Classical Philology* 41 (1930): 73–147, rpt. in *MHV,* pp. 266–324; and "Studies in the Epic Technique of Oral Verse-Making. II. The Homeric Language as the Language of an Oral Poetry," *Harvard Studies in Classical Philology* 43 (1932): 1–50, rpt. in *MHV,* pp. 325–64.

5. Often underplayed in histories of the evolution of the field is the role of Matija [Matthias] Murko, whom Parry often cited in his later works. Murko carried on fieldwork among *guslari* as early as the first two decades of this century and reported his mainly ethnographic observations in a series of publications, the most significant of which are *Tragom srpskohrvatske narodne epike: Putovanja u godinama 1930–32,* 2 vols., Djela Jugoslavenske Akademije Znanosti i Umjetnosti, knj. 41–42 (Zagreb: Jugoslavenska Akademija Znanosti i Umjetnosti, 1951), and *La Poésie populaire épique en Yougoslavie au début du XXe siècle,* Travaux publiés par l'Institut d'Etudes Slaves, 10 (Paris: Librairie Ancienne Honoré Champion, 1929). My translation of these and other of Murko's most significant works is underway and scheduled to be published in 1987 by Charles Schlacks, Inc.

6. (Cambridge, Mass.: Harvard University Press, 1960; rpt. New York: Atheneum, 1968 et seq.).

material to poems in ancient and Byzantine Greek, Old English, and Old French. Oral literature research began in earnest with Lord's book; in less than twenty-five years more than twelve hundred books, monographs, and articles have followed, testifying in their number and variety to the seminal importance of Lord's and Parry's discoveries.

At the same time that such investigations have made available to scholars a wealth of otherwise unavailable information, they have also caused serious rethinking of some very basic assumptions. For example, from the work of Havelock[7] we have learned that the Homeric epics served the society that perpetuated them as a set of oral encyclopedias, a digest of attitudes, beliefs, behavior patterns, and customs encoded in the exemplary actions of their heroes. Far from being simple folktales, the *Iliad* and *Odyssey* chronicled the oral culture's observations about itself, the kinds of observations that written cultures store in a shelf of reference books but that preliterate peoples must consign to repeated and collectively authored oral repositories. Along with this new information, however, have come new problems. For instance, the literary scholar wants to know how to edit his oral or oral-derived text and whether a written aesthetics is proper for a nonwritten text; the linguist inquires whether the fact that oral literature is actually spoken under performance conditions and is multidialectal and archaized makes any difference in its analysis as utterance; the folklorist wants to learn how to treat the many variants of a given poem and how to sense its structure; the historian wants to decide how to judge the accuracy of oral history against other sources; and the anthropologist is interested in the conditions of performance and the role of various oral forms in the cultural system as a whole. Indeed, as recent research has begun to show, the problems associated with the study of oral literature are vastly more complex than has so far been realized, and the challenge of explanation keeps pace with each fresh insight or discovery.

---

7. For example, *Preface to Plato* (Cambridge, Mass.: The Belknap Press of Harvard University Press, 1963; rpt. 1982); *Origins of Western Literacy,* Monograph Series, 14 (Toronto: Ontario Institute for Studies in Education, 1976); and *The Greek Concept of Justice: From Its Shadow in Homer to Its Substance in Plato* (Cambridge, Mass.: Harvard University Press, 1978). Havelock's major studies (including selections from the longer works) have been reprinted in *The Literate Revolution in Greece and Its Cultural Consequences* (Princeton: Princeton University Press, 1982).

This volume attempts to respond to these and other related questions by focusing the attention of leading authorities in the field on the most pressing concerns. All six essays treat in one way or another the problem of establishing an aesthetics for oral and oral-derived works, that is, of fashioning an interpretive basis for some of our major literary and religious monuments that takes into account their oral traditional roots. The broad implication, of course, that oral and written works cannot be addressed by precisely the same poetics has proved a point of controversy for quite some time, with many Homerists, for example, demanding that the *Iliad* and *Odyssey* be appraised using the same critical canons that have informed the study of Dante, Chaucer, Shakespeare, and all major writers.[8] What the present volume suggests and illustrates, however, is that the richness of the oral traditional legacy cannot be denied: in order to interpret oral and oral-derived works faithfully, we must confront just what it is about the antecedent oral tradition that affects and even determines how such texts "mean." As the authors of these essays demonstrate, while conventional literary analysis may bring us part of the way toward a full, dynamic interpretation, we cannot appreciate the truest meaning of such works as the Gospels, Homer's epics, the Old English *Beowulf,* the medieval Spanish *Poema de Mio Cid,* the Serbo-Croatian epics, the Middle High German *Nibelungenlied,* and the Middle English *Sir Gawain and the Green Knight* without assessing the contribution of oral tradition.

THE ISSUE OF ORAL TRADITIONAL CONTEXT

The contribution of oral tradition can be specifically denominated by a single term: the issue of *context.* From what context does an oral or oral-derived work emerge? Or, more productively for the latter-day scholar attempting a faithful interpretation of the work, into what context must we place (or re-place) a text in order to discover its truest meaning? One might observe that, *pace* the once-New Critics, any act of interpretation worth the name must

---

8. At the heart of the controversy is the same issue of mechanism or utility versus aesthetic design that was debated by Parry and George M. Calhoun fifty years ago; see especially Calhoun's "The Art of Formula in Homer—ΕΠΕΑ ΠΤΕΡΟΕΝΤΑ," *Classical Philology* 30 (1935): 215–27, and Parry's response, "About Winged Words," *Classical Philology* 32 (1937): 59–63, rpt. in *MHV,* pp. 414–18.

include the identification and meticulous consideration of a work's context, and that works with roots in oral tradition constitute no special case in this respect. But we should remember that contextualization of, say, a novel in the English literary tradition and an Anglo-Saxon poem involves two distinctly different processes. For the novel we can treat authorship and the authorial canon, the time and place of composition, and numerous other keys to effective criticism as givens; no one wonders who wrote *Tristram Shandy,* whether that Laurence Sterne might also have written *A Sentimental Journey,* or whether that experimentally minded author created within the tradition we construe as that of the English novel. We may argue over the significance of these and other data for interpretation of the Rabelaisian romp, but the facts of publication in printed form and of individual craftsmanship preclude any guesswork on what we take as the basic facts.

But where are these essential data to be found in the case of the oral or oral-derived work, in the present example for the Anglo-Saxon poem? Outside of a very few exceptions, such as *The Battle of Maldon,* we cannot date the Old English poetic corpus; and apart from Cynewulf,[9] a rather shadowy figure, and the Bedan Caedmon, we have no authors—none at all. To widen the perspective, we do not know who "Homer" was or even whether such a monumental figure actually lived and was responsible for the *Iliad* and *Odyssey* the ancients have attributed to him;[10] we have very little information about Mark and the other gospel-writers who made texts from oral tradition; and the authors of the *Cid, Nibelungenlied, Beowulf,* and *Sir Gawain and the Green Knight* are similarly lost to us.

On the other hand, if oral literature research has taught us anything, it is that authorship as we know it in the modern era does

9. Cynewulf's authorship of four poems known as *Elene, Juliana, Fates of the Apostles,* and *Christ II* is based primarily on a runic signature in each manuscript text which, though differently arranged, spells out what we suppose to be his name. For an analysis of the formulaic structure of the phraseology in these four poems, see Robert Diamond, "The Diction of the Signed Poems of Cynewulf," *Philological Quarterly* 38 (1959): 228–41.

10. Ancient evidence on "Homer"—his origins, ancestry, and date—is remarkably contradictory from the start, and it is instructive to remember, as J. A. Davison puts it, that "by the early fifth century [B.C.] several different cities were already claiming to have been Homer's birthplace" ("The Homeric Question," in *A Companion to Homer,* ed. Alan J. B. Wace and Frank H. Stubbings [London: Macmillan, 1969], p. 235).

not exist in oral tradition. Beginning with Parry and Lord, scholars have shown in tangible and undeniable terms how poets composing in oral tradition—*and* poets composing written materials by means of the oral traditional method—owe a great deal of what we call "authorship" to the generations of traditional poets who preceded them. The instrument of oral traditional phraseology, for instance, as highly patterned and formulaic as it is, was shaped not by a single artist or group of artists, but rather by the sum of the many individuals involved in verse-making over the decades and centuries before the semi-observable event of the text that survives to us.[11]   To take another example, the intricate and recurrent weave of details that compose a typical scene or "theme"[12]   has likewise been demonstrated to be the collectively fashioned fabric of a traditional coterie of poets, and as such illustrates at the level of narrative structure the symbiosis of poet and tradition.[13]   One senses quite clearly in the art of oral traditional verse-making the peculiar applicability of Yeats' phrase, "the poet both finger and clay."

So it is, then, that the usual notion of context as a set of verifiable authorial facts enabling effective criticism proves largely impertinent to oral and oral-derived works of literature. Quite naturally

11. Formulaic style has been particularly well studied (though not without disagreement over methods and results) in Old English poetry. See especially Francis P. Magoun, "The Oral-Formulaic Character of Anglo-Saxon Narrative Poetry," *Speculum* 28 (1953): 446–67; Robert P. Creed, "The Making of an Anglo-Saxon Poem," *English Literary History* 26 (1959): 445–54; Donald K. Fry, Jr., "Old English Formulas and Systems," *English Studies* 48 (1967): 193–204; John Miles Foley, "Formula and Theme in Old English Poetry," in *Oral Literature and the Formula,* ed. Benjamin A. Stolz and Richard S. Shannon (Ann Arbor: Center for the Coordination of Ancient and Modern Studies, 1976), pp. 207–32; and John D. Niles, "Formula and Formulaic System," chap. 5 of his *Beowulf: The Poem and Its Tradition* (Cambridge, Mass.: Harvard University Press, 1983), pp. 121–38. For an overview of formulaic studies in Old English through 1980, see my introduction, "The Oral Theory in Context," to *Oral Traditional Literature: A Festschrift for Albert Bates Lord,* ed. John Miles Foley (Columbus: Slavica Press, 1981), pp. 52–79, 107–15.

12. Lord defines the narrative formulas he calls *themes* as "the groups of ideas regularly used in telling a tale in the formulaic style of traditional song" (*The Singer of Tales,* p. 68).

13. Lord's chapter on themes (*The Singer of Tales,* pp. 68–98) explains and illustrates the compositional function of the theme in Serbo-Croatian oral epic tradition. Compare, for example, Berkley Peabody's discussion of themes in ancient Greek epos in his *The Winged Word: A Study in the Technique of Ancient Greek Oral Composition as Seen Principally through Hesiod's "Works and Days"* (Albany: State University of New York Press, 1975), pp. 168–215.

the question then arises as to what we shall substitute in its place. The answer suggested by this volume—and an exciting direction it is—consists of a new concept of tradition, a concept that suits the phenomenological reality of the situation. In their various ways, it is fair to say, the authors all prescribe consideration of their chosen texts *in an oral traditional context.* Whether that context consists of an insight into the problem of genre in ancient Greek poetry, of the influence of printed songbooks (*pjesmarice*) on oral epic in Yugoslavia and the inherent ring-structure that governs epic narrative, of the nature of the acoustic foundation underlying *Beowulf,* of the implication of various kinds of oral traditional structure for the criticism of the *Cid,* of the range of poet-audience assumptions and interactions in medieval English and Germanic works, or of the overwhelming importance of the oral roots of the Gospels and of Mark's conversion of an oral into a textual reality, all six authors invoke an oral traditional context as a prerequisite to faithful interpretation of the literary or religious work they seek to understand. In doing so they inaugurate a new era in oral literature research, an era in which we will see the stylistic analyses that have long occupied scholars in many diverse disciplines being turned to the service of aesthetic inquiry. We stand, to put it quite literally, at a significant crossroads in the history of the field; having absorbed the textual scrutiny of the last thirty years, we are ready to venture past pure analysis and to ask what that analysis means. We are ready to inquire how oral and oral-derived literatures generate meaning on their own terms, and in the process to discover layers and even worlds of meaning long buried in what Walter Ong has rightly described as a writing- and print-centered mentality. The six essays contained in this volume open up entire new vistas on the understanding of some of the most widely known and cherished works of Western civilization; if in doing so they pose more questions than they can answer, we must be grateful for the intellectual engagement of the critical and hermeneutic discourse they inspire.

INDIVIDUAL CONTRIBUTIONS

Albert Lord, the co-founder and for forty years the dean of oral literature research, opens the discourse by confronting squarely two long-disputed issues in Serbo-Croatian epic tradition, the

birthplace of this interdisciplinary field: the historical impact of
the world of literacy on the world of orality and the question of
the role of aesthetics in indisputably oral narrative recorded from
native *guslari*. First, by examining the evidence of written versus
unwritten literature from the sixteenth century onward in the eth-
nically and culturally diverse regions of Dalmatia, Serbia, and
Montenegro, he is able to show how the merging of the two worlds
was a distinctly different phenomenon in each individual case.
Early Dalmatian written literature, he finds, was exclusively the
creation of an elite, the hereditary aristocracy who composed as
easily in Latin, German, and Italian as in Croatian, while the oral
literature of the day was expressly the medium of the peasant
class, which had no opportunity to learn to read or write in any
language. No merger of any sort between the oral and literate
worlds took place until the eighteenth century, when imitations of
oral narrative were attempted by literate poets responding to the
nationalistic view of folklore felt elsewhere in Europe as well.
Lord illustrates how differently the oral-written transaction took
shape in Montenegro and in Serbia and cautions that we must be
careful in assessing the impact of writing and the world it brings
on oral cultures we know only in manuscript.

The second part of Lord's essay illustrates convincingly how the
power and memory of oral tradition and the role of aesthetics
need not be considered mutually exclusive. Using Avdo Medjedović's *The Wedding of Smailagić Meho,* he shows in tangible
terms that ring-composition, a well-established convention in
Homeric epic and *Beowulf,*[14] should be recognized not as a
mindless mnemonic employed by a poet constrained by his
medium to control the telling of his story, but rather as a meaningful level of organization inherent in the story-forms of his tradition, available for artistic epitomization, and itself resonant with
implications and poetic potential. Meho, the initiatory hero who
like his Greek "cousin" Telemachos grows gradually into the
heroic personage he must become through trial and ordeal, con-

14. The first work on Homeric ring-structure was done by Willem A. A.
van Otterlo, in his *De ringcompositie als Opbouwprincipe in de epische
Gedichten van Homerus* (Amsterdam: Noord-Hollandsche Uitgevers Maatschappij, 1948), followed by Cedric H. Whitman's "The Geometric Structure of the
Iliad," in his *Homer and the Heroic Tradition* (Cambridge, Mass.: Harvard University Press, 1958), pp. 249–84. In Old English see, for example, Niles, "Ring Composition and the Structure of *Beowulf,*" *PMLA* 94 (1979): 924–35.

stitutes the focus of many of these A-B-C-B-A patterns, and the symmetry of the elements on either side of the center establishes a narrative context of clearly drawn expectations. The poet Avdo has sensed the traditional context and, in this finest of all recorded songs from Serbo-Croatian epos,[15] he has, in Lord's words, "created and exploited [ring-composition] for artistic purposes and in order to bring into focus the ancient mythic, heroic, social, and historic values of his traditional culture."

Ruth Webber's version of the same tale of interpretation concerns the Battle of the Critics waged over the oral versus written nature of the medieval Spanish *Poema de Mio Cid,* and a veritable battle it has been. Separating themselves into "traditionalists" and "individualists," a typology that actually predates the kind of oral literature research initiated by Parry and Lord, scholars have imitated their colleagues in Homeric and Anglo-Saxon studies in contending strenuously over attribution of the *Cid* either to a poet working within the rich heritage of his tradition or to a learned craftsman virtually solely responsible for the poem. At stake, of course, is nothing less than the context into which we are to place the work in order to interpret it faithfully, and Webber fairly represents both sides of the debate in sketching the possible critical positions. Nonetheless, she does not shrink from pronouncing a particular stance untenable if available evidence indicates its implausibility; likewise, she argues effectively for what seems the soundest opinion, and that opinion often squares with the traditionalist position.

Two of Webber's most telling points concern her documentation of (1) phonological or acoustic patterning and (2) the oral nature of contemporary legal knowledge and practice at about the time of the making of the *Cid,* that is, to the end of the twelfth century,[16] only the former of which I have space to examine here.

15. For the original language text, see *Ženidba Smailagina sina,* kazivao je Avdo Medjedović, ed. David E. Bynum with Albert B. Lord, vol. 4 of Serbo-Croatian Heroic Songs (Cambridge, Mass.: Center for the Study of Oral Literature, 1974); for the English translation, see *The Wedding of Smailagić Meho,* by Avdo Medjedović, trans. Albert B. Lord with David E. Bynum, vol. 3 of Serbo-Croatian Heroic Songs (Cambridge, Mass.: Harvard University Press, 1974), which includes sections on the poet (pp. 3–12) and his originality (pp. 13–34).

16. On this point she is disputing the model of an individual poet with access to archival resources and the ability to use them as espoused by Colin Smith in his recent book, *The Making of the "Poema de mio Cid"* (Cambridge: Cambridge University Press, 1983), the most extreme statement of individualism to date.

She argues, and illustrates convincingly, that "acoustic evidence [is] among the most reliable we have in determining orality," basing her claim on the fact that oral tradition depends on sound for its very shape and existence. As Lord, Robert Creed, Berkley Peabody, and others have shown,[17] density of sound-patterning is an unmistakable feature of oral and oral-derived verse, and this evidence on the *Cid,* reflecting as it does similar analyses of Yugoslav epic, Homeric epic, Old English poetry, and numerous other traditions, helps to place the Spanish poem in the oral traditional context out of which it must have evolved. When one adds to this fundamental demonstration Webber's discussion of date, authorship, versification, rhyme, formulaic structure, historicity, social and political milieu, narrative structure, legal and biblical allusions, and aesthetic design, the appropriate critical context begins to emerge.

Gregory Nagy's presentation on the genres of lyric and epic in ancient Greek, in elegantly exploring the nature of praise-poetry and Homeric poetry through the disentanglement of *ainos* (a double-edged mode of discourse that can confer either praise or blame) and *kleos* (glory as conferred by poetry), also creates an interpretive context, or perhaps makes the present context more true.[18] By illustrating the poetic ontology of the Pindaric lyric— the layering of the proto-ordeal of mythology, the recurrent athletic or martial task, and the realization of song that binds the levels together—Nagy has supplied what amounts to a diachronic and cultural validation of individual achievement through tradition. He distinguishes this medium from that of the Homeric epic by describing how the latter form can never be personalized or turned to individual advantage or disadvantage. With reference to the lyric, it bears repeating the obverse of his thesis as well: the instance of Epinician celebration, singular and ephemeral though it must be, also (re-)validates tradition by making a connection between mythic pattern and present experience. In the so-called Age of Tyrants in ancient Greece, this personal medium was po-

17. Lord, "The Role of Sound Patterns in Serbo-Croatian Epic," in *For Roman Jakobson* (The Hague: Mouton, 1956), pp. 301–5, and *The Singer of Tales,* pp. 54–58; Creed, "The *Beowulf*-Poet: Master of Sound-Patterning," in *Oral Traditional Literature,* pp.194–216; Peabody, *The Winged Word,* pp. 66–117.

18. Of course, with Walter Ong (see his essay in this volume), we should recognize that this truer context, like all truer contexts, leaves more to be interpreted because it invigorates the textual discourse, but that is only as it should be.

liticized as the pan-Hellenic, supra-individual Homeric poems could by definition never be;[19] "only connect," the ancient Greek watchword for the apotheosis of tradition in the here-and-now event of the text, thus took on two distinct dynamics within two interrelated but separate genres.

Also of considerable significance are Nagy's ideas about text fixation in the Homeric epic.[20] If the picture he describes is true, or (to maintain our theme) "truer" than other proposals and therefore productive of more faithful interpretation and livelier discourse, then text fixation without writing is just one more example of what I would describe as the principle of *tradition-dependence:* oral traditions are similar to a degree, and—just as significantly—different to a degree.[21] I think of the still observable (or audible) Yugoslav situation, in which we must identify at least three levels of morphology in oral epic: (1) the pan-traditional (Montenegrin, Dalmatian, Serbian, or whatever), (2) the dialectal (the local tradition, practiced for example in a single village or group of villages), and (3) the idiolectal (the individual singer's own habits). Under such conditions, and given the historical and sociocultural parameters of the modern-day Yugoslav situation, a Homeric kind of text fixation giving way to a single authoritative text would be impossible. But that is only logical. Different societies, different languages, different prosodies, different mythic repositories must produce different oral traditions. Even the concept of such difference can constitute a context of sorts, after all—a comparative context. We stand on the shoulders of those who have nearly exclusively used similarities to describe the nature of oral tradition, and this concentration on cross-traditional congruency was a necessary first step in a wholly new discipline. But we are also poised at an exciting point in the history of

19. To put the same matter another way, the Homeric poems could never have served as the cultural repositories that Havelock and Ong have found them to have been had they not attained a pan-Hellenic character free of individual connections of any sort.

20. See further his "An Evolutionary Model for the Text Fixation of Homeric Epos," in *Oral Traditional Literature,* pp. 390–93.

21. Compare the thrust of my "*Beowulf* and Traditional Narrative Song: The Potential and Limits of Comparison," in *Old English Literature in Context: Ten Essays,* ed. John D. Niles (London and Totowa, N.J.: Brewer and Rowman & Littlefield, 1980), pp. 117–36, 173–78, which weighs Old English prosody and narrative structure against counterpart forms in ancient Greek and Serbo-Croatian epic.

the field. We are beginning to give oral tradition its due by recognizing its characteristic shape-shifting from one individual tradition to the next all over the world. Perhaps one day soon we shall be as interested in that Protean morphology as we have been in setting up the rules of the overall grammar.

Such a tradition-dependent morphology is precisely the central concern of Alain Renoir's comparative essay on the Old English poems attributed to Cynewulf, the Middle High German *Nibelungenlied,* and the Middle English *Sir Gawain and the Green Knight.* Proceeding further with his call for an oral traditional context for medieval poetry,[22] Renoir explains and exemplifies his concept of an "oral-formulaic rhetoric," a traditional narrative code that instills a text (whether oral or oral-derived) with an extratextual meaning or set of meanings otherwise unavailable to the reader or listener. He confronts the complex problem of what Lord calls the merging of two worlds by prescribing three criteria for effective criticism; we must determine as best we can, he says, (1) the extent to which the poet in question was steeped in the oral-formulaic rhetoric of his tradition, (2) the extent of familiarity he assumed his audience to have with that rhetoric, and (3) the extent to which he expected the audience to be composed of listeners or readers. By applying these criteria to the three rather disparate cases he selects for illustration, he is able to shed light on the complexities of Lord's merger and to argue for a poetics that can be calibrated for each given situation.

Renoir's case for a flexible oral poetics looms very large indeed at this crucial point in the history of the field, and for a variety of reasons. Certainly two of the chief reasons are his insistence on a truly comparative context for evaluation and his illustration of the innate activity of the oral-formulaic rhetoric he describes. Without giving each tradition, each text, and each implied audience its due, his essay reminds us, we fall victim to the same reductionism that has plagued oral studies almost from their inception: to wit, if a text and what can be recovered of its context do not match exactly with what has been observed of primary oral traditions in the course of fieldwork or with a canonical analog (most often

22. Especially important among Renoir's many earlier essays on establishing a methodology for comparison is his "Oral-Formulaic Context: Implications for the Comparative Study of Mediaeval Texts," in *Oral Traditional Literature,* pp. 416–39.

Homeric epic) that has rightly or wrongly been treated as the paragon of oral traditional verse-making, then we must relinquish the comparison and consider the text in question a fully literary, post-traditional work. Renoir's argument points toward a further evolution of oral literature research—in reality a much-needed complication of the first approximation of *either* oral *or* written that will foster sensitive interpretation of a whole spectrum of oral-written interaction in medieval and other texts. Hand in hand with this revolutionary thesis, so well documented by his variety of examples, goes his notion of the activity of oral-formulaic rhetoric, even in an ascertainably written work. Both theses have far-reaching implications for the hybrid or "transitional" text (more accurately now, a range of transitional texts), that is, for all works on the border between the two worlds of orality and literacy.

And it is precisely to the proximate worlds of orality (this time the pagan Germanic oral tradition) and of literacy (the new technology supplied by Christianity) that Robert Creed turns in his discussion of an originative context for the Old English *Beowulf.* Viewing the anonymous author of the version that has reached us as a "virtuoso traditional poet who may have radically reshaped the tradition in order to preserve it," Creed probes both the cultural prehistory of the poem and the evidence it provides of a delicately balanced oral idiom that served the generations who performed it as a living network of aural associations. He contends in essence that a proper appreciation of *Beowulf* includes an explicit awareness of its roots in the now-dim Germanic past and of the complex but flexible acoustic bridge that the work has built and still maintains between its many audiences and that otherwise lost past. Not unlike Eric Havelock and other scholars, he posits the poetic preservation of older mores in the timeless verse idiom of oral traditional poetry.

Just how is this preservation accomplished in a medium remarkable for its lack of written records? In answering this question Creed describes in some detail the rudimentary features of the system of acoustic patterning that underlies *Beowulf* and other Old English poetry. As have other investigators in oral traditions as diverse as ancient Greek, Old Iranian, Russian, and Vogul and Ostyak, he demonstrates how the inner structure of "sound-sharing" can support the formulation and reformulation of traditional associations through the ages. In Anglo-Saxon the primary con-

stituents of the mimetic phraseology are stress-accent and alliteration; these two prosodic features order the association of sounds
and support the recurrent phraseology we have come to call "formulaic." Using this ancient system of composition, Creed argues,
the *Beowulf*-poet refashioned his Germanic inheritance into a
bequest fitting for his newly Christian audience and the generations to follow. It was, then, this "re-making of the tale of the
beneficent heathen god into the tale of the beneficent hero that
attracted the attention of those who could command the resources
of the scriptorium." To both the very old and the very new worlds,
he contends, does the great epic *Beowulf* owe its many-layered
and lasting resonance.

I turn finally to Walter J. Ong's notions of orality and textuality,
which I find disquietingly brilliant and bristling with possibilities
for establishing new and truer contexts not only in New Testament
or biblical studies but also in oral and oral-derived literature as a
comparative whole. In probing the pretextual world of orality in
which the original *kerygma* ("proclamation, announcement") of
Jesus (and perhaps to some extent the transitional quasi-text we
call Q) existed and in which it elicited a particular noetic brand of
discourse,[23] Ong offers us a wholly revised view of the Gospel of
Mark and of all the gospels. No matter what existential force the
gospels may have for an individual, one must recognize that placing the text of Mark in the context of its oral antecedents and
assessing the extraordinary change in phenomenological import
necessarily a part of the narratizing process must affect pro-
foundly the way in which one reads and interprets the gospels as
they survive to us. By making evident the dynamics of both the
oral Jesus and his Markan remaking, Ong brings us closer to the
identity of Jesus and the experience of his teachings as presence. It
is difficult to overestimate this achievement.

One aspect of the evolution from an oral reality to the texts we

23. In "African Talking Drums and Oral Noetics," *New Literary History* 8 (1977),
411–29, Ong discusses how primary oral cultures organize thought and knowledge
around a set of repeated figures and themes; it is this kind of organization that
fosters the open-ended referentiality of oral discourse. See also his related works,
especially *The Presence of the Word: Some Prolegomena for Cultural and
Religious History* (New Haven: Yale University Press, 1967; rpt. New York: Simon
and Schuster, 1970); *Interfaces of the Word: Studies in the Evolution of Consciousness and Culture* (Ithaca: Cornell University Press, 1977); and *Orality and
Literacy: The Technologizing of the Word* (London: Methuen, 1982).

call the Gospels may be construed as the question of what may be "lost" in the transition,[24] and the question gains even larger prominence as one applies it to other literatures that underwent similar or cognate transitions. To come to grips with the "difference" in the two modes of discourse (which are, as Ong and others have shown, seldom completely separable),[25] it is necessary to appreciate first what the oral noetic economy provided for and even promoted. In primary oral tradition, there simply is no such thing as an omitted story-part, or flawed episode, or misnomer. Since the primary oral performance draws its meaning not only from the present event but equally from the diachronic and pan-geographic tradition of which it is only an instance, the process of generating meaning proceeds via metonymy, *pars pro toto*. One text recalls numerous others by synecdoche, just as one phrase or scene is always embedded conceptually in the word-hoard, in the experience of tradition. Under such conditions the oral reality of Jesus conjured for its audience not simply its present, discrete story-shape, but all story-shapes that oral tradition had gathered about this central figure. Thus does the primary oral culture create and maintain an economy of expression and interpretation that a chirographic culture can never emulate, for the post-traditional text, by cutting itself off from the generative oral tradition in pursuit of an individual identity, foregoes the metonymic power of reference inherent in the oral traditional medium. Mark epitomizes Jesus in the fashion of the written Word, and that is the way we come to know the Word, the person, and the teachings; that is *our* way. But before the textualization of Jesus in a medium we praise for its accuracy and measured referentiality, the oral *kerygma* proclaimed his presence and teachings in a vastly different, connotatively explosive mode. Something was certainly gained in the socioculturally prompted transition, and something was just as certainly lost.

*   *   *

In the manner of the bard, then, via the traditional wisdom of

24. I owe the posing of this intriguing question to Ward Parks, Professor of English at Louisiana State University, with whom I have discussed all of the essays in this volume to my considerable benefit.

25. See, for example, Ong's "Oral Residue in Tudor Prose Style," *PMLA* 80 (1965): 145–54.

ring-composition, I shall end where I began. As indicated above, this volume explores possible answers to the newly formulated question of the importance of the oral traditional roots of some of the most important literary and religious documents of Western civilization. And no matter what particular method its authors employ, or which of the more than ninety literatures now affected by this interdisciplinary field they choose to investigate, their most fundamental response seems to be unanimous: our primary responsibility as interpreters of these works is to place them in their oral traditional contexts. The specific context, we have seen, must necessarily vary for each individual situation; no monolithic model can be expected to solve such a complex problem in interpretation, any more than we could prescribe a unitary model for our most thoroughly literate texts, such as the works of Spenser, Milton, Shakespeare, and Hawthorne that justly occupy such revered places in the English-American literary canon.[26] But with a combination of philological rigor and imaginative comparison, we can fulfill the promise of these six remarkable essays and recapture essential meaning from contexts lost, in some cases, for centuries or even millennia. This, then, is our appointed task as critics and interpreters of works composed at least in part with oral traditional "words"—to hear the ages-old resonance in the structure and function of phraseology, narrative, and story-pattern, and thereby to reinvigorate the works with their original verbal energy. We must, with Homer, "raise the great song once more."

---

26. But the roots of oral tradition run very deep indeed: compare John Webster, "Oral Form and Written Craft in Spenser's *Faerie Queene,*" *Studies in English Literature* 16 (1976): 75–93; Ong, "Milton's Logical Epic and Evolving Consciousness," *Proceedings of the American Philosophical Society* 120 (1976): 295–305; Marion Trousdale, "Shakespeare's Oral Text," *Renaissance Drama* 12 (1981): 95–115; and John G. Bayer, "Narrative Techniques and the Oral Tradition in *The Scarlet Letter,*" *American Literature* 52 (1980): 250–63.

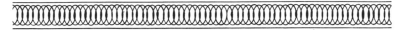

2
THE MERGING OF TWO WORLDS: ORAL AND WRITTEN POETRY AS CARRIERS OF ANCIENT VALUES
Albert B. Lord

In this paper I will investigate several specific cases of the merging of the world of orality with that of literacy as it is manifested in the development of oral traditional poetry. The world of "orality" is a world of talk. One literally *hears* of what has happened in the past, as well as of what is happening in one's own day. It is that simple. Yet perhaps not quite so simple. Sometimes, in the past as well as in the present, the "talk" is song, a specially conventionalized medium that serves to filter out some sounds, to amplify others, and generally to give them all a new artistic form. And what it does for the sounds it does also for the ideas and images that it is serving to communicate. The images, and the ideas too, are refracted in the mind's eye, an eye that sees *images* directly rather than through letters and written words. Thus sounds carry ideas and images without any other intermediary in the process of communication.

All sounds are comparatively variable; within a measurable range they are "the same." From the position of the receiver, sounds within that range may be recognized as "the same" even if they actually are not, and even if the receiver is vaguely aware of some difference. Dialects have been formed, languages differentiated, in part because of this principle, this characteristic of sound; for such variability tends to produce sound changes. The principle of fluidity of text—of which more later—may be thought of as being generated by this principle of sound. This characteristic of

sound, the fact that its variability is understandable within a range of limits, belongs to all types of discourse; it is basic to "orality."

Whatever degrees of specialized ordering and distinctiveness may occur in different types of speech, the fundamental characteristic of variability will not be destroyed, because at each step—in the oral world, in the world of artful speech before codification—the ordering has a range, and the distinctiveness is within a range of possibilities as well. We might, indeed, call this period of orality one of precodification. Since we live in a period of codification, it is difficult for us to divest ourselves of the concept of the prescribed and to grasp the concept of variability or, better, of multiformity. *Variability* is a possible term, if one understands by it that there is not the urge to use exactly the same words one used the last time that one expressed a given idea. One does not think about it. One may use the same words as the last time, but the last time was no more formative than any other time. Alternatives, options, have been developed over generations, and the speaker or singer recapitulates the process in his own experience. This concept of variability and multiformity is present in varying degrees in all types of oral discourse; it is inherent in sound itself.

If we take three regions in Yugoslavia and compare the climate of written literature with the climate of oral traditional literature in each, we will note considerable variety. In Dalmatia there was a rich Renaissance literature, with a strong Italian influence. In Serbia medieval works continue into the eighteenth century; vernacular secular literature appears only at the very end of that century, really beginning in the nineteenth century with Milovan Vidaković and Dositej Obradović. In Montenegro there was the influence of Russian letters in the late eighteenth and early nineteenth centuries, more specifically that of the Russian monasteries and of such writers as Pushkin.

But what has that to do with the singers? If a singer in Montenegro learned to read, was he immediately immersed in Russian literature? Of course not, because Russian letters influenced the literary elite in Montenegro, insofar as literary circles existed there, and the singer who learned to read would not readily enter into these circles. Singers are usually in rural areas, frequently, but not exclusively, in mountainous regions, often among herders.

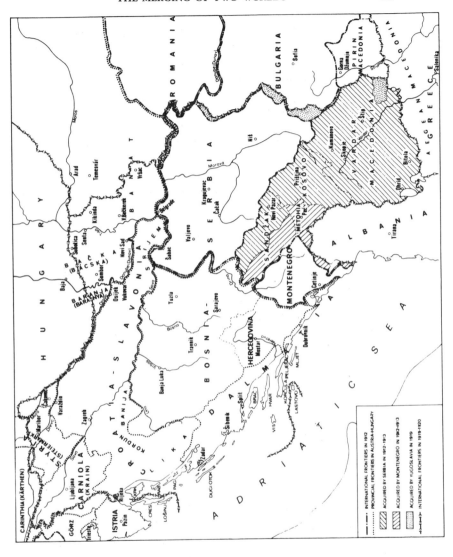

Constituent areas of Yugoslavia. Reprinted from Ivo Banac, *The National Question in Yugoslavia: Origins, History, Politics*. Copyright © 1984 by Cornell University Press. Used by permission of the publisher.

The singer's world must change for the merger to take place, or else the singer himself must change worlds. It happens both ways, of course. In the case of the early nineteenth-century prince-bishop of Montenegro, Petar II Petrović Njegoš, the singer traveled—to Dalmatia (Kotor) and then to Russia. But he always returned to Cetinje, where a miniature of the world of literacy—a special kind of literary life—was created by the monastery, and it was there that he lived and wrote. He had moved into the other world from the one into which he was born.

In some societies, such as that of the Moslem Slavs in the days of the Turkish Empire in what is now Yugoslavia, writing in the literal sense was done by professional scribes, and the rest of the population, both upper and lower classes, did not either read or write. These societies are, or were, entirely oral, and their literature was oral. What schools there were, such as the *medrese,* were religious; this was true also in the Christian segment of the population. The schools were attached to mosques or churches and monasteries, and the teachings and learning were religious. These schools produced small islands of a restricted literacy. Reading matter consisted of Scripture and, in more advanced classes, liturgical works.

In what follows I will examine what there was of poetry in both worlds, that of orality and that of literacy, first on the Dalmatian coast in the first half of the eighteenth century, and second in Montenegro in the first half of the nineteenth century. Then I will review the situation of the two worlds in Yugoslavia in the first half of the twentieth century, and how it came to be so, by tracing its roots in the 1870s, 1880s, and 1890s.

Our windows—or should we say listening posts?—before the eighteenth century are few, precious, but quite inadequate so far as oral traditional epic, or even oral traditional lyric, is concerned. What is to be noted, however, is that whatever texts we have from those centuries are not insecure flounderings in search of a style. Their style is already highly developed when it first appears in the *Ranjin zbornik* (for lyrics) in the early sixteenth century and in Petar Hektorović's *Ribanje* (for both the long-line *bugarštice* and lyrics) in 1556. The formative period for that style must have been in the distant past—how distant we do not know—but perhaps as far back as the time when South Slavic differentiated itself from East and West Slavic, particularly from the former.

What we have recorded of oral traditional poetry from the sixteenth and seventeenth centuries comes from the Dalmatian coast. This is not surprising, because written literature was richer there than elsewhere in the South Slavic area at that time. The Christian eastern part of that area was still, culturally, in the Middle Ages, under Ottoman rule. On occasion, on the coast, someone, like Đore Držić or Hektorović in the sixteenth century, showed an awareness of the traditional culture, which seems to have penetrated west from the interior. The rest is a blank page, or silence, but that is normal for oral traditional poetry, which, by definition, is oral and is "written down" later and almost by chance or for reasons that have little to do with itself. We know that oral traditional poetry existed in its own world in those centuries, but the two worlds were separate. The world of written literature on occasion showed that it knew of the other world, for example the world of Hektorović's fishermen, or, in the next century, the seventeenth, that of Ivan Gundulić's idealized Serbian peasants in his long epic poem, *Osman,* but the denizens of that world seem to have been unaffected by the world of written literature, because they did not read, or, more important, belong to the elite class. Strangely enough, it was that class and that world of literacy that used the world of orality, thus creating a bridge between the two worlds, and not vice versa.

It was toward the end of the seventeenth century that the bridge really began to be built. It was then that the private collections of oral traditional songs began to be made, which were not to be published or have an "audience," or group of readers, larger than what the family, or neighborhood, or monastery might afford, a limited reading public, a class by itself.

These collections give us some idea of what the content and to some extent the form of the songs of the world of orality were in the area of Dubrovnik or of the Bay of Kotor at the end of the seventeenth and the beginning of the eighteenth century. The earliest of these are the first fourteen songs in the famous Dubrovnik manuscript from the Franciscan monastery of Mala Braća (Little Brothers). They are a varied lot, illustrating the types of subjects current at that time and one of the current forms. They are all *bugarštice,* songs with lines of fifteen or sixteen syllables. Some of them are preceded by elaborate titles, sometimes referring to Mavro Orbini's *Il regno degli Slavi* of 1601. But these titles are to be attributed to the person who put the manuscript together, giving the manuscript as a whole the title "Popjevke slovinske skupljene g. 1758 u Dobrovniku" (Slavic songs gathered in 1758 in Dubrovnik).

The long-line poems in this manuscript and elsewhere, as well as the epic decasyllabic poems of the oral tradition, are in meters that were not used in the literary works of the fifteenth and later centuries. Here is a real difference, though of a specialized sort, between the poetic world of orality and the poetic world of literacy in Dalmatia during its brilliant Renaissance period. Some of the earliest poems in the written literary tradition were translations from Latin, using a Latin meter; for example,

> U se vrime godišća,
> In hoc anni circulo,
> In this time of year,

which is still sung as a Christmas carol even today.

The two most common literary meters in written Dalmatian letters of the sixteenth to the eighteenth centuries were dodecasyllabic and octosyllabic stanzas. The following lines from the Spličanin Marko Marulić's *Judita* with their peculiar rhyme scheme and earthy realism illustrate dodecasyllabic couplets rhyming at both the middle and end of the line:

> Da tko spovidati sva more čudesa?—
>   od konjske bahati zemlja se potresa,
>   ništar ne poresa, ni trava ni žito,
>   kuda vojska plesa, po sve ono lito.
> Tad lačan korito prasac ostavljaše,
>   zvire strahljivito bigat ne umijaše.
>   na zemlji padaše ptica sa visine,
>   kad zavapijaše vojska iz dubine.
> Od praha magline dvizahu se gori,
>   kako no oblačine kad mrče po gori,
>   seli tere dvori, poljem kada gode,
>   u dne al u zori, paljihu se hode.
>
> Who could relate all the wonders?
>   The earth trembled from the pounding of horses' hooves,
>   nothing could grow, either grass or grain,

where the army pranced, during all that time.
Then the greedy pig eager to leave its trough,
  looking about fearfully, could not flee away.
Birds fell from the heavens to the earth,
  when the army shouted from below.
Swirls of dust rose aloft,
  like great clouds when darkness comes on the heights.
Villages and castles along the way,
  in full day or at dawn, were set afire when the
  army passed.

Although one will find the earth trembling at the pounding of
horses' hooves in traditional epic—though not in this purely written literary meter, of course—I do not recall pigs, even when
frightened, unable to move from their troughs from piggishness.

The dodecasyllable was used also by Šiško Menčetić, a lyric
poet of the early sixteenth century, in such Petrarchan sonnets as:

Glasom ja dan i noć prizivam krieposti,
  jer slavit za svu moć rad bih tve lieposti.
Raju sja danica od zvizda najsvitlja;
  takoj ctiš a nica medj vilam svih liplja.
Akvile krieposti nitko nas ne ima,
  ter se tve lieposti pozirat ne prima;
cjeć ako tko gleda veseli tvoj obraz,
  stvori se od leda ter kopni kako mraz.
Jer sjaje promineš i kud se ti ozriš,
  svitlostju prosineš ter suncem sva goriš.
Od raja dar imaš, da t' lička zorom zre:
  liepo vil vazimaš, ka godi s tobom gre.
Za to je svak vesel, obraz tvoj videći,
  za to je svak dresel, srcem ga slideći.
Ar si drag viditi, moj venče gizdavi,
  nu jes trud živiti željah ljubavi.

Day and night I call aloud for strength,
  for I would gladly praise your beauty with all my might.
The day star shines in paradise, the brightest of stars:
  thus you bloom and blossom more beautiful among all vilas
  [mountain spirits].
None of us has the strength of an eagle,
  that he can look upon your beauty.
For if anyone gazes on your happy face,
  even if made of ice, he melts like frost. ›

Because you rival great brilliance wherever you look,
you shine with radiance and are afire as the sun.
You have the gift from paradise that your face glows at dawn:
You assume the beauty of vilas when one walks with you.
For that reason everyone is happy, looking on your face,
for that reason everyone is sad, following it in his heart.
Because it is lovely to see you, my beautiful garland,
but it is a burden to live with the desires for you.

Our first oral traditional epic texts are imbedded in this same written literary meter in Petar Hektorović's *Ribanje:*

Malo povozivši, pri ner se umori,
riči potočivši, Nikola govori:
"recimo po jednu, za vrime minuti,
bugaršćinu srednu, i za trud ne čuti;
da srbskim načinom, moj druže primili,
kako meu družinom vasda smo činili;"
koko da se utiče, jer biše od volje,
sam Paskoj pokliče ča može najbolje:
PASK.   "Dva mi sta siromaha dugo vrime drugovala,
lipo ti sta drugovala i lipo se dragovala,
lipo plinke dilila, i lipo se razdiljala,
i razdiliv se, opet se sazivala.

Having rowed a little, before becoming tired,
pouring forth his words, Nikola spoke:
"Let's each of us tell off, to pass the time,
a fine song, that we may not feel our labor,
and that in Serbian measure, my dear comrade,
as in company we have always done."
As he girded himself for the task, for he was in a good humor,
Paskoj himself shouted as loudly as he could:
PASK.   "Two orphans were friends together for a long time,
they were good friends and fond of one another,
well did they divide the booty, and well split it up,
and having split it, they would call one another again.

These texts dramatically, as it were, juxtapose the written literary with the oral traditional literary, demonstrating the distinctions, while at the same time putting the two styles together side by side in the same poem.

The octosyllable may appear to be more ambiguous, since it is used both in oral traditional poetry and in the written literature of the period under consideration. But the literary octosyllable par excellence, which is the only one I will illustrate here, is not the same as the traditional one. One has only to compare the well-known lines of Hanibal Lucić:

Jur nijedna na svit vila
lipotom se već ne slavi,
jer je hvale sve skupila
vila ka mi srce travi.
Ni će biti, ni je bila,
njoj takmena ka se pravi.
Lipotom se već ne slavi
jur nijedna na svit vila.

No vila on earth
can any longer be praised for beauty,
for all praises have been garnered
by the vila who enchants my heart.
There will not be, nor has there been,
any to compete with her.
There can no longer be praised for beauty
any vila on earth.

or in the next century, the opening lines of Gundulić's *Osman:*

Ah, čijem si se zahvalila,
tašta ljudska oholasti?
Sve što više stereš krila,
sve ćeš paka niže pasti!

Of what have you boasted,
vain human pride?
The higher you spread your wings,
the lower will you fall back again!

with

Puhni mi, puhni, ladane,
Dodi mi, dodi, dragane,
U moje dvore bijele!
Dovedi doga za sobom!
Svezi ga ruži za grane!
Neka mu ruža miriše!
Neka mu duša uzdiše!

Blow, blow, cold wind,

Come to me, beloved,
Into my white dwelling!
Bring your white horse with you!
Tie him to the rose tree's branches!
Let the rose's fragrance envelop him!
Let his spirit be filled with longing!

to realize that they come from quite different worlds, and that
there are octosyllables and there are octosyllables!

So the world of "literacy" is removed from that of orality, far
removed, indeed, for its inhabitants can read and write poetry in
Latin or in German or Italian as easily as in Croatian. Writing
belongs to the hereditary aristocracy, often educated in the universities of Bologna or Padua, or those of other Italian cities, or to
the clergy in the monasteries. The aristocracy wrote Petrarchan
sonnets; pastoral drama in verse flourished in Dubrovnik in the
seventeenth century, performed in the courtyards and gardens of
the palaces. Long poems on religious subjects, such as Vetranić's
"Pelegrin" in the fifteenth century and Palmotić's "Kristijada" in
the sixteenth, or Gundulić's "Suze razmetnoga sina" (The tears of
the Prodigal Son), were far removed from oral traditional poetry.
Marinism, a movement of elaborate literary conceits associated
with the Italian poet Marini, had its influence on the latter poem.
There was little social mobility in Split, or Dubrovnik, or Šibenik,
or Zadar. We all have often used the phrase *the singer who learned
to write,* but these words have little meaning here, because the
singer belonged usually to the peasant class and he did not learn to
write unless he moved out of that class, but this was impossible
because the aristocracy was hereditary. The aristocracy also provided many members of the clergy.

The Dalmatian world of written literacy was largely produced
by its port and ships. The people of the coast were in touch with a
large world. A wealthy, more cosmopolitan bourgeoisie was interested in its families and its cities, such as Split, or Šibenik, or
Dubrovnik, or Kotor. The villages in the hinterland, on the other
hand, were self-contained in many ways. They made their own
clothes. You could spot the countryman in the marketplace
because he dressed differently. And so his culture was different.
This symbol of distinctness, not limited, of course, to Dalmatia,
has been gradually disappearing in this century. The "national
costume," "the folk costume," is kept for tourism, and taken from

the museums for folk festivals—it is an indication that those who once wore such clothes were different. It is an instructive parallel to the position of oral traditional epic. One no longer practices it, but it is displayed now and again for tourists or for purposes of national identity.

Given the very elite character of Dalmatian literature in the sixteenth and seventeenth centuries, in both form and content, it seems very doubtful, to say the least, that it had any influence on the oral traditional literature. It was an extension of the Italian Renaissance rather than a product of native rhythms, and when it very occasionally looked at those native rhythms it was as something foreign and, perhaps, quaint. Gundulić's *Osman,* the greatest epic in the Dalmatian Renaissance, was modeled on Tasso's "Gerusalemme Liberata." In its eighth canto it presents a highly romantic picture of Serbian peasants singing and dancing and tells the subjects of the epics they listened to. And in the third canto it lists other subjects as the sultan's messenger travels to the River Marica, where the poet pauses to tell of Serbian and Bulgarian stories connecting that river with Orpheus, who bequeathed his power in song to the Slavic tongue. So, the poet says, the Serbs and Bulgars have put into song the deeds of Alexander the Serb, of Stefan Uroš and the other Nemanjići, of Kobilić and his slaying of the sultan at Kosovo. Mihail Svilojević is mentioned, in this passage, as well as Kraljević Marko and Lauš (Vladislav) in Buda and Krakow, Vojvoda Janko, King Matijaš, Skenderbcy, and others. These two catalogs—in the eighth and the third cantos—are like the table of contents of the Dubrovnik manuscript, which was begun at the end of the same century (the sixteenth). The literary poet—and his world, therefore—shows a knowledge of the traditional songs, referring to them in his highly written literary masterpiece, but making no attempt at imitation or at using the traditional meter or language.

That is a phenomenon that belongs to the end of the century, it would seem, or perhaps more correctly to the beginning of the eighteenth. That is when the two worlds, hitherto coexisting side by side, began to merge. The forces at work elsewhere in Europe leading to collecting and imitating oral traditional songs and other genres, such as "folklore," began to have their influence in these regions also, especially in the latter half of the eighteenth century.

The story was completely different in neighboring Montenegro.

Let us look at the situation there in the first half of the nineteenth century, using the poet Petar II Petrović Njegoš as a guide. Njegoš was born Rade Petrović in 1813 in the village of Njeguši in Montenegro. Petar was the name he assumed when he took orders and became a monk in 1831. In 1830 he succeeded his uncle, Petar I, as prince-bishop, *vladika,* of Montenegro. He was Montenegro's greatest poet.

Njegoš would have seen no books or newspapers when he was a boy in Njeguši. He would have heard men tell of the past, of the past they had lived through, of the past they had heard of from their fathers and grandfathers, who were telling of what they remembered from their own experience and of what they had heard. Some of this was just talk. But on the lips of some of the talkers the accounts took the form of ordered discourse with a lexicon of humanistic history, eloquent or pedestrian depending on the ability or talent of the individual and on the quality of the tradition of telling history in the community, of Njeguši in Njegoš's case. Njegoš was interested in these stories of the past. They were not stories, you understand, of the past of the human race, not great panoramas of history. They were of tribal and local happenings, especially of the conflicts with the Turks, but also of feudal raids between families and tribes.

Njegoš heard guslars—epic singers—recounting some of this history in song. For how long tribal and family history had been told in traditional song we cannot tell. It is possible that it is a very old tradition, but our first texts from Montenegro are from the first quarter of the nineteenth century, and the events told of belong for the most part to the eighteenth century, even though there were some Serbian figures of earlier centuries whose songs had found their way to Montenegro. But I am getting ahead of my story.

From these songs and from the prose stories as well Njegoš learned of justice, of social and moral standards, of heroism, which was beginning to become a cult, and of loyalty to family, tribe, church, and Christianity. In *The Singer of Tales* I wrote that the traditional epic was the entertainment of the men in the parts of Yugoslavia where the tradition still persisted. This was true, but there was another dimension to the traditional songs of the guslars. There were ancient mythic patterns preserved in what passed in Njegoš's day as history. There were return songs that had become attached to Serbian or Montenegrin heroes, but the narrative patterns were ancient and mythic. There were songs of dragons and vilas associated with Marko Kraljević, who lived at the end of the fourteenth century. And from the same time there were probably songs of the battle of Kosovo in 1389. All these, or songs like them, Njegoš heard as a boy. He learned to sing himself, at an early age no doubt. No books were needed for this, although books had begun to appear in Montenegro and the writing down and written creation of the songs had begun.

His world of sound, his oral traditional world, was beginning to change. But the process was slow. Two figures emerge here of great importance to Montenegrin culture and to young Njegoš. These were his uncle and his tutor.

Djilas writes that Njegoš's father used to make up songs and sing them to the gusle.[1] The idea of his making up the songs may simply be Djilas's concept from his own day about guslars, but it does indicate at least that Njegoš's father sang to the gusle. Sima Milutinović published one of his songs in his *Pjevannija* in 1833, No. 20 "Haračlija Crnogoraca." It is a story of sheep-stealing by Hamza Kapetan in Nikšić from Tomanović Nikac, or Nikac od Rovine. Nikac stops the stealing, recovers the sheep, kills thirty Turks, and takes seven or eight prisoners. There was nothing unusual about Njegoš's father singing to the gusle, because we are told from other sources that almost every house in Montenegro had a gusle.[2] Although that may be an exaggeration, and itself a sign that the cult of the gusle was then well under way, there is undoubtedly some truth in it. Gusle and singing were common.

Njegoš learned to read and write in the monastery in Cetinje in 1825, probably from one of his uncle's secretaries, we are told,[3] because when he went to the Bay of Kotor shortly after that to a tutor, Tropović in Topla, he could already do so. Djilas stresses that, in spite of all this, Njegoš was mainly self-taught, as were all his tutors, including his uncle, Bishop Petar. The world of literacy that was beginning to touch young Rade's traditional world of

1. See Milovan Djilas, *Njegoš: Poet, Prince, Bishop* (New York: Harcourt, Brace and World, 1966).
2. See Vuk Stefanović Karadžić, *Crna Gora i Boka Kotorska,* Srpska književna zadruga, Kolo XXIV, br. 161 (Beograd, 1922).
3. See Djilas, *Njegoš,* and Vido Latković, *Petar Petrović Njegoš* (Beograd: Nolit, 1963).

orality was a very limited one. Yet, significantly for us, one of the areas in which literacy was used was in the writing down of poetry in epic decasyllabics, whether by dictating or actually composing in writing. Bishop Petar had secretaries, and some of the songs, or poems, in Milutinović's *Pjevannija* came from him. He may well have dictated them.

As a youth Njegoš learned to sing traditional epic songs to the gusle. And he began to make up songs himself at an early age, at any rate before he was twenty. Milutinović published five of them in the second edition of his *Pjevannija* (1835) with a note to the first indicating that Njegoš wrote it before he became *vladika*, which was in 1833. The events of the first of these songs took place in 1828 and of the second and third in 1832. These then were new songs. He did not learn them from anyone. He made them up himself.

As Latković pointed out,[4] five of these songs are "folk epics," one of which, "Mali Radojica," is traditional and has been published in a number of versions, including one in Vuk Karadžić's *Srpske narodne pjesme,* vol. III, No. 51. Njegoš himself included one of his early poems, "Boj na Martiniće," in his anthology, *Ogledalo srpsko.* These poems are about local happenings, fitting the Montenegrin tradition of such songs. But one of those included in Milutinović's second edition of *Pjevannija* in 1837, "Nova pjesna crnogorska o vojni Rusah i Turaka, početoj u 1828 godu" (New Montenegrin Song of the War of the Russians and Turks, Begun in 1828), is different. It is longer (775 lines) and covers a much larger action than the local songs. As Latković suggests, it was probably never sung by Njegoš to the gusle, as were the others. Latković also points out that this song is on the way to being a literary poem in the style of the "folk epic," using many of its formulas and themes, but also bringing in nontraditional elements. Njegoš was beginning to move from the "folk epic" to his own individual written style.

The excellence of Njegoš's version of the traditional "Mali Radojica" was the result of his high quality as a traditional singer of epic—like Avdo Međedović's excellence within the tradition. But in "Nova pjesna crnogorska" there are new nontraditional traits, which make it possible for us to classify it as truly transitional in

---

4. Latković, *Njegoš.*

the development of Njegoš's own writing as well as in the Montenegrin tradition itself. I will set this forth now in greater detail.

The five other songs begin in traditional ways, but "Nova pjesna crnogorska" begins with the invocation to the vila to give voice to the gusle.

> B'jela vilo, moja divna drugo,
> svedi, drugo, sve u gusli glase,
> tvoje glase a u gusli jasne,
> da ih čuje koji razumije,
> razumije drago ako mu je.
> Srbalj brate, ova pjesna za te,
> ti ćeš čuti, ti je razumjeti
> ponajprije od ostalih svije.

> White vila, my wondrous comrade,
> bring together, comrade, all voices into the gusle,
> your clear voices into the gusle,
> that he who understands may listen,
> understands if it pleases him.
> Brother Serbs, this song is for you,
> you will listen, you will understand
> first of all others.

I feel sure that that invocation was the result of his tutor Sima's teachings and that the romantic cult of the gusle and its association with Serbian nationalism were comparatively new in those days of revolution for liberation from the Turkish Empire. This is new in Njegoš and in its appearance in the oral traditional epic elsewhere in Serbia and Montenegro.

The first two lines of the song proper give the date:

> Na hiljadu i osme stotine
> dvadest sedme na pola godine

> In one thousand eight hundred
> and half of the twenty-seventh year

This element began, I believe, with Kačić and is not traditional. I wrote more about this in *The Singer of Tales*. When the action of the poem begins, however, we are in traditional themes.

> sitni ferman jeste poletio
> od prostrana carstva rusinskoga
> iz bijela grada Petrovoga,

od silnoga cara Nikolaja,
Nikolaja Pavlovoga sina.

a well-writ firman flew
from the wide-flung Russian Empire
from the white city of Peter,
from the mighty Tsar Nikola,
Nikola Pavlović.

Njegoš was growing into the world of literacy, just as Montenegro itself was, and his early poetry shows him in that process of growth. In Montenegro, then, at this time the world of literacy, as I have indicated, was very limited, whereas that of orality embraced the whole society.

There *are* transitional texts in South Slavic epic, probably several kinds. Some of those I am investigating here were written by authors who were either members themselves of the traditional community or had become immersed in the traditional poetry to the point that they could compose as a member of that community, even if they had been brought up in a very written literary milieu.

If one has a knowledge of the traditional songs, not a surface acquaintance with just a few examples but a broad and deep experience of many really traditional songs in any given culture, it is possible to observe and document any new elements coming into the songs from outside to change the traditional style *and* content on all levels. But one must have an extensive experience of the oral traditional formulaic and thematic style and of the traditional content in order to recognize the new elements. Moreover, there must be sufficient material to analyze from the traditional poetry as well as from the written literary tradition. In South Slavic there is a large enough body of songs of various kinds from several historical periods both from the traditional culture and from the surrounding written literary culture to be able to document this process.

In the middle of the twentieth century, the third period I mentioned above, I can think of singers and places I have known personally; they are not abstractions, but singers with names and places and dates, as was also, of course, the case in my approach to past periods. Did the "illiterate singer" come into contact with print?

Take the Kučinari brothers Đuro and Trifko, Nikola's maternal uncles in Burmazi, srez Stolac in Hercegovina, good, but not great, singers. On occasion, such as regularly on market days, they came into Stolac, or, less frequently, went to Mostar. They would patronize a *kafana* or a *han,* since they were Christians, frequented by other *seljaci* (peasants). No newspapers, and especially no books, were to be found in those places. The men talked prices, crops, cattle, weather, and politics—as well as gossip, of course—but it was all word-of-mouth. Someone might say, "But they could have gone to the hotel in town, where there were papers." But the hotel was more expensive than the coffeehouse or less pretentious country inn (han), and country people everywhere do not like to spend any more money than they have to. Moreover, they would have been ill-at-ease, as they were when they came to visit us, because peasants do not go to the hotel, or did not in the thirties. Đuro and Trifko, however, did have a couple of contacts, at least indirectly, with the world of literacy. Their sister had married Ivan Vujnović and borne him two sons, Nikola, the older, and Đuro, the younger, named after his uncle.

Both the young Vujnovići had had four years of schooling and could read and write. It would be a mistake, of course, to conclude that they knew anything at all about written literature. Đuro, the nephew, was still living in the village as a boy of about ten or so in the midthirties, but Nikola had gone as a stone mason to Dubrovnik. In the schoolbooks they had used there were some oral traditional epics, usually from the Karadžić collection, for example, "Marko Kraljević and Musa the Highwayman." These texts might have been read to the uncles by either nephew, but if so they had little, if any, influence on the elder Đuro's song of the battle of Kosovo, which has important elements I have not found in any Kosovo songs, published or unpublished. I believe that there were Kosovo songs in the schoolbooks.

I do not know what happened to young Đuro after the midthirties, but he was engaged in writing down songs for Milman Parry,[5] supposedly from his uncles, but actually from published

5. On the field trips undertaken by Parry and Lord to observe a still-living tradition of oral epic singing as confirmation of Parry's discoveries about Homer, see Lord, "General Introduction," in *Novi Pazar: English Translations,* Serbocroatian Heroic Songs (Srpskohrvatske junačke pjesme), vol. 1 (Cambridge, Mass., and Belgrade: Harvard University Press and Serbian Academy of Sciences, 1954), pp. 3–20. For further information on the importance of the fieldwork, see John Miles Foley, *Oral-Formulaic Theory and Research: An Introduction and Annotated Bibliography* (New York: Garland, 1985), pp. 3–77.

sources. Nikola did write down songs from uncle Ðuro, including the Kosovo song I just mentioned. The world of literacy had no great effect on the Kučinari's world of orality. The latter was aware of the existence of the other world but knew extremely little of its content. There was no merger. Written literary works did not penetrate the village of Burmazi.

It was different with the younger generation, with young Ðuro and Nikola, who, incidentally, was at least fifteen years older than his brother. To both of them the world of literacy was open and had potential, and both of them knew something of the world of orality. It was around them; they were born into it. I do not know what young Ðuro did with it, except to copy songs from published books, because he was not a practitioner of oral traditional songs, although he surely at this period knew the lyric songs of his village—what we think of as folk songs, in distinction from the epic—and the "town songs"—what we might call popular songs—in Stolac and possibly Mostar. But I do know what Nikola did with his literacy. We can see its effect on his own epic songs, for Nikola was a singer. He learned to sing from his uncles and to a much lesser extent from others in the world of orality of Burmazi. Later, after he had learned to read, he also learned songs from the songbooks, when he came into contact with them. An analysis of his songs recorded by Parry as early as the summer of 1933 reveals the extent of the merger in his case, for merger it was. It would be interesting to see whether we can determine the borderline with any precision. His songs—some of them, at least—were the earliest collected by Parry,[6] and his editing and commenting on them are to be found in the early volumes of "Ćor Huso." These were not published in *The Making of Homeric Verse*.[7]

In "Ćor Huso" Parry analyzed some of Nikola's songs and compared them with the songbook versions that Nikola had read. Nikola had in fact learned his version of "Marko Kraljević and Musa the Highwayman" from one of his uncles, but he had read it

6. On the Milman Parry Collection of Oral Literature at Harvard University, the archive that includes the oral material gathered by Parry and Lord in 1933-1935 and during later trips by Lord and David E. Bynum, see n. 5, above, and Bynum, "Child's Legacy Enlarged: Oral Literary Studies at Harvard Since 1856," *Harvard Library Bulletin* 22 (1974): 237-67.

7. Adam Parry, ed., *The Making of Homeric Verse: The Collected Papers of Milman Parry* (Oxford: Clarendon Press, 1971).

later in a songbook. Here is Parry's account of the way in which Parry obtained Nikola's text:[8]

> Two nights later we again returned to the *kafana* and Nikola who evidently had been thinking about the old songs he knew sang us *Marko and Musa,* or rather, he sang only the beginning, since unlike the first evening when the *kafana* had been deserted there were a number of other workers and acquaintances of his—it was Saturday night—and he was self-conscious. Moreover, there was a great deal of noise and indifference. However, when we learned that he could write we asked him to write the poem for us, which he agreed to do. When we returned to the *kafana* for the third time, another two nights later, he gave us the manuscript of the song he had promised, but his discomfiture in regard to his friends had grown and that evening he did not sing pretending first, after much working over the *gusle* of the *kafana,* that he could not get it in order. . . .

Marko Kraljević i Musa Keserdija

Nikola	Podrugović
Vino pije Musa Keserdija	Vino pije Musa Arbanasa

U Stambolu u krčmi bijeloj.
Kad se Musa nakitio vina,

Pa mu vino u pamet udrilo,	
Tada pijan Musa besjedio:	Onda poče pijan besjediti:
"Evo ima devet godin dana	"Evo ima devet godinica,
Odkad dvorim cara u Stambolu:	Kako dvorim cara u Stambolu:
Ne izdvori' konja ni oružja,	Ni izdvorih konja ni oružja,

Ni dolame nove ni polovne.

Danas hoću jemin učiniti,	Al tako mi moje vjere tvrde,
Odvrću se u primorje ravno,	Odvrć' ću se u ravno primorje,
	Zatvoriću skele oko mora,
	I drumove okolo primorja.
Sagradiću prebijelu kulu,	Načiniću kulu u primorju,

Oko kule gvozdene čengele

---

8. The following excerpt is taken from an unpublished section of Parry's field notes, entitled *Ćor Huso;* for published sections from the same document, see Parry, ed., *Making of Homeric Verse,* pp. 437–64.

I napustit izvor vodu hladnu
Napraviću visoka vješala   Vješaću mu hodže i
                                                          hadžije."
Da ću vješat hodže i hadžije.
Otimaću trgovačko blago,
Po primorju drume zatvoriti."
Što je pijan Musa besjedio,   Što god Ture pjano
                                                          govorilo,
Ono bješe trjezan učinio.   To trijezno bješe učinilo.

While it is clear that the songbook has had some influence on Nikola's text, it is also clear that Nikola had not memorized its text.

Marko Kraljević and Musa the Highwayman

Nikola	Podrugović
Musa the Highwayman is drinking wine	Musa the Albanian is drinking wine

In Stambol in the white tavern,
When Musa had drunk his fill of wine,

The wine went to his head, Then, drunk, Musa said:	Then he began, drunk, to say:
"It is now nine years of days	"It is now nine years
Since I serve the sultan in Stambol.	That I serve the sultan in Stambol:
I've not earned a horse or arms.	I have not earned a horse or arms.

Nor a coat, new or used.

Today I shall make an oath, I shall revolt to the coastland level	By my firm faith, I'll revolt to the level coastland
	I shall close the ferries along the sea
	And the roads around the coastland
I shall build a white tower,	I shall make a tower in the coastland,

Around the tower iron hooks

And release a course of cold water

I shall erect high gallows	I shall hang priests and pilgrims."
I shall hang priests and pilgrims,	

I shall take away the
   merchants' treasure,
I shall close the roads in the
   coastland."

| What, when drunk, Musa said | Whatever the Turk spoke drunkenly, |
| That he had done when sober | That he had done soberly. |

There now followed five days in which he kept putting off our engagement by pretending that he had work which prevented him coming in the evening, although he gave me the manuscript of the *Ropstvo Stojana Jankovića* (Text 2), but by the next Saturday he and the others had become used to us and he was again willing to sing. He then sang for us the beginning of *Marko Kraljević i Vuča Đeneral,* preceded by his *pripjev.* There were other workmen present who knew how to sing and they took the *gusle* from him when he paused to rest, and sang themselves. One, a Montenegrin, sang the *pripjev* which was later sung at Budva by Simo Milić (number 426), and a Hercegovinian from Bileća sang the beginning of a *ženidba,* playing the instrument with great sureness and carrying over the last syllable of each verse, as is largely the manner of that region, but singing it gutterally way below pitch and obscuring it almost to a shout. Nikola was piqued at all this. "Pjeva trbuhom" [he sings from his belly], he remarked, and after this his attitude in singing for me became less and less one of discomfiture and more and more that of one engaged in a distinctive performance.

A few nights later at the café I gave him the duplicate of the typed copy I had made of his manuscript, which pleased him. We then asked him to sing the song again. I had told Kutuzov (on the basis of what I knew from Murko) that there would be a very great variation between the poem as he had written it in the manuscript and as he would sing it. This Kutuzov would not believe, but stated that he could note down the variations as Nikola sang. These, of course, proved to be so numerous that he could scribble only a small part of them, and then on the transposition or omission of some verses he lost the place for a while and finally gave up the attempt. Those variations which he noted on the manuscript and which he was later able to read have been noted in the following text of the poem. This procedure of comparing the manuscript with the singing discomfitted Nikola greatly.

There is no need here to remark on these variants since the examples which we have obtained this year, by means of discs, of the same song sung more than once by the same singer afford fuller and far more exact evidence on the problem of variation in the singer's rendering of the same song.

While Nikola did read some songbooks in order to pick up a song or so for his singing, I do not think that he read them for "reading pleasure." Nor did he take advantage, so far as I know, of the libraries or bookstores of Dubrovnik to acquaint himself with the works of Serbo-Croatian literature, which were richly ready at hand. But he was interested in politics and read the newspaper, *Politika,* regularly. As a Roman Catholic—although not much of a churchgoer, as I recall—he was a Croat in politics. He was not a "militant" Croat, but a devoted follower of Maček. So for Nikola the world of literacy was not the written literature, abundant as it was, but the newspaper, perhaps including whatever of literature appeared in it. Had Nikola stayed in Stolac (or Burmazi) he might have gone to the hotel and read the newspaper, but certainly the city atmosphere of Dubrovnik, particularly in Pero Arbulić's wine-shop, which he frequented, encouraged and developed that section of the world of literacy, and he loved to discuss what he read—and heard—with his friends.

A number of published books and brochures bridge the two worlds for those who wish to read them. These are the several popularly printed songbooks, frequently small paperbacks, sometimes containing only one song, a few pages. It was one of these that was the "source" for Avdo Međedović's "The Wedding of Smailagić Meho." This group of varied texts is one of the most important manifestations in the area of South Slavic oral traditional epic of the merging of the two worlds of orality and literacy. Parry bought a great many of these songbooks in 1934 and 1935, and the Parry Collection is rich in these influential publications. To the best of my knowledge, they have not been studied, and I am now going through them to segregate the various categories.

Although in what follows I will perforce because of my subject have something to say about written literature, about recording in writing of oral literature, and about imitation of oral literary style and other texts in gray areas, one must remember that during these centuries, up to the middle of the present one, a strong oral traditional literature flourished. I must stress that the effect of this activity in writing on the oral traditional songs themselves was minimal. For a long time, well into the present century—I am tempted to say up to the Second World War—what was being written down, or the imitations, affected the world of *literacy* and *not* the world of orality, which continued strong and healthy during all those years. This was especially true of the Moslem epic, which was still brilliant in the 1930s when Parry encountered it, as his collection bears witness. Our concern with the gray areas should not darken that and the rich Christian traditions.

Some of the songbooks contain bona fide oral traditional epic written down from singers, usually somewhat edited, but not necessarily. Through these little books, which often tell nothing about who dictated the songs, who wrote them down, or where, songs, or versions of songs, may become distributed in places where they were not previously known. The effect is that of the wandering singer, if you will—with the one difference, which may or may not be important, that a fixed text is thereby being propagated. To the traditional singer in the world of orality this may make no difference at all, because the reading of the text to him would be like the hearing of it from a singer, and he would treat it accordingly. That it was fixed would be of no interest to him, unless the person reading it to him indicated that this was the way it must be told or sung. Otherwise he would not hear it as fixed, even if he could read it himself, provided he was still a citizen of the world of orality. But for those in the world of literacy this printed version would likely become "the version" of the song, rather than simply one performance. To them the fixity would be important.

The earliest of these "paperbacks" that I have are two books by Jovan D. Milutinović, published in the 1870s in Beograd by N. Stefanović and Company. The first is entitled *Narodne Pesme*. This book is not part of a series, but, like a volume of a poet's poems, was published by subscription. At the end of the book is a list of the subscribers by cities, also giving their occupations. The largest group consisted of merchants, but there were a number of tavern keepers, a clerk, some teachers and farmers, a master sergeant, a house builder, a barber, and makers of moccasins, shoes, boots, and slippers. Several women bought the book for their daughters, and some men for their sons. This is a fascinating glimpse of the reading public—at least those willing to subscribe to a book—in the fourth quarter of the nineteenth century in the region north and west of Belgrade.

The songs in the little book are not traditional songs, in spite of the title, but they are national poems in the literary tradition of the lyric and satirical poet Branko Radičević. This is not surprising, since Jovan D. Milutinović clearly came from the Vojvodina, and Branko's name was on everyone's lips there. These poems belong to the cult of Serbdom. Many of Radičević's poems, including the long satirical *Put,* were written in rhymed couplets, some in octosyllables and some in decasyllables. The same is true of Jovan Milutinović, who also composes in stanzas of four, rarely also six, lines, rhyming *a a b b,* or *a a b b c c,* and inserts occasional twelve-syllable couplets. His 1874 volume has several kinds of poems, both narrative and lyric, but his little 1877 book is entirely epic. Its title is *Spev srpsko-crnogorskog rata protivu Turaka 1876 i devetodnevni bojevi Crnogoraca po dolinama Zete 1877* (Song of the Serbo-Montenegrin war against the Turks, 1876, and the nine-day battles of the Montenegrins in the valleys of Zeta, 1877). The poems are short and often consist of factual descriptions of action. For example, the "Boj na Malome Zvorniku" (pages 52–53) runs as follows.

Srpska vojska podigla se mlada,
    Pod Zvornik je došla iznenada;
Mali Zvornik čuvaju nizami,
    Regulani sve vojnici sami.
Prosu vatru srpska vojska mlada
    Na posadu tursku iznenada!
A i Turci živo pohitaše
    Sa Zvornika topom opališe.
Iz pušaka s grudobrana biju
    Srpski napad samo da odbiju.
Srbi topom na grudobran pale,
    Grudobrana sa svime razvale.
Sa svi strana juriš učiniše
    Mali Zvornik u ruke dobiše.
Još dva topa i dosta pušaka
    Beše pljena razna svakojaka.—
A nizami listom pobegoše,
    U Velji se Zvornik zatvoriše!
Tako Srbi hrabro se boriše,
    Mali Zvornik oni osvojiše!
Turska vojska kušala je bila
    Ne bi l' Mali Zvornik povratila.

Kušanje je Turke uvek skupo stalo,
   Dosta je Turaka mrtvih popadalo;—
Sada Mali Zvornik čuva vojska mlada
   I sa njime ona od danaske vlada.

The young Serbian army arose
Beneath Zvornik it arrived unexpectedly;
The troops are defending Mali Zvornik,
All regulars as soldiers.
The young Serbian army pours fire
Unexpectedly on the Turkish ambush!
But the Turks also struck sharply
And fired cannon from Zvornik.
They fired their rifles from the breastworks,
Only to fight off the Serbian attack.
The Serbs fired their cannon at the breastwork,
And destroyed the breastwork completely.
They attacked from all sides
And took Mali Zvornik into their hands.
Two more cannon and plenty of rifles
Were booty and various other things.—
The troops all fled,
Zvornik was closed in Velja!
So the Serbs fought bravely,
And won Zvornik!
The Turkish army had tried
To get back Mali Zvornik.
Trying was always costly for the Turks,
Many Turks were killed;—
Now the young army defends Mali Zvornik
And governs from today onward.

This banal and unadorned passage is a far cry from the richness of ornamentation in oral traditional poetry.

In the 1880s little songbooks began to proliferate. An excellent example is a series published by the Knjižara braće Jovanovića in Pančevo. It contained small paperbacks of forty or fifty pages each devoted to epic songs clustered around a given hero, such as Car Dušan, Ljutica Bogdan, Sibinjanin Janko, Banović Strahinja, Visoki Stefan, Serdar Stojan Janković, Vojvode Jakšići, and others, each having the additional title "u narodnim pesmama, Sa slikom." The texts were taken mainly from the Vuk Karadžić and Bogoljub Petranović collections, or others like them. They were, therefore, the best epic texts of their day, although the brochures never cited any sources. These booklets were not intended for the singers of oral traditional epic narrative but for loyal Serbs in the cities and towns who were interested in Serbian traditions, their own heritage.

The Jovanović brothers in Pančevo published a great variety of books and pamphlets. Some were intended for the Serbian Orthodox faithful, especially for young women. For them also (za žensku omladinu) they published cookbooks and books on housekeeping, and for grown young women (za odrasle devojke) *Young Women's World* (Devojački svet)! The brothers also published music for both voice and piano, including a Medley of Serbian Songs for piano (Smesa srpskih pesama) by Josif Ce. They had a line of books in fine bindings (elegantno vezane knige) including works of Serbian and foreign literatures, such as *Around the World in Eighty Days,* and a book entitled *Deklamator.*[9] This book was among those elegantly bound, obviously intended for the salons and parlors and local theatrical evenings in Pančevo, Belgrade, and elsewhere. Under the heading of "books for everyone," we find more Jules Verne, and on the back cover translations from Russian of a story by Sologub and of a historical tale by Karamzin, from Polish of a historical drama by Puzinin, from Czech of a tragedy by Kolar, and from German of "A Young Lady's Diary" (*Bolesnici,* Devojački dnevnik). It is into this literary and subliterary world of the early 1880s that the little songbooks emerged.

It was not until the world of literacy in Serbia was freed from the artificial literary language, Slaveno-srpski, that literature in the spoken Serbian language began to develop. And the impetus for that change came eventually from the world of orality. Slaveno-srpski was based on the Serbian recension of Church Slavic. Church Slavic was the language into which the Slavic apostles Cyril and Methodius translated the church books. It was the Slavic language spoken in the region of Salonica. Serbian monks modified it to some extent, thus forming the Serbian recension of Church Slavic. This became the literary language, and for a long time whatever was written in the Serbian lands was written in it.

9. Subtitled "A collection of Serbian and Croatian poems for recitation with instructions for reciting them" (an instructive note, indeed, for the worlds of orality and literacy).

Toward the end of the seventeenth century there was a great migration from the area around the patriarchate in Peć, led by Bishop Arsenije, to the Vojvodina, the region north of Belgrade. Under the impression that the purist literary Slavic was the Russian recension of Church Slavic, the leaders of this new settlement imported teachers from Russia, and it was thus that Slaveno-srpski was formed, an amalgam of the Serbian and the Russian recensions of Church Slavic. It was far removed from the spoken language of the people. Eighteenth-century Serbian literature, didactic, overprecious reading in romance for the young, especially young ladies, was written in Slaveno-srpski. Some people made a minor cult of trying to speak it, and they were later satirized in the early nineteenth-century comedies of Branislav Nušić.

Three figures played the most important role in establishing the new, indigenous literary language. They were Dositej Obradović, Vuk Karadžić, and Branko Radičević. Obradović was a transitional figure, and of these three Karadžić and Radičević were the most significant for us. Karadžić wrote a grammar and a dictionary, collected folk poetry, reformed the orthography, and brought the spoken language to the fore. Radičević put all this into practice in his lyric and satirical poetry in the vernacular. Folk speech and folk literature were catalysts in creating modern Serbian literature. The world of literacy, involved with an artificial and antiquated language no longer its own, if it ever was, turned to the world of orality for its roots. Although the parallel is not complete, one is reminded of the emergence of vernacular literatures in the rest of Europe during the Middle Ages.

The paperbacks produced in Pančevo mentioned above were of authentic oral traditional epics from the collections of Karadžić, Bogoljub Petranović, and others. Petranović also wrote several epics himself. One was published in Dubrovnik in 1894, *Pjesme o ratu rusko-turskom i o bojevima na Plevni godine 1877*.[10]

Petranović collected and published three volumes of epic songs, and there are three more in manuscript in the archives of the Serbian Academy in Belgrade, of which Widener Library has microfilms. It is not surprising that Petranović's poem on the Russo-

10. (Songs of the Russo-Turkish war and of the battles at Plevna in the year 1877), Dubrovnik: Naklada Knjižare Dragutina Pretnera, 2d ed., n.d.

Turkish war of 1877 reads for the most part like an oral traditional song; it is only sixty-six lines long. Here are some samples of its style:

O RATU RUSKO-TURSKOM
1877 god.

Aleksandar gospodu saziva,
Po izboru kneze i vojvode.
Kad gospodu na v'jeće sazvao,
Ovako je njima besjedio:
"Vi, gospodo, meni svjeta dajte,
Što da radim od Turaka kletih
I njihova cara silenoga. . . .

Alexander called his lords together,
His chosen princes and army leaders.
When he had called his lords to council,
He spoke in this way to them:
"My lords, give me your advice,
What to do about the cursed Turks
And their ruthless sultan. . . .

The Turks are threatening to slaughter their Christian subjects in the Balkans.

Tužbe su mi dodijale teške
I mene su rasplakale gorko.
Već što ćemo, moja braćo draga?
Hoćemo li braću izbaviti,
Dok ih Turci ne pokolju žive?"

Their plaints have beset me
And made me to weep bitterly.
What shall we do, my dear brothers?
Shall we rescue our brothers,
Before the Turks slaughter them alive?"

Gorčakov advises the tsar to raise an army and defeat the Turks.

"Sultan tebi poklonit se mora,
Ili svoje izgubiti carstvo,
Odseliti u Aziju s Turcim,
U njihovu domovinu staru."

"The sultan must submit to you,
Or lose his empire,

And resettle with his Turks in Asia,
In their ancient homeland."

This scene, as all who know the oral traditional epics will recognize, is perfectly traditional, in concept and in style and language. The tsar raises an army of a hundred thousand soldiers, "all heroes like living fire, horsemen and brave footsoldiers."

Ruska vojska Dunav prebrodila,
A dener'o Mihajil Skobeljev
Na svom konju Dunav preplivao.
Na njeg' Turci oganj oborili
Iz topova i bojnih pušaka,
Zastavu mu zrnjem iskrpili,
Da joj krpljač nikad ne trebuje;
Ali njega pogodili nisu, . . .

The Russian army crossed the Danube,
And General Mihajil Skobeljev
Swam across the Danube on his horse.
The Turks fired at him
From cannon and battle rifles,
Tore his banner to shreds with bullets,
So that it never needed a sewer,
But they did not hit him, . . .

Needless to say the Russians were victorious.

The poem on the battles at Plevna is 727 lines long and, in contradistinction to the preceding poem on the Russo-Turkish war, one can tell from the very beginning that it is not an oral traditional poem. Here is its opening:

Kartadina u stara vremena
Rimljanima, ljuckim divovima,
Bješe čudo sile i junaštva.
U drugome ratu puničkome
Strah zadade i slavnome Rimu,
A u trećem boju osudnome
Kartadina pade i propade,
Rimljani joj slavu ukopaše . . .

Carthage in ancient times
Was to the Romans, giants among men,
A wonder of might and heroism.
In the Second Punic War,

It put fear into glorious Rome,
But in the third and crucial battle
Carthage fell and never rose again.
The Romans buried its glory . . .

The traditional singers of the Balkans do not sing of the Second
Punic War or of Carthage. These names belong to the world of
literacy to which Petranović belonged, although because of his
deep experiences in collecting traditional epic he could write in
the style and language of the oral traditional epic as well. The two
worlds were separate and could be told apart readily enough, but
they merged in Petranović.

It is significant to note that while some of the *pjesmarice* such
as the one of Petranović just discussed, and another, *Postanak
knjaza u Crnoj Gori u narodnim pesmama,*[11] are clearly not
narodne pjesme, yet they are in the unrhymed epic decasyllable
rather than in the rhymed couplets of the world of literacy. Here is
the way the latter poem begins.

Hvala Bogu, čuda velikoga,
Što se sluči lomnoj gori Crnoj!
Prestavi se Petrović vladika,
Crnogorska pohvala i dika,
I drugoga Srpskoga naroda
Filozofska glava izabrana.
Ucvijeli malo i veliko;
Zaplaka se i staro i mlado.
Ma ako se Petar prestavio,
Nakom sebe način ostavio,
Bratu Peru bješe ostavio,
Bratu Peru i bratu Đorđiji,
I ostalim' od zemlje glavarim',

Praise be to God, it was a great miracle
That happened in rugged Montenegro!
Petrović the prince-bishop passed away,
Montenegro's boast and pride
And of the other Serbian people
Its chosen philosophical leader.
Great and small mourned;
Old and young wept.

11. Novi Sad: Srpska knižara učitelskog deoničarskog društva "Natošević," n.d.,
with no author given.

> But if Petar has passed away,
> He left behind him a legacy
> Left it to brother Petar,
> To brother Petar and to brother Đorđe,
> And to the other leaders of the land.

One word alone in this passage betrays the fact that it is not from an oral traditional song. "Filozofska" is strictly from the world of literacy. It is also to be noted that the poem is not written in rhymed couplets, yet it does not eschew them entirely. Examples are found in lines three and four, *vladika, dika;* and in lines nine and ten, *prestavio, ostavio.* One must remember, however, that occasional rhymed couplets are common enough in the traditional style. The rhyme in lines nine and ten resembles the ordinary kind in which participles rhyme naturally and the ideas they contain, of dying and bequeathing, complement each other also quite naturally. And creating a rhyme by echoing the last two syllables of Njegoš's title, *vladika,* with a word for "pride" (*dika*) is poetically effective, especially when *Petrović* in one line alliterates with *pohvala,* another word for "pride." Yet, it should be noted, the poem belongs in the world of literacy, not the world of orality. Its style and much of its language would be accessible to the traditional singer only if he were to migrate to the world of literacy. Although reading and writing are usually skills that aid in that migration, they are not absolutely necessary for the journey. The traditional singer would have to learn the ideas and attitudes of the world of literacy in order to live in that new world. He would have to think in terms of a hero who is a "select philosophical head" of a people as well perhaps as a "good hero" (dobar junak).

The published oral traditional epics and their imitations encouraged members of the intelligentsia to write more imitations. It was the Serbian thing to do, because these epics were examples of Serbian national treasure. That the treasury held counterfeit as well as genuine coinage was irrelevant. It was all in the spirit of Serbian nationalism and served the cause.

Before I close this section of my paper I must mention another interlocking tradition of oral epic in the South Slavic lands. It must be remembered that from the fifteenth century onward there were two branches of oral traditional epic in the South Slavic regions, one Christian, the other Moslem. Each had its own overt religious as well as nationalistic cause. Avdo Mededović's songs are prime examples of this. Their heroes are models of the correct behavior of the Moslem lord and of the ideals, values, and goals of the Turkish empire. Avdo's magnificent songs were long, reaching to twelve and thirteen thousand lines. Little paperbacks of Moslem epic songs appeared in Sarajevo in the 1920s published by a bookstore in Sarajevo. These included the *Smailagić Meho* that was read to Avdo Mededović, and many others. I have at hand in addition to it a songbook containing songs reprinted from Kosta Hörmann's two-volume collection and from Matica Hrvatska's *Hrvatske narodne pjesme,* Vol. 3,[12] and another songbook whose last two titles are also from Matica Hrvatska's vol. 3.[13] These represent popular editions of songs published in learned volumes. The larger volumes contained many songs, with introduction and notes, and were expensive. The little paperbacks had only a few songs, no commentary at all, and were cheap. They were like the publications already commented on from Pančevo. Since the songs themselves are from the world of orality, they were wholly accessible to its citizens, who indeed created them. In spite of the fact that they are written down and can be read, they belong to the world of orality. So they are now accessible to the world of literacy, to which they were not accessible until they were written down and published. It is an intriguing question whether the world of literacy has as great a difficulty in comprehending the world of orality as we have found that the world of orality has in understanding the world of literacy. The gap is felt on both sides. This subject is central to the problem of the relationship of the two worlds and requires far more study than it has had. *It is the accessibility of the products of the world of orality to the world of literacy that is important.* The little books described above were intended for the businessmen in the Sarajevo shops to bolster their feeling of a heritage from a Moslem heroic age, for the former Moslem officials, aristocrats, the "potomci begovi" (the once-upon-a-time beys) to remember the past glories that were once sung of in their courts, which were now relegated to, or remained only in, the coffeehouses. If the literate businessman in the small town, such as

12. *Narodni junak Lički Beg Mustajbeg* (Sarajevo: M. Milanović u Sarajevu, 1927).

13. *Junačka smrt Hivzibega Džumišića, Boj pod Banja Lukom, i Junaštvo Duralagića Meha* (Sarajevo: M. Milanović u Sarajevu, 1927).

Mededović's partner in their butcher shop, Himzo Džafić, read them to singers like Avdo, who learned new *stories* from them (not texts, you understand), that was a side benefit. Himzo was an intermediary between the two worlds.

* * *

Just as the new poems—not songs, because they were never sung—of the 1870s, 1880s, and 1890s formed a part of the written literature of their time, not of the oral traditional literature that they imitated, so the poems in the twentieth century dealing with the Balkan Wars and First World War continued that section of written literature. Maja Bošković-Stulli has used the term *pučka književnost* ("popular literature") to designate the earlier manifestations of this genre,[14] but I am not sure it can be properly applied to all of the poems I have in mind, particularly some in this century. They are not intended for the members of the "orality" community, nor actually for the elite, but for those usually reached by political or national propaganda, for these poems, particularly those around World War I, belong in a category approaching propaganda. King Alexander was hailed as the "great unifier" of the Serbs, Croats, and Slovenes in a united Yugoslavia, which was an attempt to keep the country together at a time of crisis when the king was killed.

Perhaps typical is a little paperback with the title *Nove narodne pjesme* (New Folk Songs) sung by Milovan M. Šupić of Gacko.[15] I have known Gacko well since October 1934, and the booklet intrigued me. It contains five poems—again, these were all written and never sung—four in often faulty rhymed couplets and one in octosyllables. The first is to King Alexander, the first lines of which form an encomium of the king. The bulk of the poem is a graphic account of the king's assassination in Marseilles. The octosyllabic poem is a short one to the fatherland (Našoj Otadžbini). There is a song on the formation of the first Serbian volunteer division in 1916 in Odessa and its battles in the Dobrudja, and one on the Italian-Abyssinian war, 1935-1936. The last poem in the booklet is on Austrian mobilization in 1914 and relates

14. See, for example, her "O pojmovima usmena i pučka književnost i njihovim nazivima," *Umjetnost riječi* 17 (1973): 149–84, 237–60.
15. Sombor: Jugoslavenska štampanija i papirnica, 1936.

the poet's own experiences (moji doživljaji). This consists mainly of an uninspired cataloging of the places where his division went, of being herded in and out of freight cars, and so on. It is real *pučka književnost* at its worst, just badly written literature, its only relationship to the world of orality being a pale and frequently unmetrical decasyllable and an occasional well-worn formula borrowed from the oral traditional epic.

It is now trite to say that thanks to radio and television the world of sound, or orality, has widened. Radio and television were accompanied by more drastic and wide-reaching changes to the world of orality. I recall in the sixties, as I sat in the restaurant of the new hotel in Stolac, Hercegovina, and watched a large television screen with news, feeling that the world of Stolac had changed. A vast change was taking place in social structure and way of life. Schools were multiplying; there was a concerted effort to eliminate as much illiteracy as possible in a short time. With national socialism, collectivization and other regimentation were being instituted, in the case of collectivization to be only partially successful. An agrarian country was developing new industries, and cities were growing. An exchange was beginning between the rural and urban communities, as peasants lived in their villages near the city but worked in town. Some of this had begun earlier, but at this time it was moving fast. The newspaper and, I believe, the radio—although I don't seem to remember it—were in the old hotel in Stolac in the thirties, but they did not seem to have changed the culture very much. In the fifties and sixties the change was being deeply felt.

Another aspect of cultural change was apparent in the realm of transportation. In 1963 in the Pešter area David Bynum and I were just barely able in his Volkswagen to get to the center of the plateau at Karajukići bunari, the end of the trail, over a road that was mainly a cart track. The following year we met a bus on an improved road and learned that the road was being extended across the plateau and down on the far side to Rožaje. The isolation of that singing area, as I always view such lovely places, was broken by the beginnings of what would be a new cultural invasion. I have not been back there since.

There were still some songbooks in the stores in Novi Pazar and Sjenica, but not the old ones I have described earlier. Tito had taken the place of King Alexander, and, although a concerted effort was being made by those who wrote the poems to have a

continuity of tradition, those who wrote of Tito were no more traditional people than those who wrote of Alexander.

There were still traditional singers in those days back in the villages, and traditional life was still to be found. On the road from
Stolac to Dabrica—a road over which we drove, where Parry and I
had ridden on horses over a trail—a horse frightened by David
Bynum's Volkswagen kicked in one of its headlights. There were
still places where horses shied at automobiles—one of Parry's half-
joking criteria for singing country. And in Sjenica we began to
record songs from a singer, who asked at one point that we
postpone the remainder of the recording for a day, because he had
to attend a meeting. He was an "elder" in his tribal community,
and the elders in this area still had a jurisdiction in local criminal
proceedings, even those involving murder. It was just such a traditional meeting of elders that our singer was to attend. In feuds
between families or tribes it would seem that the traditional system of justice in this predominantly peasant herding society still
was in force. Only when it failed would the "official" legal organization assert its authority.

Thus history, or pseudo-history, written for didactic purposes,
as support for nationalist causes, or for political or ideological
propaganda, had gradually over the centuries been replacing the
deeper mythic implications of the oral traditional narrative. In the
seventeenth century, the process was already under way on the
Dalmatian coast, and it acquired momentum in the eighteenth. It
was probably dominant in the nineteenth and twentieth centuries, but it had not entirely obliterated the mythic elements,
which would persist in carrying their message, however sub-
merged, as long as the traditional poetics and the traditional narrative patterns survived. Mythic themes of the initiatory hero, of
the return of a hero presumed dead after a long absence, of the
death of the substitute, became historicized and nationalized.
Age-old and worldwide patterns and symbols, stories of mon-
sters, of heroes of double birth, of the mingling of the human and
of the divine world were sometimes lost but were more often
rationalized and reinterpreted. It is to these processes as they are
manifested in poetics and story structure that we now turn.

RING COMPOSITION AND DUPLICATION IN "SMAILAGIĆ MEHO"

While much has been written about ring composition in the

Homeric poems, in Old English poetry, and in Scottish ballads, for example, there has been no analysis that I have seen of ring composition in any certifiable oral traditional epic song. Is it true that ring composition is found in true oral traditional narrative song? In what follows I will examine Avdo Mededović's "Smailagić Meho" for signs of ring composition.

The opening assembly theme of "Smailagić Meho" turns out, as a matter of fact, to be a good example of ring composition. Here is its scheme:

> 1. Description and listing of *nobles* with Hasan paša Tiro at their head.
> 2. The intervention of *Hasan paša Tiro*.
> 3. *Cifrić Hasanaga*'s speech to Meho.
> 4. *Meho*'s response.
> 3. *Cifrić Hasanaga*'s response to Meho.
> 2. *Hasan paša Tiro* has the petition prepared and gives his blessings.
> 1. Listing of *nobles* as they sign the petition and as they say farewell to Meho.

This is a perfectly acceptable ring. Even though Avdo did not plan it consciously as such, the ring pattern is there, inherent in the narrative itself, when told fully by a skilled singer. The focus of the narrative, the center of the ring, is significant in the story. It is the *narrative* and its meaning that make the ring in the first place. The narrative creates the form rather than the form shaping the narrative. The dramatic confrontation between uncle and nephew in "Smailagić Meho" with its centerpiece of the nephew's angry speech—which is to provide motivation for the entire poem, and to state the danger to orderly succession from father and uncle to son, a mythic theme—is framed in the setting of hierarchical social organization and the statement of heroic values. At the beginning of the ring, the young man has not been allowed to play any role in the activities of his society, but at the end of the scene his role in that hierarchy is defined and the first steps are taken to realize it fully. Meho's threat to disturb the social order because he is not yet a full member of it is answered by the setting in motion of the actions that will make him ultimately acceptable, namely to send him to the vizier in Buda for accreditation.

It is sometimes thought that the singer needs the ring to help him remember the episode. Actually, I believe, he needs only to tell the scene fully and well in his accustomed manner following his instinct for balancing similarities and opposites for the organization of the scene in a ring, or in some other configuration, to unfold itself and be revealed. The Russian term for performing a song is *izpolnyenye*, "filling out," "fulfilling," an excellent term for the process involved.

The balancings of corresponding elements are not necessarily, or even usually, in exactly the same words. Avdo has several formulations to express the basic idea of a passage. He makes use of a number of multiforms for such purposes. For example, in the first circle of the first ring Avdo has given a full description of the nobles of Kanidža, their numbers, and their ranks. He has a shorter form of this, and it is two versions of the shorter form that he uses in the element at the end of the circle corresponding to the listing of the assembly. It is employed as a *leitmotif* in music to suggest the whole. Here it is in lines 1039–48, when the assembly's leaders sign the petition and Hasan paša Tiro confirms it:

> Potpisa ga pedeset delija,
> A šezdeset aga kanidžkijc'   1040
> I *četiri* kanidžka *ajana*,
> Dva *dizdara*, dvan'es' *buljukbaša*,
> I dvadeset turski' *bajraktara*.
> Po mandatu turiše muhure.
> Ćatibi su mandat načinili,   1045
> Delije su potpis udarile,
> Sva gospoda turajli muhure.
> *Hasan* ga je *paša* potvrdijo,

> The fifty men-at-arms signed it,
> And the sixty aghas of Kanidža,   1040
> And the *four elders* of Kanidža,
> The *two city commanders,* the twelve *captains,*
> And the twenty Turkish *standard-bearers.*
> They put their seals on the petition,
> The scribes completed the petition,   1045
> The men-at-arms put their signatures on it,
> All the nobles put their seals on it,
> *Hasan paša* confirmed it.

It appears again after the petition has been given by the paša to Meho's uncle, who in turn delivers it to Meho, and the paša has given his blessing for the journey. Meho kisses the paša's hand and

then his uncle's (lines 1073–74). Then the others follow in lines
1075–80:

> Sivi soko na noge skočijo,
> *Hasan paši* ruci poletijo,
> Gazijsku mu poljubijo ruku,
> Pa amidži Cifriću Hasanu,
> *Dva dizdara, četiri ajana,*   1075
> I starijeg bega svakojega,
> Pa starijeg bašu i bimbašu,
> Pa starijeg svakog *buljukbašu.*
> *Bajraktari* raširiše ruke,
> Sokoli se grle sa sokolom.   1080

> The gray falcon leaped to his feet,
> He flew to *Hasan paša*'s hand,
> And kissed the hero's hand,
> Then that of his uncle Cifrić Hasan,
> The *two city commanders,* the *four elders*   1075
> And each older bey,
> The older commanders of one and of five hundred,
> Then each older *captain.*
> The *standard-bearers* stretched forth their arms,
> The falcons embraced the falcon.   1080

Note that this passage begins with the "gray falcon" (sivi soko)
in line 1071 and ends with "the falcons embraced the falcon"
(sokoli se grle sa sokolom). It is typical of Avdo that he has varied
the passage to suit the requirements of the narrative, but several of
the elements remain to reveal the basic theme.

Note also that these two multiforms of the leitmotif are themselves clustered in ring formation around the paša's blessing, a ring
within a ring, and that the whole scene ends most movingly as
tears of joy come to the eyes of all with the shared happiness of
young Meho.

To return to the story. Following the opening assembly is a brief
linking theme that takes Meho and his uncle back to the house of
his father, Smail, to report what has been happening in the assembly, of which the father has as yet no knowledge.

The next ring scene, too, is handsomely arranged and reaches
from the report of Meho's uncle to his brother Smail to the assign-
ing of Osman as Meho's companion with instructions from Smail.
At the present time I see the preparation of the horses and the

scene of departure as a separate element. It is a theme that is repeated in the two hospitality episodes on the journey to Buda, which follow.

The first item in this ring is the conversation of the two brothers, Meho's uncle and father, while Meho stands at attention doing them honor. Hasanaga, the uncle, reports to Smail what happened in the assembly, and Smail sends Meho to his mother to be dressed in the clothes sent him at his birth by the sultan. In the second circle of the ring we find, quite appropriately, Meho with his mother. It is a scene of elaborate ritual adornment, of the dressing of Meho to appear in the robes of his new role for his father's approval. There is a hint here in his mother's attitude also of the coming wedding. The center of the ring is Meho's appearance and his father's approval. Then, in the circle corresponding to Meho's ceremonial dressing is the ceremonial instructing of Meho by his father. This is followed by the preparation of the young man's new guardian, not a father figure like his uncle, but rather a special kind of companion, a sponsor, namely Osman. Osman has served Meho's father and is now assigned to serve Meho. Smail has given his son his father's position vis-à-vis Osman.

Schematized, the ring looks like this:

1. *Meho* with *father and uncle*
2. *Meho* with *mother*—ritual preparation of Meho
3. *Meho* appears for *father*'s approval
2. *Meho* with *father*—instructions
1. *Meho* with *father and Osman*—ritual preparation of Osman

Meho has passed from father and uncle to Osman.

These first two rings are to some degree duplicates. The first shows Meho in the large social group of the assembly gaining that group's approval. The second shows him in the family group, finally receiving his father's approval. With these two complementary rings completed, the singer is ready to move to the journey.

The journey, from the departure from home to the return to his father in Kanidža, is a complex tale and covers thousands of lines. The first element in it is a pair of duplicated rings both beginning with arrival at a night's lodging, reception, food, sleep, food, farewells, departure the next morning. These two episodes, well structured, well differentiated, are very important because the Christian "kmets" (head villagers) at both stops echo Bosnian

Moslem ideals. They continue presenting the values of the assembly scene, which were made more explicit in Meho's father's attitude toward the vizier in Buda. At the first stop, however, the "kmet" intimates that all is not well with the vizier and that Meho and Osman should be cautious in Buda. We are not unprepared, thanks to this incident, for the revelations about the vizier that are brought out dramatically and violently in the next episode. It is not by chance that the central pivots of the ring in this "hospitality" pair are the conversations of Meho and Osman with their hosts. There are differences of tone and of content between the two, similar as they are in other respects. They follow the same pattern:

    Arrival
    1. seen at a distance
(1) 2. guessing as to who they are
    3. realizing they are Meho and Osman
    4. instructions to household about their reception
    Reception
    1. met in courtyard
(2) 2. dismounting
    3. horses taken
    4. Meho and Osman into the house and seated
    Entertainment
    1. conversation with host (a. vizier; b. old better than young)
(3) 2. food
    3. sleep
    Preparation for Departure
    1. rising and dressing
(2) 2. down to courtyard
(4) 3. horses brought
    4. mounting
    Departure
(1) 1. gifts and farewells to household
(5) 2. riding from the courtyard
    3. riding across the plain

The Entertainment section is the central portion of the ring.

It would be fine for symmetry if under Entertainment the item *Conversation* came between *Food* and *Sleep,* but the natural order in the real world of the Balkans is conversation (while the food is being prepared), food, and sleep, and Avdo was following the order of real life.

Avdo did not invent the two stops. They were in the published text that was read to him. The names of Vuk (Vukašin; in his source Toroman Vuk) and Vujadin were not his invention either. But all his source said was that Meho and Osman were well received and well entertained. The rest is Avdo and his customary way of filling out and enriching an incident. In short, Avdo has himself created the rings by telling the tale fully.

These "hospitality" stops—unimportant in his source except as indicators of distance, but elaborated and made significant by Avdo—are only the second element in the journey sequence, which started with Departure.

In the first scene, the assembly, loyalty to the sultan on the part of the Bosnian nobles was stressed, with Meho's threatened treachery a foil for that idea, as well as, on the personal level, a decisive move in his own growing up. In the next scene, that of Meho with his family, the vizier is presented by Meho's father, Smail, as a loyal friend of the sultan. In these two pre-journey scenes the emphasis was on Meho's threatened revolt with its open warning of the possibility that he might join the Christian enemy and thus become a traitor. This is ironic—and Avdo and his audience were aware of the irony—because he will soon begin to learn who the real traitor is, whom it will be his destiny to remove. In the first hospitality scene he hears doubts expressed about the vizier. In the next scene after the two stops of the journey the whole ghastly truth of the vizier's treachery is dramatically revealed. Meho's adolescent tantrum of "I'll run away to the enemy and come back and kill you all" has been an ironic introduction to the main action and message of the song, which concern Bosnia and the Empire and the loyalty of the Bosnian nobles to the sultan.

In the scene that follows, Meho and Osman arrive at the river Klima and cross the mighty bridge onto the plain of Muhač before Buda. The plain is the setting for the crucial meeting of Meho with Fatima and his "betrothal" to her. A coach appears coming from Buda, drawn by twelve mares and surrounded by an escort of fifty soldiers, imperial Janissaries, to judge from their uniforms. The description is full and rich, as is usual with Avdo. The escorts are symbols of the might and glory of the empire. Meho and Osman wonder at them and decide to approach and find out who they are and who is in the coach. As they draw near they hear a screaming in the coach, and Meho approaches the captain of the guard and inquires politely who the occupant of the coach is. Meho, you will remember, is a Border noble, magnificently dressed and armed and magnificently and suitably accompanied by Osman. They are on equal footing with other nobles of the empire. The screaming breaks that lofty tone, and so does the rudeness of the captain, who says that Meho must be either drunk or crazy. He should move aside and mind his own business. He adds that he can see that Meho is of good family, but that he, the captain, is a member of the imperial household and has to carry out commands. Were anyone to hinder him in that he would kill him. When Osman comes up to them, the captain, calling Osman and Meho bandits, tells them to get out of the way.

Here is Meho's first test of loyalty, honor, and bravery. Osman looks at the boy to see what his reaction is. The young man's eyes are bloodshot with rage, his hair bristles, and his hand goes to his sword. Then he looks at Osman. Will his companion support him? This is a test for Osman too. Osman realizes what is in Meho's mind (this, by the way, is in the text; I am not putting thoughts into Osman's head) and reassures him in a fine speech, which ends with Osman asking Meho whether he wants to take on the fifty Janissaries or the captain. Meho replies by drawing his sword and dispatching the captain. Osman engages the soldiers. The tests of honor and loyalty between Meho and Osman have been passed. And we approach the center of the scene, and of a ring as well.

Meho, who has assured himself that Osman doesn't need him, cuts down the curtains of the coach and sees the lovely girl within, wonders at her, and asks who she is and what has happened. Her eyes are closed, and she thinks it is the captain speaking and curses him. Meho tells her she is mistaken and he wants to see her eyes. She opens them. Then she tells the long story about the treachery of the vizier in Buda and the fate of those nobles who were loyal to the sultan. Some have been killed, others, including Fatima's father, Zajim Alibey, have been exiled to Baghdad, the other extreme of the empire. Now, at last, all has been revealed. We know now what Kmet Vukašin meant when he warned Meho and Osman to be cautious in Buda.

There are at least two other levels, or interwoven strands, typical of Homer in manner, that are further brought out in this episode. Note the contrast between the two families, both of which are loyal to the sultan. The Cifrići, to which Smail and his brother Hasan belong, and of which Meho is the scion and fond hope for the future, are favored of the sultan, in direct contact with him, and in a Bosnia that is a model of loyalty. This is in contrast with the fate of the loyal family of Zajim Alibey in Buda, outside of the Bosnian center. Father and daughter are separated by traitors. The family of Zajim will die out. One family is solid and assured of a future great destiny; the other is split and destined to extinction. The balance and contrast are clear.

Another level is the personal and mythic one of the initiatory hero. This is ancient, of course, but in this story two or even three stages of growth are combined: the proving of the hero's worth as a man in battle, his gaining of a bride, and eventually his assuming of his father's position of leadership. It seems that in the processes of oral traditional narrative patterns overlap in time, and in the course of generation layers of story coalesce. The result is a fabric of great complexity and richness, when the weaver is sensitive to the nuances of his inherited material.

Sometimes starting threads may be added and mingled with the other colors in the tapestry. After Fatima has told how she had heard of Meho and that he had been marked by her parents as her husband, Meho accepts her, for he has fallen in love with her. Eventually, when Osman has disposed of the soldiers and rejoins Meho and Fatima, Meho orders him to turn the coach around and head back with it and the horses to Buda. Here is literally the pivotal point of the ring, or more accurately, of one of the several rings. And Meho says that he will take Fatima home—she is already behind him on his horse. He tells Osman that he is betrothed. The startling element is that this is not according to custom. Avdo is aware of this and adds, "if her mother agrees." Later, as we shall see, the conservative Avdo again restrains the breaking of custom. Ancient values are defended and preserved in oral traditional narrative.

A small, but significant, ring started with the appearance of the coach from Buda with its escort. Its center is the story of Fatima and the combat; its final step is the return of the coach to Buda without the escort, but with Meho. This is probably the most important episode in the song. For now we move to a balancing of Kanidža and Buda, of his family and hers, and of their fates, one with an aged father, the other with an absent one.

The episodes in Buda are contrasted with those in Kanidža in respect not only to the two families but also, as I have said, to the nobles around Hasan paša Tiro and the court of the vizier in Buda. The poem, or song, will end with Meho taking his father's place, with Fatima's father brought back from exile, and with a new and loyal vizier established in Buda, even Jahja paša, and, of course, the uniting of the families in the wedding of Meho and Fatima.

The desperation of Fatima's family with the father in exile, the daughter and only child (like Meho) given by force to the Christian general Peter, is so complete that Meho and Fatima return to her house just in time to stop her mother from plunging to her death. Compare with this the rejoicing of Meho's mother and the elation of men at Kanidža at the breakup of the assembly as they share Meho's joy.

There are similarities between the two descriptions as well, between Cifrić Hasanaga's recital of the wealth and favor of Smail and Fatima's account as she and Meho enter Buda of the wealth of Zajim Alibey. Yet Meho is a bit overwhelmed with Buda, for it is so much bigger and grander than Kanidža. The scene is enchanting, charming—to use a word I seldom employ. It is like the wonder of Telemachus and Peisistratus at the richness of Menelaus's palace.

In the development of Meho's and Osman's journey to Buda and their return, the duplicated scenes of hospitality with Vuk and Vujadin, the Christian "kmets," are balanced around the episode of the coach by the hospitality at Fatima's house in Buda. The abundant happiness of the "kmets," surrounded by sons and daughters—Nestor wise—is contrasted with the devastation and gloom of Fatima's house, offering the hospitality of sorrowful, bereaved, and threatened wealth.

But Meho's purpose in Buda is to obtain from the treacherous vizier accreditation as *alajbeg* in the Buda district of Kanidža in Bosnia. To this purpose has been added, since the encounter in the plain of Buda, the obtaining of a "nićah nama," a marriage license. So the stay of Meho and Osman in Buda, unexpectedly based at Fatima's house, is punctuated by an official visit to the vizier, whom Meho now knows is a traitor. The situation is fraught with danger, for Meho and Osman are obviously outnumbered. But right and justice are on their side, the prestige of Smail's house is great, and the fear of Bosnia and its influence on the sultan, carefully built up by Avdo from the beginning of the song, has to be reckoned with. In short, they are not alone, and Meho has already proved his mettle.

Just as the joyful and happy scenes of hospitality at the "kmets', " fused with the family picture at Smail's house, are balanced by the joyless and grim scenes at Fatima's house, so the sinister court of the vizier in Buda is balanced with and contrasted to the assembly surrounding Hasan paša Tiro.

Here, then, is the completion of a larger ring begun from the start of the song.

1. Assembly in Kanidža
2. Meho at home
3. Hospitality on the journey
4. Meho meets Fatima; Meho, Osman meet the captain and fifty soldiers
3. Hospitality in Buda
2. Fatima at home
1. The vizier's court in Buda

Is this conscious patterning in a ring by Avdo? Avdo had never heard of ring composition, but I believe one may distinguish varying degrees of "conscious artistry." Meho's stay at Fatima's house in Buda, the picture of Fatima at home, is Avdo's invention. It is not in the printed source read to him. In that source, Meho leaves Fatima at her house, turning her over to her mother, and he and Osman proceed immediately to the vizier's palace. I suspect that Avdo's conscious fullness of telling has led him to create a scene that in its nature balances and contrasts with the scene of Meho at home, only the rudiments of which were in Avdo's source. He is conscious of this fullness and proud of his ability. He is also aware of the relationship of the episodes, "Meho at home," "Fatima at home," although he wouldn't call them that, or probably have any name for them at all. He uses only one term *kititi,* "to adorn," "to embellish," a song. On a lesser scale he differentiated the two hospitality episodes on the journey to Buda, with conscious art. So he did with the two family scenes. These were no mechanical repetitions of prefabricated "themes." Avdo knew what he was doing in developing them; he had developed similar scenes before in other songs. Had he not developed the "Fatima at home" episode, the ring would have been defective. It did not come about by chance; in this case only the *potential* was inherent in Avdo's published source.

Had the two hospitality episodes with the Christian "kmets" been omitted by Avdo—they are in the printed "source"—the symmetry of the ring would have been more apparent. As it is, the theme of "Fatima at home" has to double also as a hospitality theme, which it can easily do. Actually, as we saw, Avdo made good use of the two hospitality episodes, and his song would be the poorer without them.

There is clearly ring composition in Avdo Mededovic's "The Wedding of Smailagić Meho," and Avdo has created and exploited it for artistic purposes and in order to bring into focus the ancient mythic, heroic, social, and historic values of his traditional culture.

3
THE *CANTAR DE MIO CID:*
PROBLEMS OF INTERPRETATION
Ruth H. Webber

What follows is an attempt to demonstrate what can happen to the interpretation of a work when there is a division of opinion among critics as to whether it is of oral traditional origin or composed in writing by a learned poet. The work in question is the *Cantar de Mio Cid,* Spain's only medieval epic that has come down to us in more or less complete form.

This is not meant to be a review of the traditionalist-individualist, or, if you will, neotraditionalist-neoindividualist, controversy that has centered around this epic poem, but rather an inquiry into the critical techniques applied and an assessment of their validity and of the premises on which they have been based in the most recent stages of this debate. In order to undertake such an inquiry, I have had to place myself in the uncomfortable position of taking issue with the conclusions of a number of capable and erudite scholars whose work I esteem. Because I am an unabashed traditionalist, my own bias has undoubtedly emerged despite my intention to present the problems as objectively as possible.

The great gaps in the history of the Spanish epic caused by a lamentable lack of extant texts have perforce given rise to hypothesis. The relation of these hypotheses to what we can ascertain about the few texts we do have is the subject of a considerable part of this essay. There is so much room for varying interpretations that disagreement manifests itself at every turn. The coincidence of the recent publication of Colin Smith's *The Making of the*

"Poema de mio Cid,"[1] which offers the most extreme statement to date concerning authorship and authorial intentionality in the poem, provides an appropriate focal point for much of this discussion. Colin Smith is a dedicated epic scholar whose every word merits close scrutiny and the evidence he amasses thorough consideration.

The *Cantar de Mio Cid (CMC)* tells first of the exile of the hero, the Cid, by King Alfonso VI, and his subsequent victories against the Moors culminating in the taking of Valencia, which brings about the king's pardon and the marriages of the Cid's daughters to the Infantes of Carrión. Then a family tragedy ensues. The Infantes, who have lost face by their cowardice, cruelly beat their wives by way of revenge and leave them for dead. After the rescue of the wives, the Cid, with the support of the king, successfully brings about the condemnation of the princes in court, after which they are gravely wounded in combat and the daughters are remarried to royal spouses.

The *CMC* is found in a mid-fourteenth-century manuscript that bears the date 1207. There has been prolonged discussion as to whether the date is that of the copy, that on which the text was committed to writing for the first time, or that of the composition of the work. Because of the curious spacing of the Roman numerals, which could indicate that a *C* had been removed, some theorize that the date should be 1307. Ramón Menéndez Pidal posited that the work was first put into writing around 1140.[2] Against the persuasive array of arguments he assembled, there must be weighed considerable additional evidence, all of which inclines toward an early-thirteenth-century date for the single text we possess.[3]

For traditionalists, of whom Jules Horrent is a worthy spokesman, the date is an interesting but not significant archaeological fact, since our text was but one in a chain of successive versions.[4] For individualists, however, it is critical, since for them

1. Colin Smith, *The Making of the "Poema de mio Cid"* (Cambridge: Cambridge University Press, 1983).
2. Ramón Menéndez Pidal, *Cantar de Mio Cid* (Madrid: Espasa-Calpe, 1944), 1:22.
3. For an excellent summary of the dating question from Menéndez Pidal on, see Derek W. Lomax, "The Date of the *Poema de Mio Cid*," in *"Mio Cid" Studies,* ed. A. D. Deyermond (London: Tamesis, 1977), pp. 73–81.
4. Jules Horrent, *Historia y poesía en torno al "Cantar del Cid"* (Barcelona: Ariel, 1973), pp. 310–11.

it represents the date of composition. For Colin Smith, that composition was by the Per Abbat (Pedro Abad—Peter the Abbot) whose name appears in the explicit "Per Abbat le escriuio." Smith argues, basing one hypothesis upon another, that since Pedro Abad was the first author of his kind and since he was trained as a lawyer, he would automatically have used the *scripsit* formula with which notaries customarily concluded their documents instead of the *fecit, fiz, fizo,* or *compuso* used to indicate authorship.[5] Pursuant to this theory he searched for the name, which he deemed a patronymic, through countless archival documents. Among the many records of persons named Pedro Abad, he turned up one who in Carrión in 1223 presented at court, along with other documents, a forged diploma of 1075 in which ten out of the eighteen signatories were associated in some way with the Cid.[6] Extraordinary as this fact is, there is still another that gives pause for thought. In the *Libro de la montería,* probably written at the behest of Alfonso XI (1312–1350), there appear topographical references to the "Cabeça de Per Abat" and the "Cabeça del Cid" in adjacent locations somewhere between Ávila and Toledo.[7] Whether these are valid testimonials of authorship or merely reflect the popularity throughout the thirteenth and fourteenth centuries of this version of the *CMC* to which the name of Pedro Abad was affixed cannot be determined.

Faced with the impasse of author versus copyist and original text versus one version out of many, the only recourse is to go back to the text itself. If the fourteenth-century manuscript is to be accepted as a reasonably faithful copy of the 1207 text, it has to be conceded at the same time that it contains a number of copyists' errors that indicate that it is several removes from the original. There are modifications in the language as well that are detrimental to the assonance, apparently resulting from the desire to update anachronisms, like *muort* > *muert,* which represent a pre-thirteenth-century linguistic stratum.[8] In addition, the text gives evidence of more fundamental kinds of layering. We need only recall Menéndez Pidal's epoch-making study written when he was ninety, "Dos poetas en el *Cantar de Mio Cid*," in which, based primarily on versification, he detected two different poetic tradi-

5. Colin Smith, *Estudios cidianos* (Madrid: Planeta, 1977), pp. 17–19.
6. Ibid., pp. 26–28.
7. Smith, *The Making,* p. 69.
8. Menéndez Pidal, *Cantar,* 1:28–33.

tions, one of which he assigned to a poet of Gormaz and the other to a poet of Medinaceli, or von Richthofen's scrutiny of the text that led him to declare that the middle section, the *Cantar de bodas,* was composed before the other two.[9] Whether or not one accepts the interpretation of the evidence presented in support of either or both of these theories, they render untenable the proposition that the *CMC* as we have it emerged fresh from the pen of a professional poet in 1207.

This leads us in turn to a consideration of the difficulties that have arisen in the course of various kinds of analysis of the versification and the language of the poem.

In the earlier phases of *Mio Cid* studies, no aspect of the work was more rigorously debated than the nature of the Spanish epic two-hemistich verse of irregular length: whether it was a syllable-count line distorted by transcription, whether it was stress-timed, or whether it was simply irregular from the start. It is now generally conceded that the verses of the *CMC* are for the most part meant to be as they appear in the manuscript. Menéndez Pidal's target-count theory, by means of which he showed that the number of syllables in the hemistichs is, in order of frequency, 7, 8, 6, 9, and that in the verses, 14, 13, 15, has gained wide acceptance,[10] although from time to time there appears a new adherent of the stress principle. Years ago Tomás Navarro Tomás demonstrated convincingly how the *CMC* could be intoned (or sung) on the basis of two beats per hemistich.[11] Either the target-count or the stress principle is acceptable from the point of view of orally sung verse. In fact, they are two different ways of describing the same phenomenon, which seems not to have been perceived up to now.

Colin Smith is one who is convinced of the accentual base of the *Mio Cid* line.[12] As a part of his contention that the poet composed his work in direct imitation of certain French epics, he credits Pedro Abad with having invented a new prosodic system that then became the model for all subsequent Spanish epic produc-

9. Ramón Menéndez Pidal, "Dos poetas en el *Cantar de Mio Cid*" in *En torno al Poema del Cid* (Barcelona: E.D.H.A.S.A., 1963), pp. 140–44; Erich von Richthofen, *Nuevos estudios épicos medievales* (Madrid: Gredos, 1970), pp. 144–46.

10. Menéndez Pidal, *Cantar,* 1:86–103.

11. Tomás Navarro Tomás, *Métrica española* (New York: Las Americas, 1966), p. 35.

12. *The Making,* pp. 113–14.

tion. The use of assonance and laisse divisions was borrowed from French models, he believes, to form a system characterized by a variable number of stresses and by flexibility throughout, the result in many instances of converting French syntactical structures into Spanish.[13]   He weakens his argument, however, by insisting that Pedro Abad's system was experimental, hence somewhat defective.[14]   Logically it would then follow, since the other Spanish epic texts show the same form of versification, even the late *Mocedades de Rodrigo,* that they also are experimental and defective, or else they were also composed by Pedro Abad, which no one would care to argue.

It is quite conceivable that the French and Spanish epic verse had a common origin, whether derived from the Gothic tradition or from Latin popular verse, either one of which would have been stress-timed, and that the French evolved further into a syllable-count system with a fixed length of line, while the Spanish adhered more closely to its primitive roots and retained greater freedom throughout. Constant contacts along the medieval pilgrimage routes would have reinforced the similarities between the French and Spanish verse. There can be no disagreement with Colin Smith's characterization of Spanish epic versification, and his comments are much to the point concerning the apparent license in the Spanish laisse system with the practice, too frequent to be ignored, of intercalating in a series pairs of verses of a different assonance, which he accepts as a feature of the system.[15]   But to substitute for the concept of a Romance epic with regional variations the theory that the Spanish epic was invented by a single poet bent on translating the French system into Spanish distorts the whole process of medieval epic production and the chronology as well.

In recent years the acoustic qualities of the *CMC* have attracted the attention of several scholars. In 1972, Edmund de Chasca's study of internal rime in his *El arte juglaresco en el "Cantar de Mio Cid"* initiated a series of studies that took internal rime as a point of departure. Although de Chasca had always been a staunch advocate of Menéndez Pidal's neotraditionalism, this time he was more interested in extolling the aesthetic merits of internal

13. Ibid., pp. 114–16.
14. Ibid., pp. 106–7.
15. Ibid., p. 109.

rime, which is usually vowel rime only, than in assessing its role within the framework of oral song.[16] He summed up his argument by saying (the translation is mine), "In our poem, internal rime seems to me to be always aesthetically satisfactory, whether instinctive . . . or by evident artistic purpose."[17] The very fact that he considered conscious artistic purpose to be a valid explanation reveals a disjunction between his announced position as an oralist and his working critical perspective.

According to de Chasca, 26.5 percent of the first hemistichs in the *CMC* show internal rime. This figure was subsequently modified and reduced (de Chasca was counting internal rime in alternate as well as contiguous verses) by Ian Michael to 17 percent, leaving the latter not at all convinced that internal rime was anything more than an accidental phenomenon.[18] In a 1976 article Colin Smith stated his belief that the proportion of internal rime was too high to be the result of chance alone, claiming instead that it was one feature of an elaborate system of sound patterning.[19] He developed his theory in a set of impressive analyses under the headings of rhythm, anticipation and repetition of stressed vowels, vowel sequences, leonine rime and assonance, alliteration, and the acoustic value of place names, all of which he considered to be the product of the creative artistry of an exceptionally gifted poet.

This study provoked a response from Kenneth Adams in which he also declared that the quantity of internal rime was significant.[20] He analyzed leonine and internal assonance in terms of the frequency of certain vowel combinations in the language, reaching the conclusion that internal rime, in the *CMC* at least, suggests oral composition rather than deliberate artistic purpose. Adams continued with an appreciative analysis of several passages that are notable for their acoustic features and made an especially worthwhile contribution in his demonstration of how sound-linking is combined with other kinds of poetic devices.

16. Edmund de Chasca, *El arte juglaresco en el "Cantar de Mio Cid,"* 2d ed. (Madrid: Gredos, 1972), 219–36.
17. Ibid., p. 224.
18. Ian Michael, review of *El arte juglaresco* by de Chasca, *Bulletin of Hispanic Studies* 45 (1968): 310–13.
19. Colin Smith, "On Sound-Patterning in the *Poema de mio Cid,"* *Hispanic Review* 44 (1976): 224–25.
20. Kenneth Adams, "Further Aspects of Sound-Patterning in the *Poema de mio Cid,"* *Hispanic Review* 48 (1980): 450.

Since both Smith and Adams demurred at trying to measure specific acoustic phenomena in the *Mio Cid,* I undertook to combine quantitative with qualitative analysis.[21] Taking the first one hundred verses of the *Cantar de bodas,* the middle portion of the *CMC,* as the basis, I was able to identify and then tabulate seventeen phonic devices under the headings of end rime, second-hemistich acoustics, hemistich linking, first-hemistich acoustics, and consonantal alliteration, and to do the same for the one hundred verses of the *Roncesvalles* fragment, the only other Spanish epic text whose verses have survived in more or less their original state. The results from the analysis of the two texts are remarkably similar with one exception: the *Roncesvalles* poet preferred alliterative techniques to vowel harmonics for verse-linking purposes. The combined analyses reinforce Michael's and Adams's opinions that internal assonance has been accorded undue importance as an acoustic device. The analyses suggest that it would be more appropriate to view internal assonance as misplaced verse-end assonance. The singer, always mindful of the need to supply assonance at alternate break points, that is, at every other hemistich, lost track momentarily of which one was the verse break and assonated at the midverse caesura as well. This is borne out by the fact that internal assonance (or rime) sometimes occurs in runs of three, four, or five verses.[22]

If two different epic texts reveal the same kinds of acoustic enrichment and to almost the same degree, it is reasonable to conclude that extensive sound patterning is an essential feature of the Spanish epic tradition as well as of other epic traditions.[23] However much the harmonics of the *CMC* please us, the poem is not unique in this respect. The text we have was indeed the product of a skilled and creative poet with a finely tuned musical ear; not one who had just developed a tentative new poetic system, but rather one versed in the age-old techniques of oral composition.

These studies have served to focus attention on the exceptionally euphonious qualities of the *CMC* and its elaborate sound system. For the individualist a technique that is so effective and at

---

21. Ruth House Webber, "The Euphony of the *Cantar de Mio Cid*" in *Florilegium Hispanicum: Medieval and Golden Age Studies Presented to Dorothy Clotelle Clarke* (Madison, 1983), pp. 45–60.

22. See de Chasca's statistics, *El arte juglaresco,* p. 221.

23. See, for example, the study of Albert B. Lord, "The Role of Sound Patterns in Serbo-Croatian Epic," in *For Roman Jakobson* (The Hague: Mouton, 1956), pp. 301–5.

the same time so complex can only be accounted for by the genius of a single poet. But this is the hallmark of oral composition, which depends upon sound, making acoustic evidence among the most reliable for determining orality. The complexity beneath an appearance of simplicity of the *CMC*'s sound system is the result of its having evolved intuitively by ear and then having been continually refined through performance.

It is unnecessary to reiterate here that epic formulas and epithets in particular have been the object of considerable scholarly attention in various epic traditions and have been shown to be the basic elements with which the oral poet composed his verses, the exact form of which at any given moment was linked to metrical needs. For Colin Smith the formulas of the *CMC* are a direct imitation of French epic style, and the epithets are the product of handling that was "thoughtful and sensitive and in no way automatic."[24] Other phrases like the recurrent epithet applied to the Cid, "el que en buen ora nasco" (he who was born in a good hour), for which there are no analogues in the French epic, were, in his opinion, original creations of the author.[25] Smith is not alone in praising the appropriateness of the epithets in the *CMC*. Earlier Rita Hamilton, for example, had studied the epithets applied both to Martín Antolínez, the Cid's henchman, as well as to the Cid himself.[26] She did not deny their utilitarian function but concluded that narrative reasons determined the choice of a specific epithet. The basis for the distinction in meaning, and therefore in use, between "el que en buen ora nasco" and "el que en buen ora çinxo espada" (he who girded on his sword in a good hour) according to Hamilton is that the latter alludes to the causes of tension between the Cid and the king, the Cid having been knighted by the king's brother Sancho before the latter was treacherously slain. The difficulty with this theory is that "el que en buen ora nasco" is the more frequently used of the two aforementioned full-hemistich formulas, since it can supply the $\acute{A}$, $\acute{I}$-O, and $\acute{O}$ assonances as well as $\acute{A}$-O with a change of the verb form to *naçe, naçido,* and *naçio,* respectively, while "el que en buen ora çinxo espada" can only serve in laisses assonating in $\acute{A}$-A.[27]

24. *The Making,* p. 194.

25. Ibid., p. 195.

26. Rita Hamilton, "Epic Epithets in the *Poema de mio Cid,*" *Revue de Littérature Comparée* 36 (1962): 161–78.

27. Ruth H. Webber, "Un aspecto estilístico del *Cantar de Mio Cid,*" *Anuario de Estudios Medievales* 2 (1965): 491–92.

Therefore, in order to maintain that the sword-girding phrase was chosen because of its implicit historical allusion, one would first have to prove that a shift was made to the *Á-A* assonance in order to accommodate that particular epithet. This is not to say that there is no possibility of choice within the system. A third variant assonating in *Ó,* "el que Valençia gano" (he who won Valencia), appears several times in the second half of the poem as an alternate to "el que en buen ora naçio" after Valencia has fallen to the Cid, thus enabling the *juglar* to recall the hero's greatest achievement. There is no doubt that certain formulas were universal while others appear to have been the particular property of a given poet-singer, into which category many epithets fall.

De Chasca also succumbed upon occasion to the temptation of describing formulaic usage as a calculated poetic device attuned to its environment.[28] He was gently chided for this by Stephen Gilman,[29] and rightfully so, for Gilman was acknowledging thereby that he had been partner to the same fallacy several years before in his extended treatment of tense usage in the *CMC*.[30]

For most nontraditionalist critics as well as a few others like de Chasca and Gilman, the most disturbing problem is the apparently mechanistic nature of the oral poetic process. While de Chasca simply broke ranks with Milman Parry and Albert Lord in this regard, Gilman struggled to resolve the dilemma, saying, in reference to de Chasca: "It would have been more productive to begin by admitting the peculiarity of the *Poema*'s insufficient formulaic frequency and irregular versification and to have gone on from there. But to where? . . . to the fundamental question of whether there is only one possible kind of oral composition for narrative poetry or whether . . . there may not be a plurality of species."[31] In another study published the same year on the language of the Spanish ballads, he came closer to a satisfactory solution when he stated that ballads are composed in "the grammar of another language poetically derived from the mother tongue."[32] He could and should have said the same for the epic. It is Colin

28. *El arte juglaresco,* pp. 168–69.

29. Stephen Gilman, "The Poetry of the *Poema* and the Music of the *Cantar,*" *Philological Quarterly* 51 (1972): 6–7.

30. Stephen Gilman, *Tiempo y formas temporales en el "Poema del Cid"* (Madrid: Gredos, 1961).

31. Gilman, "The Poetry of the *Poema,*" p. 7.

32. Stephen Gilman, "On *Romancero* as a Poetic Language," in *Homenaje a Casalduero: crítica y poesía* (Madrid: Gredos, 1972), p. 153.

Smith's reluctance to view Spanish epic language from this perspective that has made it impossible for him to extend the parameters and recognize that it is also true for French epic language, the
grammar of which is more closely related to that of other epic
traditions, the Spanish in particular, than it is to the vernacular of
its own day. One manifestation of the resemblance between the
poetic grammars of the French and Spanish epic is the use of many
similar if not identical formulas, products of the same poetic need,
along with other formulas that were undoubtedly borrowed back
and forth, while still others did not cross linguistic frontiers,
whatever the reasons may have been. To conceive that a poet setting out to write an epic poem should pick out here and there
appropriate French epic formulas, either seen in writing or
remembered from having heard them sung, translate them, and
adapt them for use in a suitable prosodic as well as narrative
environment so that they give the illusion of oral verse is to create a
scenario that could never have existed.

The unwillingness of critics to recognize the subservience of
poetic diction to metrical demands because it seems to imply a
lack of artistic choice is also a question of perspective and of scale.
Any language if analyzed far enough has a mechanistic base, as all
language teachers know. Witness the paradigms we inflict on our
students. The greater the complexity of the linguistic system and
the more alternate subsystems there are, the less obvious this fact
becomes. As we have seen, the choice between "el que en buen ora
nasco" and "el que en buen ora çinxo espada" is mechanical,
being determined by the prevailing assonance. But it is important
to bear in mind that the choice is not made at that level. If the
singer had begun his verse with the hero's name and the assonance
is in Á-O, he could indeed conclude the verse with the first of the
verbal phrases just mentioned, but he could also use a simpler epithet, a noun-adjective combination like "el Campeador contado"
(the renowned champion). Or he could substitute another kind of
verbal phrase denoting a reaction, like "fermoso sonrrisando"
(smiling happily) or "de aquesto fue pagado" (he was satisfied
with that); or an action to advance the story, such as "caualgo pri-
uado" (he rode off quickly); or a short speech, like "esto fare yo de
grado" (I will do this willingly); and so forth. In sum, the singer
had innumerable options for his second hemistich, and his choice
was determined both by how he wished to continue his story and
by how it would sound.

In the question of the historicity of the *CMC* we have not progressed very far from the classic debate between Spitzer and Menéndez Pidal that took place some thirty-five years ago. The latter claimed that the *Mio Cid* was essentially a historical document and that further research would eventually reveal the veracity of every detail. Spitzer, on the other hand, insisted that the *CMC* dehistoricized or fictionalized a historical hero by placing him in a poetic frame that enhanced the legend.[33] Menéndez Pidal believed that oral transmission preserved vestiges of historical details long since forgotten whose origin was in the events themselves; Spitzer argued that history was transmuted into a Christian crusade legend. Both were right.

Research has continued apace, and some individualists continue to seek out historical documentation to prove that the *Cid* poet had been a skilled archival scholar as well as a superb artist. Aside from a few aberrant cases like that of Ubieto Arteta, who hoped to establish that the *CMC* was the work of an Aragonese poet,[34] there seems to have gradually emerged a consensus to the effect that historical facts quickly dissolved into a crucible of familiar names, places, and events in arbitrary relationships that created the illusion of historicity. For the traditionalist this is consistent with the process of folklorization also manifest in the evolution of the poem's narrative structure. For a latter-day individualist like Colin Smith, the *Cid* poet was a creative artist who felt no responsibility for recording the facts of history as he may have known them and felt free to adjust them for literary purposes.[35] Yet at another point Smith asserted that the poet had informed himself about the basic facts of the Cid's life for his framework, perhaps from a written genealogy, and had made use as well of: the *Historia Roderici,* generally considered a factual account in Latin of the Cid's military exploits written contemporaneously with or shortly after they took place; the *Cronicón de Cardeña* (known only from a text of 1327), the annals of the monastery with which the Cid was associated in the poem; and possi-

33. Ramón Menéndez Pidal, Prologue to *Poema de Mio Cid* (Madrid: Clásicos Castellanos, 1913), pp. 14–27; Leo Spitzer, "Sobre el carácter histórico del *Cantar de mio Cid,*" *Nueva Revista de Filología Hispánica* 2 (1948): 105–17. Menéndez Pidal answered Spitzer, modifying his stand somewhat, in "Poesía e historia en el *Mio Cid,*" *Nueva Revista de Filología Hispánica* 3 (1949): 113–29.

34. Antonio Ubieto Arteta, *"El Cantar de mio Cid" y algunos problemas históricos (Valencia, 1973), "Conclusiones," pp. 87–92.*

35. *The Making,* p. 137.

bly the *Chronica Adefonsi Imperatoris,* which contains the
Poema de Almería, a Latin poem written between 1147 and 1157
that alludes to the Cid and Alvar Fáñez, the Cid's companion and
counselor.[36] The investigation of historical documents by the one
who composed the *Mio Cid* and the free manipulation in terms of
artistic purpose of the information thus acquired is a hypothesis
not readily acceptable for a poet of around the year 1200. If these
documents had been available to him and if he had made use of
them, that fact would have been registered in some way.

As an adjunct to the question of historicity, there has arisen
lately the matter of topicality, whether the text of the *CMC* in our
possession contains allusions to the contemporary scene. Even
Menéndez Pidal who, as we have seen, chose the date 1140 for the
extant version did so thinking it might have been written down in
honor of a politically critical royal espousal. One could question
the appropriateness for an engagement celebration of a tale of
treacherous sons-in-law, cruel beating of the brides, and dissolved
marriages unless, of course, the version of the *CMC* in circulation
at that time had ended with the marriages of the Cid's daughters to
the Infantes.[37] Once the idea of historical distortion in the *CMC*
was acknowledged, the way was left open to consider the possibility of intentional manipulation of historical facts to reflect a
later political situation.

Although Smith did not attach special significance to the date of
1207 for the composition of the poem beyond its being the date on
the manuscript and generally acceptable on other accounts, he
was tempted to search, without success, for important betrothals
and marriages around this time.[38] Additionally, he suggested as a
reason for choosing as villains the princes of Carrión, who are
documented as being in good grace in Alfonso VI's court during
the critical period, a bitter mid-twelfth-century feud over possession of the abbey of San Pedro de Cardeña between the Spanish
Benedictines and the Cluniacs, the counts of Carrión probably
having been the supporters of the latter in their attempted take-
over of Cardeña.[39]

36. Ibid., pp. 140–49.
37. Erich von Richthofen, *Nuevos estudios,* pp. 145–46. Von Richthofen proposed that the original *Cantar* was composed of the present *Cantar de bodas*
minus the weddings.
38. *The Making,* pp. 212–13.
39. Ibid., pp. 175–76.

The precise purpose of a recent book by María Eugenia Lacarra is to demonstrate that the *CMC* is a work of personal as well as political slander and propaganda.[40] According to Lacarra, the poem was directed against the Castro family, related to and identified with the Leonese Beni-Gómez (the family of the villains of the *CMC*), who, in the last years of the twelfth and the beginning of the thirteenth century, opposed the Laras, descendants of the Cid and supporters of the Castilian monarchy. Smith was not convinced by Lacarra's argument, declaring that the identification would have been too elusive for a contemporary audience.[41] Additional opposition came from José Fradejas Lebrero in a recent essay accompanying an edition of the *CMC* put out by the city of Burgos as part of the celebration of the eleven-hundredth anniversary of the founding of that city.[42] Although Fradejas also believes that the work was written for propagandistic purposes, he found the motivation to be less hermetic than did Lacarra. For him the epic was a response to a desperate need of the moment, that of inciting the Castilians to a vigorous renewal of the Reconquest after their disastrous defeat at Alarcos in 1195. Thus, the *CMC* proffers the model of the Cid's notable victories against the Moors one hundred years earlier and displays simultaneously the attractive rewards soldiers might expect from participating in such a crusade.[43] Indeed, Castile and Navarre did join forces to definitely put to rout the forces of Islam in the battle of Navas de Tolosa in the year 1212. From the traditionalist point of view the writing down for the first time for such a purpose of a familiar oral epic long in circulation like the *CMC* is an acceptable theory. For Fradejas, however, the poem was composed at this juncture by a learned poet affecting popular style.[44]

In recent years there have been two persistent theories concerning the structural base of the *CMC,* one involving the relations between the king and his vassal concerning the question of honor, and the other involving the biographical pattern of the hero. The

40. María Eugenia Lacarra, *"El Poema de Mio Cid": realidad histórica e ideología* (Madrid: Porrúa Turanzas, 1980).

41. Colin Smith, review of *"El Poema"* by Lacarra, *Modern Language Review* 76 (1981): 716–19.

42. José Fradejas Lebrero, "Intento de comprensión del Poema de Mio Cid," in *Poema de Mio Cid* (Burgos: Ayuntamiento, 1982), 2:245–87.

43. Ibid., pp. 248–57, 270–72.

44. Ibid., p. 245.

king-vassal structure, perhaps best elucidated by Peter Dunn and by Roger Walker, accords the king the pivotal role.[45] In these terms the first half of the poem has to do with the loss and regaining of royal favor and the second with the successful testing of the king after his ill-fated decision to marry the Cid's daughters to the Infantes of Carrión. According to the biographical theory, the *CMC* is a two-part story that focuses on the hero. The first part is his exile and triumphant return; the second, the loss of his honor leading to its ultimate enhancement in a double victory, juridical and moral, over his villainous sons-in-law. Although the *CMC* chronicles only the latter part of the Cid's life, the triumphs of the aging hero, the degree to which the Cid's life came to be assimilated into the heroic canon can be best appreciated in the *Mocedades de Rodrigo,* a fourteenth-century epic about the youthful feats of the Cid.[46] According to either theory, it is, in Proppian terms, a narrative of two moves. The heroic pattern has the advantage of allowing us to see the parts as two different plots. The first is the trajectory of the Cid himself, who goes from disfavor, exile, and poverty to wealth, fame, and pardon in that order. The second, the result of gemination, is the inverse of the former with the Infantes as protagonists who fall from pride, wealth, and esteem to public shame with concomitant loss of fortune and status, making the Cid's daughters the vicarious victims.[47]

In all attempts at structural analysis of the *CMC,* the concern has been to reconcile the dichotomy between the story of the Cid's conquests, with its origin in real-life events, and the story of the daughters' fateful marriages, a product of fiction. Since the discussions about the latter have bulked so large in *Mio Cid* criticism and have led to such widely differing interpretations, it is appropriate to review them here. The sadistic punishment and then abandonment in the wilds of the Cid's daughters by their cowardly husbands, the Infantes of Carrión, who sought to avenge in this way

45. Peter N. Dunn, "Levels of Meaning in the *Poema de mio Cid," Modern Language Notes* 85 (1970): 109–19; Roger M. Walker, "The Role of the King and the Poet's Intentions in the *Poema de mio Cid"* in *Medieval Hispanic Studies Presented to Rita Hamilton,* ed. A. D. Deyermond (London: Tamesis, 1976), pp. 257–66.

46. See Archer Taylor, "The Biographical Pattern in Traditional Narrative," *Journal of the Folklore Institute* 1 (1964): 114–29.

47. Dunn also called attention to the journey in reverse as "an infamous parody" ("Levels of Meaning," pp. 112–13).

imagined insults by the Cid, have been attributed to various sources: to Lupercalian rites by Gifford; to virgin-martyr legends by Walsh, a theory recently supported by Nepaulsingh; while, according to Walker, it is a direct imitation of *Florence de Rome,* a French *chanson d'aventure.* [48] Walker's theory has caused some dissension in the ranks of the individualists, since any claim of direct borrowing must be confirmed by textual chronology. A. D. Deyermond and David Hook assembled evidence to show that *Florence de Rome* was composed later than the 1200 date claimed by Walker. [49] Smith defended Walker's assertion, saying that the *Florence* may well have been known in some earlier form now lost, [50] employing the same argument he rejected when applied by the traditionalists to earlier stages of the epic for which no texts remain.

Chronology aside, medieval tales of battered women are numerous. [51] The victims tend to fall into two categories: those who were punished by their husbands because of false accusations of adultery and those whom an evil brother-in-law sought to rape out of revenge. The *afrenta* episode of *Mio Cid* combines features of both in that the daughters are maltreated by their husbands who wish to avenge themselves on the Cid. Furthermore, these stories, which are all similar, are distinguishable from one another by one or more telling details. In *Berte aus grans piés,* it is a physical deformity, the size of the heroine's feet, while in *Florence* it is her chastity brooch and the fact she is hung by her hair. The resemblance with the *CMC* story is generic rather than specific, which suggests all these tales came out of a common store of thematic material in oral circulation throughout Romania and beyond. This is why the individualists who keep seeking textual

---

48. Douglas J. Gifford, "European Folk-Tradition and the *Afrenta de Corpes*" in *"Mio Cid" Studies,* ed. A. D. Deyermond (London: Tamesis, 1977), pp. 49–62; John K. Walsh, "Religious Motifs in Early Spanish Epic," *Revista Hispánica Moderna* 36 (1970–1971): 156–72; Colbert I. Nepaulsingh, "The *Afrenta de Corpes* and the Martyrological Tradition," *Hispanic Review* 51 (1983): 205–21; Roger M. Walker, "A Possible Source for the *Afrenta de Corpes,* " in *Medieval Hispanic Studies Presented to Rita Hamilton,* ed. A. D. Deyermond (London: Tamesis, 1976), pp. 335–47.

49. A. D. Deyermond and David Hook, "The *Afrenta de Corpes* and Other Stories," *La Corónica* 10 (1981–1982): 12–37.

50. *The Making,* p. 163.

51. See Ruth H. Webber, review of two articles by Walker, *Olifant* 7 (1979–1980): 413–16.

parallels can only find them scattered widely throughout a number of texts.[52]

The same could be said about other parallels drawn between the French and the Spanish epic under the assumption that the direction of influence was across the Pyrenees from north to south, even though the counter direction can be documented as well. French epics cited as the source for *Mio Cid* borrowings include: *Ogier* for the scene of the Cid's departure from Bivar, *Doon de la Roche* for his arrival in Burgos, the *Couronnement de Louis* for Jimena's prayer, the *Chanson de Roland* for the appearance of the archangel, *Berte aus grans piés* for the Cid's family viewing Valencia from the castle heights as well as for the lion episode, the *Roland* for the courtroom scene, and so forth.[53] Colin Smith does not believe that the *Cid* poet necessarily consulted French epic manuscripts, but rather that he "combined and recreated, taking hints and producing echoes, always his own man with his own story to tell. This suggests that he composed from the resources of a rich memory and of a poetic imagination in which French materials had been molded anew and recombined"—all of which would have amounted to a description of oral poetic processes had Smith not added as his final words: "before he ever set pen to parchment."[54]

More of the same can be said for the other stories that have been assimilated into the Cid's adventures, for example, the ruse of the richly decorated chests filled with sand that the Cid pawned on the eve of his departure into exile for money to support himself and his men. Another version, as is well known, is found in the *Disciplina clericalis* of Pedro Alfonso,[55] a contemporary of the Cid, in which the protagonist is a pilgrim returning from Mecca who has to deceive the man with whom he left his money for safe-keeping in order to get it back. Despite the great popularity of Pedro Alfonso's Latin story collection and the fact that manuscripts are to be found in libraries all over Europe, given the dis-

52. Smith, *The Making,* pp. 161–64.
53. Colin Smith, "Further French Analogues and Sources for the *Poema de mio Cid,*" *La Corónica* 6 (1977–1978): 14–21, and *The Making,* pp. 158–66.
54. *The Making,* p. 157.
55. Pedro Alfonso, *Disciplina clericalis,* ed. and trans. Angel González Palencia (Madrid: Editorial Maestre, 1948), no. 15, "Ejemplo de los diez cofres," pp. 38–40 (Latin), 133–36 (Spanish).

crepancies between the two versions, it is easier to believe that the *Cid* poet could have come to know it through oral sources than that he knew it from a manuscript of Pedro Alfonso's work, as Colin Smith theorizes.[56]

Latin as well as French sources play an important role in the individualists' arguments, one of the most controversial of which involves the description of battles and military tactics. In 1975 Colin Smith proposed that the Cid's taking of Castejón by luring the inhabitants out of town and of Alcocer by pretending to march away and then doubling back had their sources in Sallust and Frontinus respectively.[57] Except for the epithets, there is probably no aspect of the traditional epic that has been more thoroughly examined by scholars than the theme of the battle, both as a total pattern and its individual phases, even broken down as far as the single lance or sword stroke.[58] The universality of the theme with its many associated motifs found from Homer through present-day Serbo-Croatian songs is impressive.

It is obvious that medieval epic battles do not reflect the then current forms of warfare. The power of tradition as a force against change was greater than that of new techniques of fighting. Sallust's account of Marius's taking the town of Capsa in Numidia and Frontinus's of a military action of Crassius in the Slave War have much in common with the accounts of the *CMC*. However, the Belgian historian Louis Chalon, after scrutinizing the evidence put forth by Smith in favor of the Sallust source, concluded that the comparison was too imprecise and the contexts too different to be valid.[59] More recently Fradejas cited Berceo's *Vida de Santo Domingo de Silos* (verses 732–39) and a passage from Judges 9:42–45 that recounts Abimelec's taking of Siquem as more likely sources than Sallust for the Castejón maneuver. Concerning the Alcocer battle, he recalled the similarity of Dozy's description of Ferdinand I's attack against Valencia in 1064 (based on Ben

---

56. *The Making,* p. 155.

57. Colin Smith, "Literary Sources of Two Episodes in the *Poema de mio Cid,*" *Bulletin of Hispanic Studies* 52 (1975): 109–22, and *Estudios cidianos,* pp. 109–23.

58. See Jean Rychner, *La Chanson de geste: Essai sur l'art épique des jongleurs* (Geneva, 1955), pp. 139–41.

59. Louis Chalon, "Le poète du *Cantar de mio Cid* s'est-il inspiré de Salluste?" *Le Moyen Âge,* 4e serie, 33 (1978): 479–90.

Bassám, a contemporary Arab chronicler), which reports the same tactic to entice the inhabitants to leave the city.[60] In short, these same military ruses have been used and reused since time immemorial. The attempts to pinpoint a single textual source are unsatisfactory given the differences of detail and the obvious fact that they all represent variants of traditional battle patterns.

The foregoing areas of scholarly investigation in the *CMC* have all led to a similar dichotomy of opinion between those defending oral traditional origin and those favoring learned authorship. The single argument that Colin Smith has employed most to combat the theory of oral composition goes as follows (I quote from his concluding chapter): "Oralist critics who . . . rightly analyse the poem in terms of high art and sophistication should, I think, ponder an awesome logical impasse: can all of this complex composition *really* have been improvised by a chanting illiterate?"[61]

The bugaboo of illiteracy appears to be primarily the product of the Serbo-Croatian analogue. No one denies that in an illiterate society that is an enclave of a literate society the intrusion of literacy or even of secondary orality via radio and television is capable of inhibiting and then finally destroying oral art forms. Hence the sad fact that in the Hispanic world as in the South Slavic the sung ballad is gradually disappearing. This was not the case in the medieval world. Medieval Spanish society, no different from other medieval European societies, was illiterate, but illiteracy did not necessarily have adverse cultural implications because it did not exist alongside of or in competition with a literate society in the same way. Those who wanted to learn to read and write did so in Latin. Many cultured people did not feel that this was a necessity because they always had at hand someone to read and write for them. Just as Latin was not a spoken language except in the Church, the Romance tongues were not generally being written, except unknowingly by a few ill-trained notaries who thought they were writing Latin. Up to the end of the twelfth century in Spain there would have been no detrimental influences on oral traditional poetry comparable to those found in modern society; there would have been only other oral models. There was, in addition, nothing to prevent a minstrel from learning to read and write

60. "Intento de comprensión," pp. 282–84.
61. *The Making,* p. 216.

Latin, and doubtless some did since they came from all walks of life. The learning acquired thereby would probably have had no effect upon his linguistic prowess and poetic skills in the vernacular, although a certain amount of content could easily have seeped through. By the same token, reworkers of a text like the *CMC* once it was written down could conceivably have been able to make emendations in traditional style from their own oral memory without their literacy in Latin contaminating the results.

Let us suppose, nonetheless, that the poet/singer of our text was illiterate, hence without access to Latin schooling. What might he have been expected to know? In a fragmented society in which the individual's social mobility was severely restricted, the minstrels played a special role. They were professional entertainers who circulated freely and found eager audiences among all social classes, from the royal court down to the lowliest hamlet. Among them the singers of epic songs and of saints' lives formed a class apart and enjoyed more esteem than most of their cohorts,[62] esteem that would have brought with it access to the more cultivated segments of society. Through the breadth of their experience and many and varied contacts with both their own countrymen and pilgrims from abroad, they would have acquired a store of knowledge far beyond that of the average person. But here Deyermond would object, saying: "It is very doubtful whether this [learned authorship] can be adequately disposed of by the theory of a *juglar* who picked up some ecclesiastical and legal knowledge from his audience, . . . since what is involved is not specific pieces of knowledge but habits of mind which could only be the result of long training."[63] Deyermond underscored the two areas in which the individualists find the strongest evidence in favor of a learned poet as author of the *CMC,* knowledge of the Bible and knowledge of the law. Both are problematic from the traditionalist point of view.

Even Fradejas, who is willing to give oral and written culture equal weight in the elaboration of the *Mio Cid,* nevertheless categorized the Bible solely as a learned source.[64] Some progress has

---

62. Ramón Menéndez Pidal, *Poesía juglaresca y orígenes de las literaturas románicas* (Madrid, 1957), p. 38.

63. A. D. Deyermond, "Tendencies in 'Mio Cid' Scholarship, 1943–1973," in *"Mio Cid" Studies,* ed. A. D. Deyermond (London: Tamesis, 1977), p. 23.

64. "Intento de comprensión," p. 282.

been made in dispelling this idea by making known the familiarity that all social classes had with the Bible from oral teaching; preaching in the vernacular; the "people's Bible," that is, forms of pictorial representation like paintings on church walls, sculptured scenes, crèches, tableaux;[65] and the incorporation of biblical accounts along with saints' lives into the mass of storytelling materials in oral circulation.

Concerning Jimena's prayer, in which the specific biblical content is dense, the fact that the poet simply combined in his own way a series of prayer formulas repeatedly used in the medieval epic tells us nothing about his biblical knowledge per se, nor does it carry any implications about related learned sources, as Colin Smith suggested.[66] A more open view is shown by David Hook in his discussion of the lion episode, when he admitted that the similarities with Matthew 8:23–27 might well be unconscious or even fortuitous.[67] In the matter of biblical phraseology in the *CMC,* Colin Smith's arguments are plausible.[68] They bring to mind Walter Ong's statement about the overwhelming orality of the mindset in the Bible, which when read aloud at liturgical services, even though imperfectly understood, could have imposed its patterns upon a receptive ear.[69] The whole problem of direct and indirect biblical influence calls for further exploration.

The question of medieval man's knowledge of the law is no more easily resolved. The great capacity and efficiency of memory in an oral culture are axiomatic. In medieval society, as in any society, a certain amount of specific legal knowledge was necessary for survival in a given milieu. At most social levels this information was imparted orally, and all would have had access to and familiarity with public legal procedures. The dispute has to do with whether the amount and kinds of legal expertise demonstrated by the *Cid* poet constitute a decisive proof of learned authorship.

Militating against the contention of the British Hispanists (and

65. R. L. P. Milburn, "The 'People's Bible': Artists and Commentators," in *The Cambridge History of the Bible,* ed. G. W. H. Lampe (Cambridge: The University Press, 1969), 2: chap. 7.
66. *The Making,* pp. 160–61.
67. David Hook, "Some Observations upon the Episode of the Cid's Lion," *Modern Language Review* 71 (1976): 554–55.
68. *The Making,* pp. 185, 199.
69. Walter J. Ong, *Orality and Literacy* (London and New York: Methuen, 1982), p. 75.

others as well) that the author of the *CMC* was a trained lawyer is what can be ascertained about the state of jurisprudence during the period the *CMC* is presumed to have been composed. In Spain the great medieval codes of law had not yet been compiled. Castile, where the old Visigothic code, the *Forum judicum* (*Fuero juzgo*), was never promulgated, virtually lived without laws until the thirteenth century, when very slowly they began to be written down.[70] It was customary law that prevailed even where municipal charters (*fueros*) existed. Law was determined by usage and habit and preserved by oral transmission. It depended on personal testimony and the memory of the community as to what had been done in the past, thus being strictly local in character. The need for lawyers or for a legal profession in the modern sense had not yet arisen. The whole community participated in judicial procedures, which were public, and decisions were oral. As a matter of fact, the *CMC* itself gives testimony to the oral character of the legal process and to how legal knowledge was transmitted. Both the king and the Cid had in their retinue *sabidores* (verses 3005, 3070), and *coñosçedores* were designated for the Infantes' trial (verse 3137). These were men who knew the law and whose responsibility it was to distinguish right from wrong (verse 3138).

Lacarra's extensive and rigorous investigation of later codifications of the law under the assumption that they described usage already long in effect together with numerous royal documents revealed fundamental agreement with the *CMC* as to legal institutions, principles, and general procedures but continual discrepancies of detail, not only between the codes and our text but among the codes themselves as well. Although she was willing to conclude that the *Cid* poet's extensive knowledge of the law caused him to set up in juridical terms the narrative crises of his poem,[71] it is not at all evident that this knowledge goes beyond what an alert minstrel would have routinely acquired during the course of his wanderings. It is even less clear how an educated poet could have gone about studying customary law in all of its manifestations should he have so desired.

A more productive perspective was offered by R. Howard Bloch. Bloch views both medieval vernacular literature and the

---

70. Galo Sánchez, "Para la historia de la redacción del antiguo derecho territorial castellano," *Anuario de Historia del Derecho Español* 6 (1929): 262.

71. *El "Poema,"* p. 96.

customals as a reflection of a period of social transformation in which they played a part. A trial in a *chanson de geste,* for example, constituted "a ceremonial demonstration of the principles by which the community defined itself."[72] It was a mirror image of reality in which both reality and its fictive counterpart took the form of public performance. Bloch found chronicled in the epic the attempt by the king to suppress private wars of vengeance and replace trial by combat (*judicium Dei*) with judicial procedures, an important step in the long struggle by monarchy to curb the power of the nobility.

Within the frame of reference proposed by Bloch, the results of Lacarra's study of the *CMC* have a special pertinence. She brought out a fact that has not usually been recognized, that the Infantes of Carrión were brought to trial and found guilty, not of abandoning their wives, but of carrying out an act of private vengeance against the Cid.[73] The triumph of public law over the right to take justice into one's own hands was a new concept that had only begun to manifest itself in late twelfth-century *fueros.* The outcome of the trial in the poem would then represent an early stage in the transition from private to public law, since, at the conclusion of the judicial proceedings, a trial by combat is called for and carried out. Such anomalies were not unusual, Bloch observed, during the prolonged process of change, later stages of which are reflected in the courtly romance. Lacarra also detected in the *Mio Cid* a condemnation of the institution of *ira regia,* the right of the king to execute summary justice on a noble, in this case the Cid himself, without the victim's being able to defend himself. No legal solution, however, is offered in the poem; only the implicit criticism of the injustice of the king's act based on slander. That this was another issue of moment is evidenced by decrees that came out of the *Cortes* of León in 1188 curtailing the arbitrary powers of the king in such instances.[74]

In a recent study of the Count of Barcelona episode in the *CMC,* Ivy Corfis followed Bloch's lead and, after consulting the same French customals, concluded that the count's hunger strike after

---

72. R. Howard Bloch, *Medieval French Literature and Law* (Berkeley: University of California Press, 1977), pp. 8, 3.

73. *El "Poema,"* p. 99.

74. Ibid., p. 98.

his ignominious defeat by the Cid had legal implications.[75] Although her evidence is very suggestive, it unfortunately cannot be taken as proof since the validity of customary law (*usus terrae*) is by definition restricted as to time and place.

Other passages cited as evidence of the more than fortuitous legal expertise of the *Cid* poet include the detailing by a little girl before the Cid's barred door in Burgos of the penalties to be imposed by the king should anyone render him assistance. Yet the interdiction and its violation are recurrent folklore motifs. A similar proclamation by the king in a late twelfth-century French epic, *Floovant,* forbidding the vassals to give his son silver, gold, arms, horses, or food under threat of losing their lands and possessions and having their arms and legs chopped off is an almost exact counterpart of the *Mio Cid* passage except for the substitution of limbs for eyes.[76] Other counterparts can be found in the Spanish ballads.

Even in default of all of the foregoing, the whole argument in favor of a learned legal foundation is undercut by the failure to take into account a vital legal point that would have involved both civil and canon law: how the Cid's daughters were free to remarry while their husbands were still alive. Colin Smith passed over it quickly.[77] Lacarra faced the dilemma but was unable to supply documentation resolving the conjugal tangle, leaving it to be deduced that abandonment was sufficient cause for the dissolution of a marriage.[78] Once more it is demonstrated that what is represented in our text goes back to matters of custom and precedent.

As for the problem of the informed, responsible interpretation of the *Cantar de Mio Cid,* it is apparent that the most informed minds are unable to reconcile their differences and reach a consensus as to what that interpretation should be. We are grateful that the battle of the critics has stimulated some fine research in a number of specialized areas. At the same time, it has not infre-

---

75. Ivy A. Corfis, "The Count of Barcelona Episode and French Customary Law in the *Poema de Mio Cid*," *La Corónica* 12 (1984): 169–77.

76. *Floovant: chanson de geste,* ed. F. Guessard and H. Michelant (Paris, 1859), verses 147–53.

77. *The Making,* p. 79.

78. *El "Poema,"* p. 57.

quently confused the issues and changed investigative strategies to combative ones, causing objective scholarship to be temporarily lost in the jousting. The intensity of the debate has drawn attention away from equally challenging problems, among them that of defining the aesthetics of oral poetry, which I should like to see once more come to the forefront of scholarly discussion and investigation.

4
ANCIENT GREEK EPIC AND PRAISE POETRY: SOME TYPOLOGICAL CONSIDERATIONS
Gregory Nagy

There has been much interest expressed recently about parallelisms between medieval European epic poetry and latter-day African praise poetry. In light of this interest, it may be useful to examine a situation in which epic and praise poetry coexist in one culture. Such a situation existed in the archaic and Classical periods of Greek civilization, as documented most clearly in the epic poetry of Homer and the praise poetry of Pindar. I propose to survey the relationship between these two kinds of ancient Greek poetry, illustrating both convergences and divergences in form and function. The illustrations, it is hoped, will lead toward a clearer understanding of the universal characteristics—let us call them typologies—of epic and praise poetry.

I shall begin by considering how these two distinct media of epic and praise poetry, in terms of their inherited diction, refer to themselves. Then I shall consider also how they refer to each other, and how these references reflect on the evolution of these media.

From the epic poetry of Homer, we see that this medium refers to itself as *kleos* (plural *klea/kleea*), that is, 'glory' *as conferred by poetry*.[1] From the praise poetry of Pindar, on the other hand, we

---

1. See, for example, *Iliad* 2.486, 11.227, as discussed in G. Nagy, *The Best of the Achaeans: Concepts of the Hero in Archaic Greek Poetry* (Baltimore: Johns Hopkins University Press, 1979), pp. 15–18. Pindar's *Olympian, Pythian, Nemean,* and *Isthmian* Odes will be cited as *O., P., N.,* and *I.* I wish to thank N. F. Rubin and W. Sale for their sound advice.

see that this medium likewise refers to itself as *kleos*,[2] but that it can also refer to itself as *ainos* or *ep-ainos*.[3] Unlike the word *kleos,* the word *ainos* is more exclusive in its applications. As we see from Pindar's traditional diction, the *ainos* as a medium is ostensibly restricted to the following:

1. the *sophoi,* those who are 'skilled' in understanding poetry[4]
2. the *agathoi,* those who are intrinsically 'noble'[5]
3. the *philoi,* those who are 'near and dear' to the poet and to each other[6]

In other words, the *ainos* of Pindar presupposes a restricted audience who

1. understand the *message* of the *code* that is the poetry
2. have been raised on the proper ethical standards that are the *message* that the *code* of the poetry teaches
3. are socially connected to the poet and to each other, so that the *message* of the *code* may be transmitted to them and through them: *communication through community*

In this tripartite scheme, I have set up the distinction between *code* and *message,* using the terminology of the Prague School of Linguistics,[7] in order to drive home a point that the poetry of Pindar's *ainos* consistently makes about itself: the *ainos* is a code that carries the right message for those who are qualified and the wrong message or messages for those who are unqualified. By way of its self-definition, the *ainos* is predicated on the ideology of an ideal audience, listening to an ideal performance of an ideal composition. But at the same time it is also predicated on the reality of uncertainties in interaction between performer and audience in the context of the actual performance of a composition: the *ainos*

2. For example, Pindar *N.* 7.61, as discussed in Nagy, *Best of the Achaeans,* p. 223.

3. For a survey of passages, see M. Detienne, *Les maîtres de vérité dans la Grèce archaïque,* 2d ed. (Paris: François Maspero, 1973), p. 21.

4. See Pindar *I.* 2.12–13. Note too the discussion in Nagy, *Best of the Achaeans,* pp. 236–38.

5. See Pindar *P.* 2.81–88; see further, at the end of the same poem, lines 94–96; also *P.* 10.71–72, at the end of another poem.

6. See (again) Pindar *P.* 2.81–88. Note too the discussion in Nagy, *Best of the Achaeans,* pp. 238–42.

7. See also R. Jakobson, "Linguistics and Poetics," in T. Sebeok, ed., *Style in Language* (Cambridge, Mass.: MIT Press, 1960), pp. 350–77.

of Pindar is by its very character ambiguous, both difficult in its form and enigmatic in its content. As a difficult code that bears a difficult but correct message for the qualified and a wrong message for the unqualified, the *ainos* communicates like an "enigma"—to use an English word that was borrowed from and serves as a translation for the Greek *ainigma,* which in turn is an actual derivative of *ainos.*[8]

By contrast with the praise poetry of Pindar, the epic poetry of the Homeric *Iliad* and *Odyssey* makes no such claims to exclusiveness and does not qualify as a form of *ainos.* Whereas both the epic poetry of Homer and the praise poetry of Pindar qualify as *kleos,* only praise poetry, to repeat, qualifies as *ainos.* On the other hand, whereas all praise poetry may qualify as *ainos,* not all examples of *ainos* are praise poetry. For example, the word *ainos* can also refer to a speech of admonition, or *par-ain-esis.*[9] Or again, it can designate animal fables, such as those used by Archilochus to admonish his friends or blame his enemies.[10] As a double-edged mode of discourse, the *ainos* can admonish or blame as well as praise.[11] Moreover, the *ainos* can assume a variety of poetic forms: it is recited by rhapsodes in such formats as the iambics of Archilochus[12] and the elegiacs of Theognis,[13] while it is sung and danced by choral groups in the Aeolic and "dactylo-epitrite" meters of Pindar. In other words, it is better to think of the *ainos* as a mode of discourse, not as a genre. Still, the point is that the genre of Homer's epic and the genre of Pindar's

---

8. The noun *ainigma* is derived from the verb *ainissō,* "make riddles," which in turn is derived from *ainos/aineō.* Note the use of *ainissō* in Theognis 681–82, where the poet says that he is cryptically communicating with the *agathoi* and that the hearer will recognize the impending doom about which he is communicating—if the hearer is truly *sophos.* For more on this passage of Theognis, see G. Nagy, "Theognis and Megara: A Poet's Vision of His City," in T. J. Figueira and G. Nagy, eds., *Theognis of Megara: Poetry and the Polis* (Baltimore: Johns Hopkins University Press, 1985), pp. 22–81; esp. pp. 22–36.

9. See H. Maehler, *Die Auffassung des Dichterberufs im frühen Griechentum bis zur Zeit Pindars,* Hypomnemata 3 (Göttingen: Vandenhoeck & Ruprecht, 1963), p. 47; see also Nagy, *Best of the Achaeans,* pp. 238–39.

10. For example Archilochus fr. 174 (M. L. West, ed., *Iambi et Elegi Graeci* [Oxford: Oxford University Press, 1971], vol. 1).

11. See Nagy, *Best of the Achaeans,* pp. 281–88.

12. Note the self-reference to the poem at hand by way of the word *ainos* in Archilochus fr. 174.

13. Note the self-reference to the poem at hand by way of the word *ainissō* in Theognis 681–82.

praise poetry are differentiated by the absence and presence, respectively, of self-definition in terms of *ainos*.

How, then, does the fact that the *kleos* of epic does not define itself as *ainos* make this *kleos* different from the *kleos* of praise poetry? In order to comprehend the difference, we must first consider the implications of the word *kleos* itself. In the epic poetry of Homer just as in the praise poetry of Pindar, *kleos* denotes the act of praising,[14] but in epic the praise takes place by the very process of narrating the deeds of heroes, predominantly in the third person. In praise poetry, the praise is more direct: here, too, *kleos* denotes the act of praising, but the praise applies to the here-and-now, narrated in the second person. In the epinicians, or victory odes, of Pindar, for example, the victories of athletes who competed in the great pan-Hellenic Games (Olympian, Pythian, Nemean, Isthmian) are celebrated on the occasion of the victors' return from the Games to their native cities. The praise poetry of Pindar, then, is occasional. By contrast, the epic poetry of the Homeric *Iliad* and *Odyssey* is distinctly not occasional: unlike the praise poem, it does not praise anyone in the here-and-now of its own performance. The praise of Homeric poetry is restricted to the heroes of the distant past.[15]

By contrast, the praise of Pindaric poetry is not restricted to the victorious athletes of the poet's here-and-now. The word *kleos* in Pindar's praise poetry applies equally to the athlete of the present and the hero of the past.[16] Moreover, what is being praised about the athlete is ideologically parallel to what is being praised about the hero. In the inherited diction of praise poetry, what an athlete undergoes in his pursuit of victory is a *ponos* (ordeal),[17] also called a *kamatos*,[18] and these same words apply also to the life-and-death struggles of heroes with their enemies, man and beast

14. Consider the use of the verb *kleiō*, derivative of *kleos*, at, for example, *Homeric Hymn* 32.19. See again *Iliad* 11. 227, cited at n. 1.

15. This is not the case with all epic poetry: see, for example, W. Radloff, *Proben der Volksliteratur der nördlichen türkischen Stämme* V: *Der Dialekt der Kara-Kirgisen* (St. Petersburg: Commissionäre der Kaiserlichen Akademie der Wissenschaften: Eggers et Co., 1885), pp. xviii–xix; see also J. Svenbro, *La parole et le marbre: Aux origines de la poétique grecque* (Lund: Studentlitteratur, 1976), pp. 17–18.

16. There is a striking example in Pindar *N.* 9.39–42.

17. See Pindar *O.* 5.15, 11.4; *N.* 4.1; *I.* 5.25.

18. See Pindar *P.* 5.47, *N.* 3.17.

alike.[19]   There is a parallel situation with the partial synonym
aethlos, from which *āthlētēs* (athlete) is derived: besides meaning
'contest' (the neuter *aethlon* means 'prize won in a contest'),
aethlos also means 'ordeal' and is applicable both to the efforts of
the athlete in the present and to the life-and-death struggle of the
hero in the past.[20]

In decidedly not making a distinction between the *kleos* due to
an athlete of the present for his athletic event and the *kleos* due to a
hero for his heroic deed, the ideology of Pindar's praise poetry is
parallel to the ideology of the athletic games in which the athletes
earned their *kleos.* The ideology of the Games, including the four
great pan-Hellenic festivals known as the Olympian, Pythian,
Nemean, and Isthmian Games, is fundamentally a religious one:
each festival, held on a seasonal basis into perpetuity, is predicated
on the death of a hero, on an eternal proto-ordeal, as it were, for
which the seasonally recurring ordeals of athletes, in principle
ongoing to eternity, serve as eternal compensation.[21]   This
religious ideology, clearly articulated in Pindar's poetry,[22] is
matched by the religious ideology of the poetry itself: each ordeal
of each victorious athlete, compensating for the proto-ordeal of
the hero who struggled and died, demands compensation of its
own in the form of song offered as praise for the athlete.[23]   And the
song in turn demands compensation from the victorious athlete

19. For *ponos,* see Pindar *P.* 4.178, 236, 243; for *kamatos,* see Pindar *N.* 1.70.
See also N. Loraux, "*Ponos:* Sur quelques difficultés de la peine comme nom du
travail," *Annali del Seminario di Studi del Mondo Classico, Naples: Archeologia
e Storia Antica* 4 (1982): 171–92.

20. For the *aethlos* of an athlete, see Pindar *I.* 5.7; for the *aethlos* of a hero, see
Pindar *P.* 4.220, *I.* 6.48.

21. See F. Pfister, *Der Reliquienkult im Altertum* (Giessen: Alfred Töpelmann,
1909), pp. 496–97, and A. Brelich, *Gli eroi greci* (Rome: Edizioni dell'Ateneo,
1958), pp. 94–95.

22. Note the motivation for the founding of the Rhodian athletic festival known
as the *Tlēpolemeia:* it was in response to a death, the deranged slaying of the half-
brother of the grandmother of Tlepolemos by her grandson (Pindar *O.* 7. 27–32). In
the words of Pindar, the institution of the athletic games is a *lutron,* "compensation," for this catastrophe (*O.* 7.77).

23. In Pindar's own words, the occasion of a victory ode is a *lutron* 'compensation' for the *kamatoi* 'ordeals' of the athlete (*I.* 8.2). Just as the ordeal of the athlete,
to repeat (see n. 22), is a formal *lutron* for a primordial death, so also the Pindaric
victory ode is a formal *lutron* for the athlete's ordeal.

and his family, to be offered to the composer of the song.[24] This aspect of the chain of compensation, which is clearly articulated throughout the poetry of Pindar, has been consistently misunderstood by latter-day Pindarists as if it were a blatant illustration of Pindar's mercenary Muse: when Pindar says that he owes it to his patrons to create a song, he is misunderstood as referring merely to a contract between patron and poet, entailing services to be performed and to be paid for. This is to ignore the sacral aspect of the very concept of value in archaic Greek society.[25] But, besides this general objection in principle, I offer a specific counterproposal. Any material compensation for the composer of an epinician song of praise in honor of a victorious athlete is but the final stage in a sacral process of ritual compensation: the athlete's deed literally demands to be requited in song, and the realization of the song in turn demands to be requited by way of some favor, material or otherwise.

There were of course other contemporary deeds, besides those of athletics, that could have demanded requital in song of praise. The most obvious category that comes to mind is victorious deeds in war, which are in fact denoted by the same terms used for victorious deeds in athletics: in the diction of Pindar and elsewhere as well, a man who fights in a war undergoes an ordeal as denoted by the words *ponos, kamatos, aethlos*.[26] So once again we see a collapsing of distinctions between the *kleos* due a hero and the *kleos* due a man. Only, in this case, both hero and man are potentially getting *kleos* in return for the same activity, a martial struggle. The internal evidence of poetic diction can be reinforced by external evidence: as we can see from the facts collected by Angelo Brelich on the institution of warfare in archaic Greece, fighting in wars was indeed a ritual activity, parallel to the ritual activity of engaging in athletic games.[27] Accordingly, the com-

24. Just as the athlete's compensating for the primordial death is a *ponos,* so also the poet's compensating for the athlete's ordeal is a *ponos* (e.g., Pindar *P.* 9.93).

25. On which see L. Gernet, "La notion mythologique de la valeur en Grèce," in *Anthropologie de la Grèce antique* (Paris: François Maspero, 1968), pp. 93–137; but see also Loraux, *"Ponos,"* 188n87. I reserve for another occasion a confrontation with other interpretations, for which see R. Descat, "Idéologie et communication dans la poésie grecque archaïque," *Quaderni Urbinati* 38 (1981): 7–27, esp. pp. 25–27.

26. See Pindar *I.* 8.1–16.

27. A. Brelich, *Guerre, agoni e culti nella Grecia arcaica* (Bonn: Halbelt, 1961).

pensation for deeds of war through songs of praise, just like the compensation for deeds of athletics, can be considered a vital link in a ritual chain.

But the picture is drastically affected by other developments in the history of archaic Greek civilization. With the evolution of the *polis,* or city-state, and the concurrent evolution of the *phalanx,* an army of citizen-soldiers, the factor of communal effort in warfare tends to counteract the factor of individual aristocratic enterprise. Thus the opportunity for individual feats of war, let alone the opportunity for celebrating them, is considerably reduced. The best chance for any individual distinction would have been afforded by actually getting killed in war (Pindar's *Isthmian* 7 gives us a vivid depiction).

But even here the evolution of the city-state produces a drastic effect. The archaic *polis* discourages, often by way of actual legislation, the glorification of the individual in the context of funerary practices in general and funerary praise poetry in particular. The very art-form of the poetic epigram, in which performance is replaced by the written record, is in fact a reflex of the strictures imposed by the *polis* against songs of praise in the context of funerals.[28]

Such restrictions on the glorification of the individual are a reflex of a much larger-scale phenomenon, in which the institutions of the city-state are in the process of evolving from and conflicting with the institutions of the tribal society that preceded it. In the process of the detribalization of the *polis,* inherited ideologies and practices having to do with ancestors—a key determinant of aristocratic individuality—were drastically curtailed. For one, the inherited ideologies about ancestors as encoded in genealogical traditions became differentiated into mythological genealogies of heroes and historical genealogies of immediate ancestors. This process was, of course, intensified by a universal tendency to mythologize remote as opposed to immediate ancestry: in any genealogical tradition, the distancing of a given ancestor from the here-and-now progressively reintegrates him into the current patterns of mytho-poeic thinking in the here-and-now. In any case, with the advent of the city-state, heroes became

28. M. Alexiou, *The Ritual Lament in Greek Tradition* (Cambridge: Cambridge University Press, 1974), pp. 104, 106.

differentiated from ancestors.[29] With this differentiation of
inherited ideologies came a parallel differentiation of inherited
practices: the institutional worship of ancestors became differentiated into two separate but related practices, the cult of heroes
and the worship of immediate ancestors.

In the course of archaic Greek history, the gap produced by
these differentiations could be bridged only by individuals who
developed the political power to rise *as individuals* above the
institutions of the city-state. And this could not really happen
until the so-called age of tyrants and thereafter, when tyrants and
tyrantlike personalities (like the Alcmaeonids of Athens) finally
succeeded in making a breakthrough into our recorded history as
real historical figures.

Toward the end of this phase of archaic Greek history, enter the
figure of Pindar. He and his contemporaries or near-contemporaries—figures like Simonides and Bacchylides—made their own
breakthroughs into our recorded history by virtue of being pro-
tégés of powerful families of tyrants or quasi-tyrants. The poetry
that celebrated such families could become fixed as individual
poetry, exempt from the process of ongoing recomposition-in-
performance that would have characterized any poetry transmitted through the ever-evolving city-state. While these poets owe
their fame *as historical individuals* to their patrons, the tyrants
owe their fame at least partly to these same poets, who enhance
the breakthrough of their patrons into the remote past of the
heroes. The poet Ibycus says this explicitly, as he tells the tyrant
Polycrates of the ever-lasting *kleos* that is to be conferred on him
by the poet's song, which is also called *kleos:*

καὶ σύ, Πολύκρατες, κλέος ἄφθιτον ἑξεῖς
ὡς κατ᾽ ἀοιδὰν καὶ ἐμὸν κλέος

You too [as well as the heroes just mentioned in the song], Polycrates, will have *kleos* that is unwilting, in accordance with my
song, my *kleos.*[30]

The double use of *kleos* here reenacts the notion of reciprocity

29. See E. Rohde, *Psyche: Seelencult und Unsterblichkeitsglaube der Griechen,*
2d ed. (Freiburg: J. C. B. Mohr, P. Siebeck, 1898), 1:108–10; also Brelich, *Gli eroi
greci,* 144 n. 202; Nagy, *Best of the Achaeans,* p. 115.

30. Ibycus, *Poetae Melici Graeci,* ed. D. L. Page (Oxford: Clarendon Press,
1962), 282a.47–48.

built into the word: the patron gets fame from the praise of the poet, whose own fame depends on the fame of his patron in the here-and-now.

But the poet effects the fame of his patron not merely by recording the subject's accomplishments or qualities in the here-and-now but also by linking him with the heroes of the past. This linking can even be directly genealogical. Thus, for example, the praise poetry of Pindar confirms the political claim of the tyrant Theron of Akragas, to the effect that Theron is descended from Polyneices, a hero of the Seven against Thebes epic tradition.[31]

The situation is altogether different with the poetry of epic. By the time of the age of tyrants, the epic traditions of the Greeks, as represented by the *Iliad* and *Odyssey* of Homer, had reached a stage of evolution where they had already become too fixed—let us say crystallized—to be substantially responsive to the political exigencies of tyrants. The emergence of the Homeric poems in the form of fixed texts, as I have argued at length elsewhere, is the consequence not of a single event, such as the writing down of the poems, but rather of an evolutionary process whereby the pan-Hellenic diffusion of the Homeric traditions, concomitant with ongoing recomposition-in-performance at international (inter-*polis*) festivals, led gradually to a uniformity at the expense of a multiformity of versions.[32] While a multiformity of localized versions would benefit the localized concerns of tyrants, the uniformity of the Homeric poems could in the end become an obstacle to the tyrants' current political ideologies: we recall the testimony of Herodotus (5.67) to the effect that Cleisthenes, tyrant of Sicyon, banished the public performances of Homer in his city on the grounds that the contents were partial to Argos, a city that was at that point an enemy of Sicyon. With its universal or pan-Hellenic stature, then, the poetry of Homer would not accommodate the localized needs of the audience, and we cannot expect it to be responsive to such considerations as the genealogies of powerful patrons. In the epic poetry of Homer, the gap that separates the heroes of the past and the men of the present could not and would not be bridged. Little wonder, then, that heroes could lift stones that two of us today could not even manage to budge (*Iliad* 12. 445–49)!

31. Pindar O. 2.41–47.
32. See G. Nagy, "Theognis and Megara," p. 35 § 17 n. 3.

As for the praise poetry of Pindar, it does more than just confirm the extension of the genealogies of powerful families into the heroic past: as we have already seen, the *kleos* of victorious athletes who come from such families is pointedly equated with the *kleos* of heroes as they are known from epic.[33] But the praise poetry of Pindar does not claim to be descended from the epic of Homer—which would have matched the way in which his patrons may claim to be descended from heroes praised by the narration of epic poetry. To repeat, the *kleos* of Pindar praises not only the victors of the present but also the heroes of the past, and this praise of heroes is treated as intrinsic to the medium of praise poetry. In the words of Pindar, the medium of epinician praise poetry existed even before the Seven against Thebes (*N.* 8. 48–51): by implication, praise poetry was praising heroes even before the events recorded by epic.[34] In the praise poetry of Pindar, Homer figures as but one in a long line of poets who are masters of *kleos*. By implication, then, the *kleos* of Homer is but an offshoot of the *kleos* that survives as the praise poetry of Pindar. Unlike the *kleos* of Homer, however, the *kleos* of Pindar extends into the here-and-now, linking the heroes of the past with the men of the present. In the diction of Pindar, the very concept of *nea* or *neara* 'new things,' as Andrew Miller has recently shown, applies not to poetic innovations but to poetic applications of the past glories of heroes to the present glories of men who are being praised in the here-and-now.[35]

The built-in conceit of Pindaric poetry, that its praise collapses the distinction between heroes of the past and men of the here-and-now, accentuates the occasionality of the medium. Which brings us back to the self-definition of this medium as *ainos*—a self-definition not shared by Homeric poetry. As we have seen, contemporary feats of athletics are particularly appropriate for celebration by the *ainos* as a form of poetry that purports to close the gap between the heroic past and the historic present, in that the very activity of athletics is from the standpoint of religious ideology a present-day ordeal that reenacts, in a perpetual series

---

33. See again n. 16, above.

34. See A. Köhnken, *Die Funktion des Mythos bei Pindar* (Berlin: de Gruyter, 1971), pp. 34–35; Nagy, *Best of the Achaeans*, pp. 227–28.

35. A. Miller, "*Phthonos* and *Parphasis: Nemean* 8.19–34," *Greek, Roman and Byzantine Studies* 23 (1982): 111–20, esp. p. 114.

of seasonal festivals, the primordial ordeal of the hero. We see the same ideology depicted in the Funeral Games of Patroklos in *Iliad* 23, where the Games are instituted as compensation for the death of the hero Patroklos and where, as Cedric Whitman has noticed, the athletic activity of each character in some way reenacts the martial activity of his own heroic career.[36]

As we have also seen, contemporary feats of war would have been equally appropriate for celebration by praise poetry, had it not been for the evolution of the *polis*. Moreover, even if we discount for the moment the emphasis that the *polis* placed on the communal effort as opposed to individual aristocratic enterprise, any celebration of martial feats still raises the problem of inter-*polis* politics: what is a success for one *polis* will be a failure for another, so that it becomes difficult for any military victory to achieve pan-Hellenic recognition in poetry. By contrast, the victories of athletes at the four great pan-Hellenic Games are by definition recognized by all Hellenic city-states. It should come as no surprise, then, that in the case of military victories, the one notable exception meriting pan-Hellenic recognition in poetry was in fact a pan-Hellenic victory: I refer to the Greek victory over the Persians in 479 B.C., as for example celebrated by Pindar in *Isthmian* 8 (alongside the central topic of that composition, an athletic victory by an Aeginetan in the Isthmian Games of 478 B.C.). The special appropriateness of athletics to praise poetry is best illustrated by Pindar's claim, as already noted, that epinician praise poetry had existed even before epic. We may add that the Seven against Thebes, in the same Pindaric context, are represented as having engaged in an athletic contest specifically before they embarked on their famous war. This athletic contest, serving as prototype for the Nemean Games, would have been celebrated by the prototype of Pindar's current Nemean Ode in honor of the current victor at the Nemean Games.

The ideology of the athletic games, as expressed in the epinician praise poetry of Pindar, may even be said to be a sort of compensation for the historical differentiation between heroes and ancestors, in that the *kleos* of the hero and the *kleos* of the athlete converge precisely in the context of praising the athlete's immedi-

---

36. C. H. Whitman, *Homer and the Heroic Tradition* (Cambridge, Mass.: Harvard University Press, 1959), p. 169.

ate ancestors. By upholding the values of the epic heroes, the victor is represented as simultaneously upholding the values of his own immediate ancestors. In one particularly striking passage, Pindar expresses this simultaneity in the actual words of a dead hero, who is represented as speaking from the dead about the martial victories of his son. The son, who is from the standpoint of his father's words still a living hero, is Alcmaeon, one of the Epigonoi, the sons of the Seven against Thebes, who succeeded in destroying Thebes. The father is Amphiaraos, son of Oikles, one of the original Seven against Thebes who had failed at what their sons later succeeded. The theme of these heroes is introduced in the context of praising the athlete Aristomenes of Aegina for his victory in wrestling at the Pythian Games of 446 B.C. I begin the quotation with the words of the poet in praise of the victorious Aristomenes for the glory that this athlete has conferred upon his immediate ancestors, the patriliny of the Meidulidai:

αὔξων δὲ πάτραν Μειδυλιδᾶν λόγον φέρεις, | τὸν ὅνπερ ποτ' Ὀϊκλέος παῖς . . . αἰνίξατο . . . (43) ὧδ' εἶπε μαρναμένων· | "φυᾷ τὸ γενναῖον ἐπιπρέπει | ἐκ πατέρων παισὶ λῆμα . . ." (55) τοιαῦτα μὲν | ἐφθέγξατ' Ἀμφιάρηος. χαίρων δὲ καὶ αὐτὸς | Ἀλκμᾶνα στεφάνοισι βάλλω.

Making praiseworthy the house of the Meidulidai, you carry with you the words that once the son of Oikles said [said as an *ainos*]. . . . Thus he spoke about those who fought: "The will of the fathers shines through from them, in what is inborn in the nature of their sons." . . . Thus spoke Amphiaraos. And I also take joy in casting a garland at Alcmaeon. (Pindar *P.* 8.38–57)

The word *pateres* in this passage means not only "fathers" but also "ancestors." The latter meaning, I submit, emerges more clearly as the ode progresses:

ἐπάμεροι· τί δέ τις; τί δ' οὔ τις; σκιᾶς ὄναρ | ἄνθρωπος. ἀλλ' ὅταν αἴγλα διόσδοτος ἔλθῃ, | λαμπρὸν φέγγος ἔπεστιν ἀνδρῶν καὶ μείλιχος αἰών. |

Creatures of the day. What is a someone? What is a no one? Man is the dream of a shade. But when the brightness given by Zeus comes, there is at hand the shining light of men, and the life-force gives pleasure. (Pindar *P.* 8.95–97)

I interpret *skiās onar,* "dream of a shade," as a recapitulation of the earlier words of the dead Amphiaraos about his living son: the *skiā*, "shade," is a dead person (we know well such a meaning of *skiā* from Homeric diction), who is literally dreaming—that is, realizing through his dreams—the living person. It is as if we the living were the realization of the dreams dreamt by our dead ancestors. And this link of the victorious athlete to his ancestors, to repeat, is celebrated through the glories of heroes.

The "glories of heroes" are the *klea andrōn* of epic, as represented by epic. But the "glories of heroes" need not be epic alone: they can also be *ainos,* even as represented by epic. I think of *Iliad* 9, when old Phoenix gives his admonition to Achilles in the format of an *ainos* (specifically, *parainesis*):[37] he refers here to his own discourse as *tōn prosthen . . . klea andrōn | hērōōn,* "glories of men of the past, heroes" (9. 524–25). As I have attempted to show in detail elsewhere, the actual message of what Phoenix then says turns out to be—from the standpoint of Achilles and the *Iliad* itself—the very name of Patroklos, *Patro-kleēs,* "he who has the *klea* [glories] of the ancestors."[38] In the Homeric theme of Patroklos, the differentiation between heroes and ancestors has not yet happened. In this theme, the praise of ancestors and the praise of heroes are as yet one. So, too, in the poetry of Pindar in praise of athletes: the praise of their ancestors is realized in the praise of heroes. It seems fitting, then, that the death of Patroklos requires as compensation the ultimate athletic event of Homeric poetry, the Games of *Iliad* 23.

The Iliadic theme of Patroklos is too intricate to be treated adequately here, and I bring it up, albeit all too briefly, for the sole purpose of isolating an instance in which epic refers to the format of the *ainos* without actually identifying itself with it. We can find other instances as well, especially in the *Odyssey,* and each time we may observe the same pattern: whereas epic can refer to the format of the *ainos,* it is not an *ainos* itself.

Which brings us back, one last time, to the self-references of *ainos* as praise poetry. As we have seen, praise poetry both calls itself *kleos* and explicitly identifies itself with the *kleos* of epic. It is as if praise poetry were the primordial form of epic. This is in fact what Aristotle says, that epic is descended from praise poetry

37. See Maehler, *Die Auffassung des Dichterberufs,* p. 47.
38. Nagy, *Best of the Achaeans,* pp. 111, 114–15.

(Poetics 1448b32–34). It is also what epic itself seems to be saying in situations where one character, in praising another, predicts that this praise will become the *kleos* heard by future audiences. Even the sporadic instances in Homeric poetry in which a hero is addressed in the second person give the impression that the third-person narrative of epic is but a transformation of the second-person direct address of praise poetry. But, however we may want to formulate the transformation of epic poetry *as a derivative form* from praise poetry *as a parent form,* we must keep in mind that, while the derivative form was evolving into the generalized and universally accessible medium of Homeric poetry, the parent form was in the meantime evolving into the specialized and restrictively difficult medium attested in the epinician poetry of Pindar.[39]

39. It goes without saying that the evolution of the parent form, as represented by Pindaric poetry, is crystallized much later than that of the derivative form, as represented by Homeric poetry. For a valuable discussion of epic and praise poetry in early Indic society, see M. Dillon, *Celts and Aryans* (Simla: India Institute of Advanced Study, 1975), p. 54.

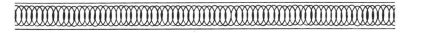

5
ORAL-FORMULAIC RHETORIC AND THE INTERPRETATION OF WRITTEN TEXTS
Alain Renoir

Simplicity and difficulty are by no means antithetical, and their intimate coexistence in respect to a variety of tasks is usually taken for granted. For example, even though I am no Sisyphus, what I must do in order to roll a one-thousand-pound boulder up a hill is absolute *simplicity,* but I lack the muscular strength to perform the task, so that the *difficulty* may correctly be said to be too great for me, and the enterprise both simple and difficult. By the same token, the interpretation of oral traditional poetry by a properly trained scholar is both extremely simple and extremely difficult.

Within this essay, I use the term *oral traditional poetry* to refer to metrical utterances composed orally by a poet working within a tradition of oral rhetoric and subject matter for the benefit of a live audience accustomed to listening to this kind of composition. In order to avoid unnecessary ambiguity in the initial section of my argument, I am further assuming—but only for the moment— that neither poet nor audience has been directly exposed to the written word and that the scholar has forgotten to put new batteries in the tape recorder, so that we are left with no tangible record of the performance.

Now, it has been over two decades since Albert Lord first taught us that, under circumstances akin to those which I have arbitrarily formulated, the audience reacts actively to the ongoing perform-ance and the performance is in turn affected by the reactions of the audience.[1] The task facing the scholar is, accordingly, perfectly

1. Albert B. Lord, *The Singer of Tales* (1961; New York: Atheneum 76, 1974), pp. 14–17.

simple: he or she needs only listen to the performance and observe the interaction between audience and performer in order to understand the utterances being strung out by the latter. If the composition happens to be formulaic as well as traditional—and these two conditions tend to go hand in hand—then our hypothetical scholar may even anticipate both the audience's reaction and the performer's next statement. As Stanley Greenfield and Adrien Bonjour first suggested in the 1950s,[2] and as John Miles Foley has demonstrated more recently by emphasizing the importance of archetypal elements,[3] familiarity with an oral-formulaic system leads the listener to construe some formulaic utterances within a context which automatically brings to mind associations likely to influence interpretation; and students of the subject know that the presence of a given oral-formulaic element may likewise lead the same listener to expect certain things to occur or at least to be mentioned.

Simple common sense tells us that an audience used to Homeric verse and listening to a performer composing or reciting the sixth book of the *Odyssey* would be affected, consciously or otherwise, by the formulaic epithet "white-armed," which serves here to describe King Alcinous's cute young daughter—"Ναυσικάα

2. Stanley B. Greenfield, "The Formulaic Expression of the Theme of Exile in Anglo-Saxon Poetry," *Speculum* 30 (1955), has argued, "The association with other contexts using a similar formula will inevitably color a particular instance of a formula so that a whole host of overtones springs into action" (p. 205). Adrien Bonjour, "*Beowulf* and the Beasts of Battle," *PMLA* 71 (1957), argues that the affective use of formulaic themes makes the audience see things "in advance, and thereby implies deeper connotations" (p. 556). Donald K. Fry, "The Heroine on the Beach in *Judith,*" *Neuphilologische Mitteilungen* 68 (1967), puts the same idea in a slightly different light when he suggests that formulaic themes may "prove to be a mnemonic device as much for the audience as for the poet; they provide the audience with a supply of associations" (p. 181).

3. John Miles Foley, "Formula and Theme in Old English Poetry," in Benjamin A. Stolz and Richard S. Shannon, eds., *Oral Literature and the Formula* (Ann Arbor: Center for the Coordination of Ancient and Modern Studies, 1976), notes that the presence of formulaic elements is likely to affect our reaction to "speech and character by locating them with relation to archetypal paradigms" (p. 218). The point is brilliantly developed in Foley's "*Beowulf* and the Psychohistory of Anglo-Saxon Culture," *American Imago* 34 (1977), where he argues that the "repeated and collective experience of performed epic poetry" in a traditional oral society educates the audience "by presenting them time and again with a verbal montage of the group's poetic models and thereby with the data which these models encode" (p. 134).

λευκώλενος" (6. 101)⁴—but which we know from the *Iliad* to be associated with Queen Helen (3. 121), whose regal beauty is such that she is easily mistaken for one of the immortal goddesses (3. 158). We may likewise suppose that listeners familiar with early-Germanic traditional poetry and hearing a performer reciting or composing the section of *Beowulf* in which the Geats reach the Danish coast might not inconceivably pick up on the mention of shining sea cliffs (222ᵃ)⁵ and realize that these shining cliffs are the key element of a well-known oral-formulaic theme labeled "the Hero on the Beach," in which a hero (here, Beowulf) in the presence of retainers (here, the other Geats in the boat) at the end or beginning of a journey (here, the sea voyage) stands near the boundary between two areas (here, the water and the land) in the presence of something that shines (here, the cliffs) and is in some kind of obvious or latent danger (here, the expected fight with Grendel). The realization might further prepare them emotionally for, and perhaps even help them anticipate, the kind of killing which subsequently takes place in Heorot, since David Crowne, who first identified the theme, has demonstrated that it usually occurs before a scene of slaughter or a mention thereof.⁶ A similar argument can be formulated in respect to a traditional Yugoslav audience listening to a traditional return song, since Lord has shown that the hero of this kind of poem normally proves tem-

---

4. Quotations and citations from the Homeric poems are from *The Odyssey,* ed. and trans. A. T. Murray, 2 vols., Locb Classical Library (1919; Cambridge, Mass.: Harvard University Press, 1975, 1976), and *Iliade,* ed. Paul Mazon et al., 4 vols. (Paris: Belles Lettres, 1947–1949).
5. Quotations and citations from *Beowulf* are from *Beowulf and Judith,* ed. Elliott Van Kirk Dobbie, Anglo-Saxon Poetic Records 4 (New York: Columbia University Press, 1953).
6. David K. Crowne, "The Hero on the Beach: An Example of Composition by Theme in Anglo-Saxon Poetry," *Neuphilologische Mitteilungen* 61 (1960): 362–72. Crowne's essay assumed that the hero must necessarily be standing on a beach, but subsequent investigation has suggested that any confine between two areas meets the requirements of the theme. See, for example, my own footnote to Crowne's essay, "Oral-Formulaic Theme Survival," *Neuphilologische Mitteilungen* 65 (1964): 70–75, and Donald K. Fry's "The Heroine on the Beach in *Judith,*" *Neuphilologische Mitteilungen* 68 (1967): 168–84. A list of salient studies of this theme may be found in my "Oral-Formulaic Context: Implications for the Comparative Criticism of Mediaeval Texts," in John Miles Foley, ed., *Oral Traditional Literature: A Festschrift for Albert Bates Lord* (Columbus: Slavica Publishers, 1981), p. 438, n. 42. To this list, one should add Alexandra Hennessey Olsen, "Guthlac on the Beach," *Neophilologus* 64 (1980): 290–96.

porarily unrecognizable at the time of his homecoming, and we may accordingly suppose that the audience in question would expect him to go unrecognized for a time.[7]

Since the foregoing list could be extended almost at will and innumerable examples are readily detectable to the trained observer, the task facing prospective interpreters under the conditions which I have outlined is unquestionably simple. Yet, it is by no means easy, and the primary cause of the difficulty may well lie in the fact that, as Foley has reminded us, modern scholars are not the products of oral traditions, even though they may have come to study such traditions as part of their advanced training.[8] Consequently, they must usually fall back on conscious analysis in order to acquire the understanding which the poet's intended audience has unconsciously developed through repeated exposure from early childhood onward. However simple the process may be, the task of analyzing the many elements which constitute the symbiosis of an oral performance will usually require a staggering amount of painstaking work, which may well consume more time than is available to an individual scholar or even to a research team.

In addition, even the most thorough, accurate, and complete analysis may occasionally lead to substantial misinterpretations when we deal with materials or situations whose interpretation depends on the kind of automatic emotional reactions which one develops only through active participation in a given cultural context. A personal anecdote will illustrate the principle. Many years ago, I happened to see a motion picture in a small provincial town in Mexico. I recall that the opening scene was comical and that the audience reacted accordingly. A few minutes into the show, however, the plot included a middle-aged woman who had won an automobile at a lottery. Because she did not know how to drive and was too poor to afford the upkeep, she had no use for the prize and only wanted to be left alone, but the lottery representative who had brought it to the door of her tenement would not take no for an answer. There he was, center-screen, addressing the assembled neighborhood and extolling the befuddled woman's accomplish-

---

7. Lord, *Singer of Tales,* for example, pp. 250–54.

8. John Miles Foley, "The Oral Theory in Context," in Foley, *Oral Traditional Literature,* points out that we initially approach the study of literature "from our point of view as a very literate, typographic culture" (p. 27).

ment in having reared two sons to manhood. As he kept pointing to her and repeating with increasing emotion and frequency the words "una madre Mexicana," he was so caught up in his own hollow rhetoric that I was put in mind of the actor whose over-blown emotions prompt Hamlet's account in Shakespeare's play:

> . . . all his visage wanned,
> Tears in his eyes, distraction in his aspect,
> A broken voice . . .
>
> (2.2. 538–41)[9]

Naturally, I construed the scene as a spoof and reacted accordingly. But I was wrong; or, at any rate, I was out of step with the rest of the audience, for my brief snicker was the only one in the room: except for my own, there was not a dry eye in the audience, and the tears came gushing anew with every reiterated mention of the "madre Mexicana."

The truth is that I was raised in a culture with little appreciation for sentimentality in mimesis and that my formal literary training and subsequent experience on the faculty of various departments of English have not encouraged me to develop this kind of appreciation. In addition, I was then totally unacquainted with a particularly popular class of Mexican motion pictures in which sentimentality seems to be valued for its own sake. I have seen several such motion pictures since my initial fiasco, and I have learned to appreciate the affective function of sentimentality; but my appreciation remains artificial insofar as it is the reasoned product of analysis rather than a genuine emotional reaction like that of the intended audience, and my interpretation must necessarily fall short in this respect.

The same phenomenon applies to orally composed South Slavic narrative poetry, where we are only too readily disturbed by repetitions and inconsistencies which seem to pass unnoticed by both the performer and his audience.[10] By analogy, we may assume

9. William Shakespeare, *The Tragedy of Hamlet Prince of Denmark,* ed. Williard Farnham (Baltimore: Penguin Books, 1961), p. 85.

10. For example, Lord, *Singer of Tales,* tells of a singer who claimed the ability to reproduce another singer's performance precisely as he had heard it but could see no contradiction between his statement and the fact that his version was different from the original: "he was singing the story as he conceived it as being 'like' [the other] story, and to him 'word for word and line for line' are simply an emphatic way of saying 'like'" (p. 28).

that the original audiences of the Homeric poems would not have been bothered by the constant reiteration of formulaic epithets like "godlike Odysseus" ("δῖος Ὀδυσσεύς" / "Ὀδυσσῆος θείοιο") or "Odysseus of many wiles" ("πολύμητις Ὀδυσσεύς"),[11] but we know that this kind of repetition, especially when apparently uncalled for by the action, so bothered Julius Caesar Scaliger that he felt compelled to chastise the poet with such vigor that his example was followed by later critics, who went on complaining about Homeric contradictions and repetitions well into the eighteenth century.[12]

Whether the *Iliad* and the *Odyssey* must be considered products of oral or of oral-derived composition is irrelevant within the framework of the arbitrary assumptions I constructed above, but it is important to note that most modern students have heard enough about oral-formulaic composition to know not to be bothered by its repetitions and incongruities. Yet, as in the case of my own appreciation of sentimental sections in Mexican movies, the understanding must necessarily remain artificial in a majority of cases: We know that the repetitious elements and seeming inconsistencies associated with oral-formulaic rhetoric are quite acceptable, and we have no wish to be thought so unsophisticated as to admit that they may still bother us a little. Yet, in our heart of hearts, most of us still consider these things oddities, even if these oddities fascinate us so much that we must study them and write about them. The fact is that it takes a mixture of literary sensitivity, scholarly devotion, and years of immersion in the materials and their traditional context before the oddities cease to be oddities. In fact, it takes someone like Albert Lord himself to gain enough familiarity with oral-formulaic performances to study the poetry with the highest scholarly rigor while bringing to it the genuine appreciation of the intended audience. To repeat once again my initial point, the nature of the task is simple but the difficulty involved in the accomplishment is so great that only the

11. Milman Parry, *The Traditional Epithet in Homer,* trans. Adam Parry, in Milman Parry, *The Making of Homeric Verse,* ed. Adam Parry (Oxford: Clarendon Press, 1971), tabulates the uses of "δῖος Ὀδυσσεύς" (p. 11) and discusses them in context (see pp. 10–14).

12. For a history of such misunderstandings of Homer's rhetoric, see Howard Clarke, *Homer's Readers* (East New Brunswick, N.J.: Associated University Presses, 1981), pp. 106–55 ("Homer Criticized"), esp. pp. 117 (Scaliger), 125 (Jean Terrasson), and 151 (François Hédelin).

chosen few may occasionally make bold to hope for the total success that will finally elude them anyway. As for the rest of us, we had better be satisfied with striving for very partial success if the overall research in the discipline is ever to reach the ultimate goal of explaining beyond reasonable doubt the symbiotic processes whereby oral literature is produced, appreciated, and transmitted.

By now, everyone has surely noticed a glaring flaw, if not in my argument, certainly in my choice of materials. Although I have postulated a situation in which there was no place for the written word, I have nevertheless illustrated some of my points with references to Homeric Greek and Old English materials which we know only from the written records and about the actual composition of which we can only surmise. My inconsistency illustrates a problem which faces diachronic scholars in contrast to their synchronic colleagues. Whether the latter be Milman Parry and Albert Lord recording South Slavic singers in the twentieth century or the scribes at the Monastery of Whitby transcribing the songs of Cædmon some thirteen hundred years earlier, they are both in a position to observe the performance and to attempt assessing whether what they hear is a genuine oral composition or merely the recitation of a memorized text. In contrast, the former have no means of observing the performance personally, have usually no access to a reliable account of that performance, and must accordingly work from a written record without knowing for certain whether the text on the page corresponds to what any particular performer ever composed and whether it should be considered the product of oral or written composition or of a combination of both. Everyone concerned with traditional poetry, for example, knows that the text of the Homeric poems was substantially different before Aristarchus's edition and presumably even more so before Pisistratus's recension,[13] and Germanists have been arguing for a century about the proper order of lines in the *Hildebrandslied*,[14] for any text that has been copied and

13. For a convenient outline of the vicissitudes of the text and contents of the Homeric poems, see J. A. Davidson, "The Homeric Question," in Alan J. B. Wace and Frank H. Stubbings, eds., *A Companion to Homer* (London: Macmillan and Co., 1962), pp. 234–65, with the contributions of Pisistratus and Aristarchus discussed on pp. 238–40.

14. I have discussed this problem in some detail in my "The Armor of the *Hildebrandslied*: An Oral-Formulaic Point of View," *Neuphilologische Mitteilungen* 78 (1977): 389–95.

recopied is likely to be affected by substitutions, deletions, additions, and all kinds of other changes which make it difficult to determine what was there in the first place. As for the mode of composition, an observation of Donald Fry's in respect to Old English poetry applies to other literatures as well: as long as we know how to recognize the main features of a given oral-formulaic tradition, we can usually tell whether a particular text from the distant past was composed in accordance with that tradition, but we have yet devised no test to determine to everyone's satisfaction whether the actual act of composition took place orally or in writing.[15]

In other words, diachronic scholars must turn to surmise more often than their synchronic colleagues, with the double result that their task tends to grow more complicated and their conclusions less compelling. The complications further multiply when we deal with ancient texts which we assume to have been composed in writing but which nevertheless contain indisputable elements of oral-formulaic rhetoric. Here, a new and complex dimension is added to the problem because we often have no means of establishing whether the poem was intended for private reading or for public delivery, or to assess the degree to which either the poet or the intended audience or both were intellectually and emotionally steeped in the implications, suggestions, and connotations of the tradition of oral rhetoric used for the composition of the written text.

Another anecdote will illustrate the latter point. On a recent visit to Hollywood, I was impressed by the quantity of apparently expensive imitations of classic vintage cars that adorned the streets. The phenomenon first came to my attention while I was walking along and happened to notice in a row of parked cars ahead of me a glimmer of blue that reminded me of the blue which the 2.3-liter Bugatti had made famous on automobile racing circuits the world over in the late 1920s and early 1930s. I dashed ahead to find myself looking at what I can only call a gross caricature of the lovely car whose memory had flashed through my

15. Donald K. Fry, "Cædmon as a Formulaic Poet," *Forum for Modern Language Studies* 10 (1974), notes, "A consensus seems to be emerging that written Old English poetry used oral forms, but no reliable test can differentiate written from oral poems" (p. 227); reprinted in Joseph J. Duggan, ed., *Oral Literature: Seven Essays* (New York: Barnes and Noble, 1975).

mind. True, the color was correct, the radiator seemed a fair approximation of the original, and the two leather straps that held the hood down left nothing to be desired; but the resemblance ended there. The rear end was too long, the tires were too big, the wheels looked too heavy, and the seats were too soft and thick; in other words, whereas everything about the original car was delicate and firm, everything about the copy was heavy and soft.

The owner, who fortuitously showed up during the course of my inspection, was so delighted to find someone interested in what turned out to be his new acquisition that he obligingly offered to let me look under the hood. As may be expected, the massive power plant bore no resemblance to the trim motor of my nostalgic memory. The greatest disappointment was the electronic ignition, for aficionados fondly recall the unshakable aesthetic principles which kept Ettore Bugatti devising finer and finer magnetos long after all other automobile manufacturers had shifted to the Delco system. I could not refrain from mentioning how much fun the original system had been for the drivers of the time, but my interlocutor had never heard of a magneto. All he knew was that he had paid a hefty sum to a local manufacturer of copies of classic automobiles, that he was absolutely enchanted with his purchase, and that he did not mind mechanical improvements as long as the overall appearance produced the desired illusion. It was clear that he loved the idea of owning a copy of a Bugatti but did not know what a Bugatti was and would have been at a total loss if someone had substituted the real thing for the copy in his possession.

But what of the manufacturer? In view of the evidence, he or she must necessarily be one of two things: *either* a real connoisseur of Bugattis who had consciously decided to adapt his or her favorite vintage car to the taste of Hollywood just as Benihana of Tokyo has adapted Japanese food to the American taste while making certain that the outward aspect remains somewhat Japanese *or* someone who knew no more about Bugattis than my interlocutor and simply had the bright idea of cashing in on local snobbism by copying a picture or a museum display. I personally incline toward the latter scenario because the same company manufactures copies of all kinds of vintage cars, and I doubt that anyone could be a truly competent connoisseur of more than a very few of them.

Likewise, it has been pointed out that John Keats's poem *La*

Belle Dame sans Merci follows precisely the rules of courtly love outlined by Jehan le Maire de Belges in the fifteenth century.[16] Yet few of us would call the poem medieval, and most of us find it rather typical of Romantic medievalism. I readily confess having no notion of how much firsthand knowledge and understanding of Jehan le Maire de Belges and the medieval poetry of courtly love may be attributed to Keats, but I think we can assume the majority of his readers to have been quite innocent of both. We may even suppose that many who liked the poem would have been terribly bored if they had been made to wade through Chrestien de Troyes or Gottfried von Strassburg. Anyone who doubts the possibility will do well to glance at some of the opinions which Keats's contemporaries and near-contemporaries expressed in respect to medieval poetry. The point is that, just as the owner of the would-be Bugatti enjoyed his car without looking for such features of the original as were missing and as he would not have understood anyway, so the readers of Keats's would-be medieval poem presumably enjoyed it without looking for such features of medieval courtly love as were missing from it and as they would not have understood anyway. Likewise, just as it would take a psychiatrist to figure out the cognitive and emotional context within which the manufacturer of the would-be Bugatti thought up his or her enterprise, so it would be very difficult to figure out how cognitively and emotionally intimate Keats may have been with the tradition and conventions behind his poem.

It would make little difference in the principle, incidentally, if the automobile manufacturer had produced an exact replica of a Bugatti and Keats had produced a convincing replica of a medieval poem. To be sure, the chances are that the car would have proved too uncomfortable and operationally surprising to sell in Southern California at the end of the twentieth century and that the poem would have proved too hard to read and rhetorically surprising to sell in England at the beginning of the nineteenth. Yet both would have remained replicas—however technically competent—of artifacts belonging to traditions that had ceased to be meaningful; and such experiments must not be confused with active participation in an ongoing tradition. Lord has made a sim-

16. L. G. Locke, "Keats' *La Belle Dame sans Merci,*" *The Explicator* 5 (1946): 1.

ilar observation in respect to so-called folk festivals in Yugoslavia, where singers deliver without ever consulting the text all kinds of apparently formulaic songs which they may have composed earlier in writing or memorized from legitimate collections of oral poetry. In his own words, "In spite of the fact that the songs themselves are often oral poems, we cannot consider such singers as oral poets."[17]

The illustrations which I have invoked thus far have in common the fact that they are recent enough to be subject to the documentation methods of modern scholarship. Much as I will stand by my earlier contention that few of us could ever ascertain the exact cognitive and emotional context within which a human being puts together an automobile or a poem, I am fully aware that scholars have gathered a formidable amount of evidence concerning what Keats had done, read, seen, and heard at any time of his brief life; I further assume that an interview with the manufacturer of vintage-car replicas would enable me to guess whether he or she was really intimate with the 2.3-liter Bugatti, and no one in the world would dare argue that Lord would need more than the briefest confrontation to assess the extent to which a pseudo-oral poet might be steeped in the real thing. Most regrettably from the diachronic scholar's point of view, such means of documentation are seldom available once we go back to the Middle Ages or earlier.

Because the large-scale uniformity brought about by the age of technology pervades everything we see, we can often gauge the state of a culture by its external manifestations, and we have come to expect cultural and social changes to follow hard upon technical innovation. In the industrialized world, the combination of the public-address system and the electric guitar has radically altered musical sensitivities within two generations, and the unprecedented progress of air and ground transportation since the Second World War is similarly changing what used to be considered the normal pattern of life in the United States. More to the point, anthropology has shown that the intrusion of modern technology into a primitive society can bring a healthy oral tradition to a sudden end. The traditional singer in a primitive village can be

17. Lord, *Singer of Tales*, p. 14.

readily discarded in favor of a battery-operated radio because the
push of a button is all it takes to call in the new rhythms.[18] Contrary to this situation, change was slower in the old days. In a situation similar to the one I have sketched, the counterpart of the
battery-operated radio would have been a written statement,
which could not have been deciphered and enjoyed until someone
had learned how to read; and the average human being had neither
the time nor the opportunity to do so. The result was that the
inroads of a new culture into an older one could remain mere
inroads for a long time and that the old and the new could coexist
for generation after generation within the same society and at
times within the same person. Even if we wished to discount the
story of Cædmon as too miraculous to be significant, the famous
letter Alcuin wrote to the Bishop of Lindisfarne in 797 would leave
little doubt that in that year the native tradition of oral Germanic
poetry was thriving in the monastery along with the imported literacy.[19]

The coexistence of an oral and a written tradition within the
same person has been recently attested by Jeff Opland's study of a
Bantu poet highly educated in the Xhosa oral tradition as well as in
the European written tradition and capable of producing superior
poetry in both; and Opland has cited at least one occasion when
the poet in question tried his hand at composing in writing traditional oral Xhosa poetry. Although I have serious reservations
about the significance of the following addendum, it seems worth
mentioning that I was not the only one to find this written version
of oral composition decidedly inferior to poetry which the same
poet had composed orally and which had been simultaneously
recorded on tape, and he appeared to be firmly of the same opin-

18. Richard Chase Smith, quoted by Cynthia Gorney in "Peruvian Jungle Culture
Is Recorded by American," the *Oakland, Calif. Tribune/Today*, 5, July 1981, p.
B-12, speaks of having witnessed the almost instantaneous disintegration of an
oral tradition under these circumstances. In a book in progress (*The Gypsy on the
Doorstep: A Study in Arab Epic and Identity*, chap. 3), Bridget Connelly reports
her observations of traditional oral singers whose performances cease to be in
demand in Egyptian villages as soon as more fashionable sounds are made available
by progress and who move to Cairo to perform in nightclubs but no longer train
anyone to continue the tradition after their death. Related information will be
found in Connelly's "Three Egyptian Rebab Poets: Individual Talent and Poetic
Design," forthcoming in *Edebiyàt*.
19. Alcuin, "Letter 81," in William Wattenbach and Ernst Duemmler, eds., *Mon-
umenta Alcuiana* (Berlin: Weidmann, 1873).

ion.[20] Nobody is likely to put blind faith in either Ingulf or William of Malmesbury when they claim that King Alfred once passed himself off as an oral poet,[21] but we ought to give both of them credit for having hesitated to write down as a relatively recent historical fact something their readers would have considered absolutely impossible. We may therefore suppose that eleventh- and twelfth-century England found nothing drastically abnormal in the concept of a highly literate person being likewise a skilled oral poet; and it seems likely that a principle which applies to such different times and places as twentieth-century Africa and medieval England ought to be general enough to apply to other places and times whenever the circumstances are right.

To a certain extent, the relationship I posited earlier between oral performers and their audiences also takes place between writers and their readers, but the resultant symbiosis is both indirect and delayed. Whereas the oral performer can modify an ongoing performance to suit the reactions of the audience,[22] the writer can do no such thing until the critiques have been printed and the sales reports are in. The observation applies to serial writing as well. We know that when William Makepeace Thackeray was writing *Vanity Fair* public reaction prompted him to change the relative emphasis he had intended to place on Amelia and Becky respectively,[23] but the fact remains that he could rewrite only the *next* installment after having assessed the readers' reaction to the *previous* one. He had no means of changing a given installment

20. Jeff Opland, "The Installation of the Chancellor," a lecture delivered at the University of California, Berkeley, under the auspices of the Committee on Mediaeval Studies, in spring 1981. On the occasion discussed by Opland, the poet started out reading from his prepared text but was so dissatisfied with the result that he discarded it and went on composing orally. In his lecture, Opland played tapes of the performance and distributed transcripts and translations of both versions.

21. Ingulf (one of William the Conqueror's secretaries) tells the story in his *Historia Croylandensis* (London, 1595), p. 495. William of Malmesbury retells it in his *De Gestis Regum Anglorum,* ed. William Stubbs, 2 vols., Rolls Series nos. 90:1 and 90:2 (London, 1887–1889), 2:126. An up-to-date discussion of the episode may be found in Jeff Opland's *Anglo-Saxon Oral Poetry* (New Haven: Yale University Press, 1980), pp. 156–57.

22. See Lord, *Singer of Tales,* pp. 16–17, for a discussion of oral performers modifying their ongoing performances to fit the circumstances.

23. On the basis of William Makepeace Thackeray, *Works,* 17 vols., ed. George Saintsbury (London: Oxford University Press, 1908), II: 528, Gordon N. Ray, in *Thackeray: the Uses of Adversity* (New York: McGraw-Hill, 1955), has noted, "During the course of *Vanity Fair*'s serial publication, Thackeray had been hard put to defend Amelia from his readers" (1:424). I thank John H. Raleigh for this reference.

while the public was first reading it. Nevertheless, most writers will visualize their intended readers and write accordingly, even though the results may subsequently show that they have missed the mark; and the principle applies to the scholar as well as to the poet or the novelist. The Germanic philologist at work on a general introduction to *Beowulf* for the benefit of college sophomores will neither write the same way nor emphasize the same problems as when writing yet another note on the missing opening of the *Muspilli,* intended to be printed in some obscure journal for the benefit of the other two or three philologists interested in the same problem. Regardless of the nature of the works under scrutiny, there is much to be said in favor of John Niles's admonition in respect to *Beowulf* that "critics need to take into account the audience" of the poem.[24]

If there be any validity to the foregoing observations, then modern scholars attempting to interpret an ancient poem composed in accordance with a tradition of oral-formulaic rhetoric but presumably composed in writing must attempt to work in the light of three considerations whose factual bases are often impossible to establish, as the following outline will illustrate.

(1) *The extent to which the poet was cognitively and emotionally steeped in the relevant oral-formulaic tradition.* If we accept the credibility—though not necessarily the veracity—of Bede's assertion that Cædmon used to isolate himself in his cell to "ruminate"[25] over his materials before coming out to dictate the resultant poem to the scribes, we have to assume the possibility that an oral-formulaic poet also trained in the art of writing could do the same thing but dictate the composition to himself or herself, or even skip the dictation and simply write down the words instead of voicing them. In contradistinction, we can also assume the possibility of someone trained in the art of writing but having subsequently learned all the mechanics of oral-formulaic rhetoric in order to compose a formulaic poem, and students of Old English know that the feat was brilliantly performed by Robert Creed

---

24. John D. Niles, *Beowulf: The Poem and Its Tradition* (Cambridge, Mass.: Harvard University Press, 1983), p. 205.

25. Bede, *Baedae Opera Historica,* ed. J. E. King, 2 vols. (New York: G. P. Putnam's Sons, Loeb Classical Library, 1930), 2:146, uses the expression "quasi mundum animal ruminando" (bk. 4. chap. 24).

in 1959.[26] Although both compositions might well reveal the same formulaic density, the chances are that they should not be interpreted according to the same standards. Because one cannot readily unspeak and change a line already spoken in front of a live audience, revision is not normally part of oral composition, and we may accordingly suppose that the first poet would adhere to the established pattern and merely record the words spoken aloud or silently before the audience in his or her mind's eye; because revision is a natural feature of written composition, however, we cannot safely suppose that the second poet would resist the temptation to revise a word, a line, or a whole passage whenever a better idea would occur belatedly. Even more important is the probability that the first poet would sense from experience the affective impact of certain oral-formulaic elements within a given context and would shape the text accordingly, while the second poet might not have such experience to draw on automatically and might therefore shape the text according to the principles of written rhetoric. Regardless of formulaic density, we should be wary of interpreting the second poem as a strictly oral-formulaic composition, since some of the most obvious oral-formulaic features might prove as irrelevant to interpretation as the color of the paint and the shape of the radiator were to the Bugatti replica I discussed earlier.

(2) *The extent of the familiarity the poet was assuming the intended audience to have with the relevant oral-formulaic tradition.* Just as we may assume that the manufacturer of pseudo-Bugattis would attempt to produce more exact replicas if he or she thought that these would meet with increased approval on the part of the prospective customers, so we may assume that a hypothetical success conscious poet equally competent in both oral and written composition would choose his rhetorical devices in view of the tastes and aptitudes of the intended audience. Anticipation of an audience thoroughly steeped in and appreciative of

26. Robert P. Creed, "The Making of an Anglo-Saxon Poem," *ELH* 26 (1959): 445–54; reprinted in Jess B. Bessinger, Jr., and Stanley J. Kahrl, eds., *Essential Articles for the Study of Old English Poetry* (Hamden, Conn.: Archon Books, 1968), pp. 363–73; Donald K. Fry, *The Beowulf Poet: A Collection of Critical Essays* (Englewood Cliffs, N.J.: Prentice-Hall, 1968), pp. 141–53; Martin Stevens and Jerome Mandel, eds., *Old English Literature: Twenty-two Analytical Essays* (Lincoln: University of Nebraska Press, 1968), pp. 52–61.

oral-formulaic rhetoric but nonetheless in need of a written text would probably yield a written poem whose rational interpretation would depend primarily on our understanding of the conventions of oral-formulaic rhetoric. In contrast, anticipation of an audience afflicted with longing for the old style of poetry but nonetheless unaccustomed to that style and unlikely to appreciate it would probably yield a poem whose outward form would be oral-formulaic but whose rational interpretation would depend primarily on an understanding of the conventions of written rhetoric.

(3) *The extent to which the poet was expecting the audience to be primarily composed of listeners or of readers.* Although this consideration is by no means as important as the other two, we ought not to forget that a poet composing for the eye as well as for the ear will occasionally take advantage of devices not available to colleagues composing for the ear only, and that a poet composing for public and possibly mimetic delivery may likewise have recourse to devices not available to colleagues composing for private or semiprivate reading. Quite obviously, the interpretation of George Herbert's *Easter Wings* requires that we see the text as it is displayed on the page, and that of Vachel Lindsay's *The Congo* would surely prove unsatisfactory if we did not experience or at least imagine the attendant sounds and mimicry. By a similar principle, we may suppose that a poem designed to be read aloud to a small elite audience in the quiet privacy of elegant quarters—say, the way the "romaunce . . . of Thebes" is read aloud to Criseyde and her friends in Chaucer's *Troilus and Criseyde* (2. 100)[27]—will use rhetorical devices different from those found in a poem designed to be delivered before a large and heterogeneous crowd at a marketplace. In many respects, the former situation is tantamount to a silent reading by a single person, even though the reading takes place aloud.

Within the suggested framework, the range of possibilities would extend *from,* at one extreme, a poem written by someone ill at ease with oral-formulaic rhetoric and composing on the assumption that the finished product will be read silently by a

27. All quotations and citations from Chaucer's works are from *The Works of Geoffrey Chaucer,* ed. Fred N. Robinson, 2d ed. (Boston: Houghton Mifflin Co., 1957). The abbreviation *GP* refers to the *General Prologue of the Canterbury Tales,* and the abbreviation *PP* to the *Parson's Prologue.*

reader totally unfamiliar with oral tradition *to,* at the other extreme, a poem written by someone thoroughly steeped in all aspects of oral-formulaic rhetoric and composing on the assumption that the finished product will be read aloud before a large audience thoroughly familiar with oral tradition. Although both poems would be oral-formulaic in outward style but actually written and might conceivably exhibit the same formulaic density, they should not be interpreted according to the same standards unless we wish to misunderstand one or the other or both and be disappointed at not finding what we would like to see there while objecting to features which make no sense to us. The trouble here is that, as already mentioned, we do not often have enough access to empirical facts regarding the actual composition of a given poem, so that we must infer these facts from the text itself. The result is only too often a circular argument: because a given text has some oral features, we assume oral composition, and, because we assume oral composition, we approach the business of interpretation from the point of view of oral tradition; or we reverse the process because we know the text to have been composed in writing. Fortunately, texts occasionally provide cues which may enable us to reconstruct a few extrinsic facts with a modicum of certainty, as the following three examples will illustrate.

My first example is that of the Old English poet Cynewulf. Linguistic evidence points to early ninth-century Mercian as the possible time and dialectical origin of his poetry, whose overwhelming and frequently acknowledged debt to written and presumably Latin sources has encouraged us to imagine him as a highly literate cleric.[28] In fact, the only thing about him which we seem to know is his name, which is signed in runes functionally interwoven with the text near the end of four poems.[29] In the words of Daniel Calder, the foremost Cynewulfian scholar at the end of the twentieth century, "He emerges from the ano-

---

28. For instance, Cynewulf tells us near the end of *Elene* that he found his materials in books (1254b: "swa ic on bocum fand") and in writings (1255b: "on gewritum"). All quotations and citations from Cynewulf are from the *Anglo-Saxon Poetic Records,* as follows: the *Fates of the Apostles* and *Elene* from vol. 2 (*The Vercelli Book,* ed. George Philip Krapp [New York: Columbia University Press, 1932]); and *Christ II* and *Juliana* from vol. 3 (*The Exeter Book,* ed. George Philip Krapp and Elliott Van Kirk Dobbie [New York: Columbia University Press, 1936]).

29. *Fates of the Apostles,* 98b–105b; *Elene,* 1257b–69b; *Christ II,* 797a–807a; *Juliana,* 704a–8b.

nymity of Anglo-Saxon poetry long enough to sign his name and then disappears again into that great obscurity he shares with the other scops who have left no trace."[30] My previous arguments should have made it clear that I question the thrust of Larry Benson's assertion that, "when we know that a poet was literate, used written sources, and intended at least part of his poems for readers, as in the case of the signed poems of Cynewulf, we should assume written composition."[31] Yet I must side with the majority in accepting his verdict in respect to the signed poems. Since the runes are made to function as alphabetic symbols within the context of the signature but as logograms within the context of the narrative, the audience has to *see* the physical appearance of the text on the page in order to make out the signature, and it would have been extremely difficult for the poet to stretch this visual riddle over as many as thirteen lines (see *Elene,* 1257–69) without *seeing* what he was doing. In addition, we must note that the composition of this kind of visual game makes it necessary for the poet to think primarily in terms of the proper selection and positioning of individual words, and these two concerns are typical of written rather than of oral composition.[32] One might, of course, object that most of us can compose a limerick without pen or paper and nevertheless get the right words in the right places with the help of pauses and hesitations. This fact was taken into consideration by Francis Peabody Magoun in 1955, and he convincingly argued that such accomplishments, along with the verses which Milton and

30. Daniel G. Calder, *Cynewulf,* Twayne English Authors Series 327 (Boston: Twayne Publishers, 1981) p. 18. For date and dialect, see, for example, David M. Zesmer, *Guide to English Literature from Beowulf through Chaucer and Mediaeval Drama,* College Outline Series 53 (New York: Barnes and Noble, 1961), p. 56, as well as Stanley B. Greenfield, *A Critical History of Old English Literature,* 2d printing (New York: New York University Press, 1968), p. 109.

31. Larry D. Benson, "The Literary Character of Anglo-Saxon Formulaic Poetry," *PMLA* 81 (1966): 340.

32. Francis P. Magoun, Jr., "Bede's Story of Cædman: The Case History of an Anglo-Saxon Oral Singer," *Speculum* 30 (1955), points out that the use of formulaic *phrases* "distinguishes the verse of the orally composed poems of unlettered singers" (p. 52) and argues that the composition of poems "word by word" (p. 53) would be impossible in the oral composition of "a poem of any substantial length" (p. 53). One must likewise note that the conscious search for the proper selection and positioning of individual words is a basic concern of authors striving for originality; but, in his *Singer of Tales,* Lord notes in respect to the oral poet that originality "is a concept quite foreign to him and one that he would avoid if he understood it" (pp. 44–45).

Coleridge are known to have composed orally, should be considered the product of written composition performed without the actual assistance of writing materials rather than the product of genuine oral-formulaic composition.[33]

Within my framework, the evidence outlined thus far prompts us to classify Cynewulf as a poet composing in writing for the benefit of readers. Since we cannot rationally assume Cynewulf to have been unaware that the subject matter of his signed poems—the stories of Ellen, of Juliana, of the fates of the Apostles, and of the Ascension of Christ—seemed made-to-order for the kind of public reading to which clerical congregations were enjoined to listen,[34] we may modify our classification to say that, in addition to being obviously intended to be read, the poems must have been composed with the realization that they would also be heard by fairly large audiences. Although regrettably doomed to defy empirical demonstration, this supposition draws circumstantial support from Fry's argument that some Old English formulaic poetry dealing with religious subjects may have been recorded "ahead of time and recited from memory."[35]

Three additional considerations must come into play before we can attempt such classification as may enable us to approach interpretation from a relatively secure position. *First,* as demonstrated by Robert Diamond, Cynewulfian diction is so heavily formulaic as almost to equal that of the most traditional Old English poetry.[36] *Second,* in a particularly convincing section of a major study of Cynewulfian poetics, Alexandra Olsen has argued that Cynewulf not only used the techniques of oral-formulaic rhetoric but did so with a dexterity and effectiveness suggestive of com-

33. Magoun, "Bede's Story of Cædman," p. 53.

34. For instance, Alcuin, in the letter already cited ("Letter 81"), enjoins clerics to listen to the reading of holy matters rather than to vernacular poems ("sermones patrum, non carmina gentilium").

35. Fry, "Cædmon as a Formulaic Poet," p. 227.

36. Robert E. Diamond, "The Diction of the Signed Poems of Cynewulf," *Philological Quarterly* 38 (1959): 228–41, finds that 62.7 percent of the verses in the signed poems "are demonstrably formulaic" (p. 234). Francis P. Magoun, Jr., in his pioneering essay, "Oral-Formulaic Character of Anglo-Saxon Narrative Poetry," *Speculum* 28 (1953): 446–67, has examined the opening twenty-five lines of *Beowulf* and found 66 percent of the verses to be demonstrably formulaic and 74 percent to be probably formulaic (pp. 449 and 464–65); he was cognizant of Diamond's research (n. 22, pp. 457–58), which was still in progress.

plete immersion in the tradition behind those techniques.[37] *Third,* both in the same study and in an independent article, Olsen has shown that, in addition to being potentially exposed to oral-formulaic poetry in the monastery, Anglo-Saxons could almost certainly learn how to compose it there, at least under certain circumstances.[38] The conjunction of these three considerations with the facts and arguments advanced just before them is admittedly not enough to establish the precise cognitive and emotional state of mind of Cynewulf while he composed the signed poems. Until new evidence turns up, however, it is enough to permit us to assume the strong probability that he was both highly lettered and thoroughly steeped in the tradition as well as in the techniques of oral-formulaic rhetoric, and that he wrote for an intended audience which—whether composed of a single reader or of a group of listeners—would be familiar enough with the tradition to appreciate the devices of its rhetoric.

I submit that we should do well to approach the texts accordingly if we expect our interpretation to make sense and be as rewarding as it ought to be, and I believe that a glance at the opening section of *Elene* will illustrate the point. Here, we need only read down to line 23 to come across the statement that, as Constantine and his Barbarian enemies assemble their respective troops, "the spears shone, the woven battle corslets" (23b–24a: "Garas lixtan, / wriðene wælhlencan"). Within the context of the Western European tradition of written rhetoric in which most of us have grown up, the information seems perfectly inconsequential. We are glad to know that the warriors take good care of their equipment, and we may even hope that they will be awarded the Good Conduct Medal for doing so, but we do *not* think of the information as a functional element of the narrative technique, and we are likely to go on reading without giving it further

37. Alexandra Hennessey Olsen, *Speech, Song, and Poetic Craft: The Artistry of the Cynewulfian Canon* (Bern: Peter Lang, 1984); see, for example, chap. 2, pp. 46–47, for illustrations of Cynewulf's mastery, already pointed out by Donald K. Fry in his "Themes and Type-scenes in *Elene,* 1–113," *Speculum* 44 (1969): 41–44.

38. Alexandra Hennessey Olsen, in "Old English Poetry and Latin Prose: The Reverse Context," forthcoming in *Classica et Mediaevalia,* writes, "If Bede was, indeed, as most scholars agree, the author of the *Death Song,* he had learned how to compose formulaic vernacular songs. Since he entered the monastery at the age of seven and was not a much-travelled man, the only place where he could have learned the formulaic method was in the monastery of Jarrow" (ms. p. 3). See also *Speech, Song, and Poetic Craft,* p. 11.

thought. Within the context of the Germanic oral-formulaic tradition, however, the evocation of flashes of light produced by corslets and spearheads automatically alerts us to the possibility that
what we have here is a key part of the theme of the Hero on the
Beach, just as the mention of shining cliffs alerts us to the presence
of the same theme near the beginning of *Beowulf.* The fact is that,
as Fry was the first to point out,[39] the theme is very clearly there,
and the expectation of slaughter that goes with it is by no means
disappointed, for the battle which follows (109b–47b) turns out to
be especially fierce.

Nor is it likely that a reader familiar with the Germanic tradition
of oral-formulaic rhetoric would be surprised at the violence and
magnitude of that battle, for the theme of the Hero on the Beach is
here interwoven with another theme usually associated with car-
nage on a large scale. It was first identified by Magoun, who called
it the "theme of the beasts of battle"[40] because it usually consists
of the appearance of a wolf, an eagle or hawk, and a raven—or at
least one of these—in connection with an armed troop about to
fight a battle which it will win. In *Elene,* the beasts first appear
three lines after the initial occurrence of the flashes of light
already mentioned:

> Fyrdleoð agol
> wulf on wealde,   wælrune ne mað.
> Urigfeðera   earn sang ahof . . .
> (27b–29b)

the wolf in the forest sang a song of battle; he did not conceal the
battle-secret. The dewy-feathered eagle raised up its song . . .

From the point of view of profane modern readers, we seem to
have here a blatant example of so-called medieval naiveté and narrative ineptness, since we usually assume that even the worst
Western novel or motion picture would hesitate to give the buz-
zards and coyotes enough anthropomorphic foresight to guess
that a major battle is about to take place. From the point of view of
an audience familiar with the appropriate tradition, on the contrary, we have a superbly timed cue which, when mentally super-

39. Fry, "Themes and Type-scenes," pp. 35–45.
40. Francis P. Magoun, Jr., "The Theme of the Beasts of Battle in Anglo-Saxon
Poetry," *Neuphilologische Mitteilungen* 56 (1955): 81–90.

imposed upon the initial cue found three lines earlier, so heightens the tension and the anticipation with which we approach the subsequent narrative that we are fully prepared to appreciate the treatment of the action therein.

This kind of manipulation has prompted Fry to observe that formulaic elements provide the poet with "rich sources of association, structure, and unity" and to conclude that in the first 113 lines of *Elene* "Cynewulf uses them all in a brilliant tour de force of formulaic art."[41] Olsen further argues that this kind of functionally effective formulaic dexterity is in evidence throughout the entire poem and is typical of the signed corpus.[42] A glance at one of her observations will illustrate the degree to which we can trust her high opinion of the centrality of the Germanic oral-formulaic tradition to the poet's achievement. The initial appearance of the Beasts of Battle occurs in connection with the description of the Barbarian army, and this connection is historically wrong, since we need not read the rest of the poem to know that the Barbarians were defeated by Constantine and we have already noted that the theme normally occurs in connection with the prospective victors. What is historically wrong, however, turns out to be momentarily and psychologically correct: at this point, the formidable Barbarian army (35a: "fyrda mæst") so outnumbers the diminutive Roman troop (48b–49a: hie werod læsse / hæfdon") that we must expect the former's victory and that Constantine is "afraid, disquieted by terror" (56b–57a: Cyning wæs afyrhted, / egsan geaclad"). Clearly, the Beasts of Battle are here connected with an army which shows all the signs of victory within the immediate time frame of the action. But, now Constantine has his Christian revelation, and no sooner has he ordered a standard similar to the "cross of Christ" (103b: "Cristes rode") to be carried before his troops than the Beasts of Battle reappear (110b–13a), this time on the side of the Romans, who march to immediate victory.[43] The switch is brilliantly executed and the message perfectly clear; but it is clear only to those readers or listeners who understand the

41. Fry, "Themes and Type-scenes," p. 45.

42. In *Speech, Song, and Poetic Craft,* Olsen says in regard to *Elene* that "we must fully understand the theme of speech and song in the epilogue when we study the poetic language of the whole poem" (p. 45) and makes similar points on the preceding pages.

43. Ibid., pp. 46–47.

relevant oral tradition. Readers trained exclusively in the written tradition will merely wonder why so many animals are swarming all over the page.

In view of the bulk of the convincing evidence of which I have given a mere sample, we have to agree with Olsen when, after comparing the poem with its Latin original and the other vernacular adaptations thereof, she writes, "Although the differences in plot and characterization are slight, and although there is influence from the Latin rhetorical tradition, *Elene* differs in its 'tellyng' from other versions of the legend, because it was composed in accordance with the dictates of a formulaic tradition."[44] Before going on to my next example, I want to call attention to her acknowledgment that the influence of Latin rhetoric may be detected in the midst of the overwhelmingly Germanic oral-formulaic tradition of Cynewulf's composition. From the point of view of interpretation, I believe that this influence of written rhetoric, however slight it may be, is probably what differentiates the oral-formulaic poem composed in writing for an audience attuned to oral-formulaic tradition from a similar poem composed orally before a live audience under the circumstances which I posited at the outset of this essay. To put the same thing in slightly different terms, I believe that interpreters approaching works which can be classified as I have done the signed poems of Cynewulf might do well to take as a temporary starting point the assumption that, for pragmatic purposes, these works ought to be treated like oral compositions, and yet not quite so.

My second example is that of the anonymous Middle-High German *Nibelungenlied,* which scholars date in the early thirteenth century[45] and assume to be the product of written composition by an Austrian poet. At any rate, it is composed in the Der-von-Kürenberg stanza, which we associate with courtly written poetry. The poem nevertheless contains so many features traceable to the practices of Germanic oral-formulaic rhetoric that Franz Bäuml and Edda Spielmann, who consider it a written epic in every sense of the word, nevertheless write, "Oral tradition . . . served as a basis for the written composition of the transmitted

---

44. Ibid., p. 42.
45. See, for example, the introduction to the B-text by Karl Bartsch, ed., *Das Nibelungenlied,* 12th ed., rev. Helmut de Boor (Leipzig: F. A. Brockhaus, 1949), p. v. All quotations and citations from the poem are from this edition.

text by a literate poet for a literate audience."[46] Especially in view
of the fact that the evidence of the *þiðrekssaga* has prompted
scholars to surmise the possibility of a lost written text between
the oral tradition and the *Nibelungenlied,* it would be difficult to
assess with any accuracy the degree to which the poet and the
intended audience may have been familiar with the oral-formulaic
tradition within which early antecedents had presumably been
composed. Since the overall courtly tone of the poem, the choice
of a courtly stanzaic form, and the incorporation of French materials bear out the common assumption that the poet was aiming at
a courtly audience,[47] and since it seems likely that courtly Austrian audiences of the time would have been more eager to display
their appreciation of the fashionable literary forms imported from
France and Provence than to expose such familiarity as they may
have had with the older Germanic forms being replaced by the
newcomers, we must be permitted to doubt that the author of the
Nibelungenlied would have intentionally composed that epic in
such a manner that only readers and listeners steeped in those
older forms could have interpreted the work and appreciated the
narrative mastery which had gone into its composition.[48]

Regardless of the validity of my argument, it should not be construed as implying that the oral-formulaic features of the
Nibelungenlied are the result of sheer coincidence. On the contrary, I suspect that they are there at least partly because of history
and the poet's intention. As Walter Ong has demonstrated, elements of traditional oral rhetoric have found their way into Tudor

46. Franz H. Bäuml and Edda Spielmann, "From Illiteracy to Literacy: Pro-
logomena to a Study of the *Nibelungenlied,*" *Forum for Modern Language Studies* 10 (1974): 249. For a somewhat different emphasis, see D. G. Mowatt and Hugh
Sacker, *The Nibelungenlied: An Interpretative Commentary* (Toronto: University
of Toronto Press, 1967), who argue, "The general style of the *Nibelungenlied* certainly accords with Lord's specifications" (p. 20).

47. The various elements in the *Nibelungenlied* have been discussed by
Friedrich Panzer, *Studien zum Nibelungenliede* (Frankfurt: Verlage Moritz Die-
sterweg, 1945), esp. pp. 5–86 and 109–78. Especially in respect to the genesis of the
poem, the views in Panzer's indispensable work should be compared with those in
Andreas Heusler's classic study, *Nibelungensage und Nibelungenlied* (Dortmund:
F. W. Ruhfus, 1923).

48. Even Mowatt and Sacker, who emphasize the formulaic aspect, point out in
their *Interpretative Commentary* that the poem was composed at a time when the
old ways were "subordinated to worldly chronicles, romances and the new vogue
for French love-songs" (p. 23).

prose.[49] Yet there is little reason to believe that Renaissance writers had been reading Parry and Lord four centuries ahead of time, so that I would rather think that they had been studying Homeric Greek and that some of it had rubbed off on them or that they had been influenced by Latin or earlier English texts containing vestigial elements of oral-formulaic rhetoric.[50] We likewise recall how those nineteenth-century writers who turned to medieval or pseudomedieval genres and topics wrote in a manner typical of their own time but nevertheless sprinkled their texts with forms and devices which their audiences would have associated with the Middle Ages: Dante Gabriel Rossetti, for instance, presents us with an archaic "blessed damozel" presumably because it sounds more medieval than an idiomatic equivalent like "lucky maiden"; William Morris calls Sigurd "Fafnir's-bane" presumably because it does more to evoke his intended readers' quaint notion of the North Germanic past than would "the killer of Fafnir"; and Keats, whom we have already seen emulating a medieval pattern, is surely acting on the same principle when he asks "what can ail thee, Knight at arms . . . ?" instead of something like "what's the problem, Mister?"[51] The fact is that a writer attempting to bring up-to-date a topic or story from the past must usually present the materials in a manner familiar to the audience but may find it advisable to throw in just enough archaisms correctly or incorrectly reminiscent of the old ways to lend the enterprise an air of legitimacy without making the result uncomfortably hard to understand.

Since the *Nibelungenlied*-poet was retelling an old Germanic story for the benefit of the thirteenth century, he or she must by

49. Walter J. Ong, "Oral Residue in Tudor Prose Style," *PMLA* 80 (1965), shows that certain "oral elements . . . in Tudor prose are akin to those in the *Iliad* and the *Odyssey*" (p. 153).

50. Olsen, "Old English Poetry and Latin Prose," convincingly argues the probability that "the Old English poetry composed, copied, and recited in English monasteries affected the Latin prose written therein," with the equally probable result that "themes and images from the vernacular influenced Latin works and were later re-borrowed by the authors of other vernacular works" (ms. p. 1).

51. John Keats, "La Belle Dame sans Merci," in Alexander W. Allison et al., *The Norton Anthology of Poetry,* rev. ed. (New York: W. W. Norton & Co., 1975), p. 709; William Morris, trans., *Volsunga Saga: The Story of the Volsungs and Niblungs,* ed. Robert W. Gutman (New York: Collier Books, 1962), p. 30; Dante Gabriel Rossetti, "The Blessed Damozel," in *Norton Anthology,* p. 852.

necessity have faced the same problem as the authors mentioned above, whether consciously or not and although the chronological gap was much narrower. We must therefore acknowledge the probability that our poet acted according to either or both of the principles which I have outlined. He or she may have been unwittingly influenced by formulaic devices in an earlier version of the story or in other works commonly heard, read, or studied; and he or she may likewise have consciously adopted some of these devices in order to lend this otherwise modern work an air of archaic legitimacy. If my surmises make any sense, we are back to the manufacturer of pseudo-Bugattis who equips his up-to-date machines with powerful engines and all the latest devices designed to produce the comfort and driving ease expected by the customers but who includes enough features of the original car to produce the appearance of archaic legitimacy and may not even realize that the copy has lost the fundamental qualities of the original. But, of course, there is a difference insofar as the Hollywood Bugattis are childish toys while the *Nibelungenlied* ranks among the towering masterpieces of world literature.

In the light of the foregoing argument, I think that we may tentatively approach the *Nibelungenlied* as the written work of a poet thoroughly steeped in the rhetoric of written composition but nevertheless familiar with the direct or indirect products of oral-formulaic composition and using, either wittingly or otherwise, some techniques thereof for the benefit of an audience that would associate them with the subject matter of the poem but may not necessarily be either willing or able to appreciate their functions and implications within the tradition. In other words, I believe that interpreters should initially approach the text in terms of the literary conventions in vogue at the time of its composition rather than in terms of the tradition which had applied to its antecedents a few hundred years earlier. My belief does not mean that we ought not to take full cognizance of these oral-formulaic techniques and of their possible implications, but merely that we must differentiate between what the conjunction of synchronic and diachronic scholarship has helped us find in the poem and what the intended audience was likely to find in it. Since the theme of the Hero on the Beach, which we have already seen in *Beowulf* and *Elene,* also occurs in the German poem, a comparative glance at the way in which it is handled here will make the point.

Not only does the theme of the Hero on the Beach usually occur in formulaic poetry before a scene of slaughter or a mention thereof, but it tends to do so within very few lines. In *Elene,* we count only ninety-one lines (23^b–114^a) between the initial mention of the flashes that cue us in and the beginning of the expected full-fledged slaughter. In *Beowulf,* the number of lines between the initial cue and Grendel's slaughterous entry into Heorot is much greater, but that cue comes only fifty lines (222^a–72^b) before an account of slaughter and is repeated twice (311^{a-b}, 321^b) a mere eighty lines from the first of two additional accounts of slaughter (409^b–87^a), as well as once more only sixteen lines (570^a–86^a) from yet another mention of slaughter, before a final occurrence which is connected with Beowulf's vow to fight Grendel to the death and which comes 134 lines (606^b–740^a) before the monster begins the slaughter which we have been awaiting in masterfully orchestrated suspense for over five hundred lines (222^a–740^a). Furthermore, all these instances are in one way or another connected with the main episode, to which they lead. As may be expected, the demonstrable mastery of the accomplishment more than vindicates Creed's assertion that we can successfully appreciate *Beowulf*—and, by implication, much of the Old English poetic corpus—only if we take into constant account "the traditional elements which are the very fabric of the poem,"[52] but the important point here is that the handling of the theme is typical; and one may recall in this respect that, in the *Hildebrandslied,* the cue to the same theme occurs only eighteen lines (46–63^a) before the beginning of the expected combat.[53] In all three poems, the expected slaughter begins while the audience still feels the full emotional impact of the cue.

In contrast, the *Nibelungenlied* lets 359 lines (1837:2–1927:1) come between the initial mention of the flash that cues us in and the beginning of the expected slaughter. For an audience familiar with oral-formulaic rhetoric, the appearance of the theme is obvious, and it is aptly connected with a reference to the expected

52. Robert P. Creed, "On the Possibility of Criticizing Old English Poetry," *Texas Studies in Literature and Language* 3 (1961): 106.
53. The reference is to the text of the *Hildebrandslied* in Wilhelm Braune, ed., *Althochdeutsches Lesebuch,* 11th ed., rev. Karl Helm (Halle: Max Niemeyer, 1949), pp. 72–73. I have discussed the form taken by the theme in this poem in my "Armor of the *Hildebrandslied.*"

slaughter. As Hagen and Volker are mounting guard in Etzelnburc while the other Burgundians sleep, Volker notices the flash of a helmet in the night (1837:2: "Volkêr der küene   einen helm schînen sach"), and we are told that it comes from Kriemhild's Hunnish warriors, who would like nothing better than to do the Burgundians whatever harm they can (1837:4: "die wolden an den gesten   schaden gerne hân getân"). The actual slaughter likewise begins in an absolutely unequivocal manner, as a Burgundian decapitates a Hun with a single blow and mockingly offers the deed as a wedding present (1927:3: "daz sî dîn morgengâbe"). Within twenty-one lines, countless Burgundians and at least five hundred Huns (1932:3: "fünf hundert oder baz") are lying dead in the bloodbath, and the main event of the struggle has not even begun.

To be sure, there are other shining objects and even another killing in these 359 lines, but they do not readily fit the requirements of the theme. A few lines after the initial flash, for instance, we are told that Volker wears a clear, shining, and hard helmet (1841:1–2: "Der treit ûf sînem houbte   einem helm glanz, / lûter unde herte"), but the remark is made by one of the Huns, from whose point of view we see the scene, while all the other instances of the theme already mentioned—as well as many others which have remained unmentioned—present the shining object from the hero's or the audience's point of view. We must likewise question the thematic nature—if any—of the unlocated light of dawn which enables us to see the Burgundians asleep in the guest hall (1850:1) or of Hagen's injunction that they wear bright helmets which we are not made to see:

> nu traget für die rôsen   diu wâfen an der hant,
> für schapel wol gesteinet   de liehten helme guot,
> sît daz wir wol erkennen   der argen Kriemhilden muot.
> (1853:2–4)
> Now carry, instead of roses, your weapons in your hand and, instead of bejeweled hats, your good bright helmets, since we know very well the evil Kriemhild's intentions.

Of the four mentions of shining objects which I have discussed in respect to the *Nibelungenlied,* only the first occurs in connection with all the other elements which scholars consider part of the theme of the Hero on the Beach,[54] so that the affective formulaic function of the last three is at best very doubtful. A similar case may be made in respect to the instance of killing. It occurs semi-accidentally during a joust 145 lines (1853:3–1889:3) beyond the last mention of a shining object and 209 lines (1837:2–1889:3) from the one clearly formulaic mention thereof, and it bears no apparent relationship to either of them or to the other two.

Unless I have grossly misread the materials, the foregoing observations suggest that, although we should recognize the presence of the theme of the Hero on the Beach and consider its implications in regard to the genesis of the text, we should hesitate to consider it a central element in the affective rhetoric of the poem. In and beyond the passage we have examined, the excruciating tension which mounts inexorably as we approach the tragic massacre of the Burgundians results from the poet's masterful use of the kind of written rhetoric to which most of us are used, and the oral-formulaic elements which lend the poem an air of archaic legitimacy are not used traditionally enough to help much with the interpretation. To borrow a term from historical linguistics, there are reasons for suspecting that within the immediate context of the composition of the *Nibelungenlied* the oral-formulaic apparatus had largely ceased to be productive. For this reason, I incline to think that it would be as misleading and unrewarding to approach the interpretation of the poem primarily from the point of view of oral-formulaic rhetoric as it would be to approach the interpretation of the signed poems of Cynewulf primarily from the point of view of written rhetoric.

54. In the occurrence on lines 1841:1–2, the shining object which should be perceived by the hero or the audience is perceived by an anonymous Hun (1840:1: "Ein der Hiunen recken"), and the Hun in question is on his home turf and shows no sign of having recently returned from a journey or being about to set out on one. In the occurrence on line 1850:1, we do not really see a specific shining object, but rather the general illumination of dawn (1840:1: "Do erschein der liehte morgen   den gesten in den sal"); in addition, there is no specific hero on the scene, and the awakening Burgundians are incontestably inside the hall rather than by the boundary between two areas. In the occurrence on line 1853:3, the mention of bright helmets does not imply that either we or Hagen ever see the helmets in question, and, as in the case of the previous occurrence, it seems that all the characters in the picture are inside the hall. One may likewise note that the initial cue to the theme (1837:2) occurs in the "30. Âventiure," while the beginning of the slaughter (1927:1) occurs in the "32. Âventiure," so that a separate chapter ("31. Âventiure") interrupts the continuity of action—hence, the reader's thread of association—between the cue to the theme and the expected outcome thereof.

My third and last example is the anonymous Middle English romance, *Sir Gawain and the Green Knight,* which scholars date in the late fourteenth century and assume to have been written in the West Midlands,[55] and in which we come upon a scene which puts us once again in mind of the theme of the Hero on the Beach. At the end of his quest through the Kingdom of Logre, the knight Gawain reaches a splendid castle which "schemered & schon þur3 þe schyre oke3" (772).[56] In a poem which, as Benson has demonstrated beyond question, "is deeply indebted to the tradition of oral verse,"[57] the description necessarily catches our attention because we do not normally expect castles to shimmer and shine; as students of oral-formulaic rhetoric we are therefore cued in to the possible presence of the theme. Nor are our expectations disappointed, since we see Gawain immediately thereafter admiring the "roue3 þat blenked ful quyte" (799) while he stands by the moat surrounding the castle (785–86) until he is welcomed by a whole retinue (815–19).[58] Because we have read the beginning of the story, we assume that he is in danger, since his quest is for a gigantic green knight by whom he has agreed to have his head lopped off (381–85), and we accordingly expect the kind of bloodletting which normally follows the theme.

In fact, Gawain is in no real danger, and we have to read another 1,513 lines (799–2312) before finally reaching the anticipated scene of slaughter, which turns out to be no slaughter at all by any stretch of the imagination. He is in no real danger because of his unshakable faith in the Virgin Mary (645–50), who in those days was not in the habit of letting down those who worshiped her and who in fact sees him personally through the treacherous amorous

55. For the known facts about *Sir Gawain and the Green Knight,* see, for example, Albert C. Baugh, "The Middle English Period," in Baugh, ed., *A Literary History of England* (New York: Appleton-Century-Crofts, 1948), p. 238.

56. Quotation and citations from *Sir Gawain and the Green Knight* are from the edition by Sir Israel Gollancz, EETS o.s. 210 (London: Oxford University Press, 1940). This passage (772) has been analyzed from a completely different point of view by Larry D. Benson in his masterful study, *Art and Tradition in Sir Gawain and the Green Knight* (New Brunswick: Rutgers University Press, 1965), pp. 183–84.

57. Benson, *Art and Tradition,* p. 120, which also provides a formulaic analysis of lines 1–14.

58. Since we learn later that the whole affair is arranged by "Morgne la Faye" (2446, 2452), who is Gawain's aunt, one might even wish to argue that the retainers are in fact almost his own, as is usually the case with the theme of the Hero on the Beach.

encounters that subsequently test both his loyalty and his courtesy (1768–69). As for the would-be slaughter, it consists of a symbolic nick (2312) which comes so long after the occurrence of the theme that the affective impact of the latter has grown entirely inoperative by the time we reach the former, especially since the magnificent intervening scenes in both the field and the bedroom have so captivated our attention as to stamp out whatever functional memory we might have kept of the outward appearance of the castle. In brief, the handling of the theme of the Hero on the Beach does not seem to pass muster from the standpoint of oral-formulaic rhetoric. As far as I can tell, the much-acclaimed quality of the narrative is due mostly to the poet's mastery of written rhetoric, and one may accordingly be tempted to approach the text as I suggested that we do the *Nibelungenlied.*[59]

Basically correct though it may be, the foregoing statement requires a codicil, for the English poet has provided at the outset several cues which ought to guide our initial approach to the rhetoric of the poem:

> If ȝe wyl lysten þis laye bot on littel quile,
> I schal telle hit as tit, as I in toun herde,
> > with tongue,
> > As hit is stad & stoken
> > In stori stif & stronge,
> > With lel letteres loken,
> > In londe so hatȝ ben longe.   (30–36)

The stated facts—whether actual or invented to satisfy some convention—are in the main perfectly clear. Since we are asked to *listen* (30) while the speaking voice *will tell* (31) the story *with tongue* (32), we must assume that the resulting composition is intended for oral delivery, and the assertion that it will be related as it was *heard* (31) tells us that the previous transmission has likewise been oral, just as the statement that it is *placed and securely kept in legend* (33–34) suggests a tradition. The mention of *loyal*

---

59. Taking cognizance of the oral-formulaic elements in the poem means, of course, that interpreters should take these elements into consideration whenever they happen to be relevant to the interpretation and appreciation of the poem, as illustrated in Martin Camargo's perceptive essay, "Oral-Traditional Structure in *Sir Gawain and the Green Knight*," in John Miles Foley, ed., *Current Research on Oral Literature: A Memorial for Milman Parry* (Columbus, Ohio: Slavica, 1986), forthcoming.

letters joined (35) is somewhat ambiguous because it may refer either to the poem under composition or to the earlier versions heard by the poet, but it nevertheless tells us that the referent was or is to be composed in alliterative verse and that the mode of composition must be written since the word *lettre* at that time still referred primarily to writing symbols, for which an oral poet would have little use. Finally, we are told that this system of composition is ancient, since it has been around *for a long time* (36).

The implications are not so clear as the facts themselves, but they are nevertheless difficult to ignore. The statement that the poet heard the story *in town* (31) implies that it comes from a place other than the one where we—that is to say, the poet and the audience together—are located during the performance. The mention of the antiquity of the alliterative system likewise implies that it comes from a time earlier than our own. In conjunction with the fact that, after over thirty lines of alliterative verse, the poet feels the need to call attention to the mode of versification and to provide a historical introduction to it, the foregoing observations go far toward suggesting that the poem is intended for an audience quite unfamiliar with these things and therefore in need of some kind of prefatory explanation.

Since, in addition, the passage which I have quoted follows directly upon a statement to the effect that the story which it introduces will surely tax the credibility gap (27–28), the message reads very much as if we were being forewarned that we are about to hear a surprising story appropriately told in a surprising manner. It is, after all, far preferable to warn the unsuspecting Geoffrey Chaucers in the audience that the rhetoric will be unusual because "the wordes moote be cosyn to the dede" (*GP*, 742) than to risk having the likes of the Parson of the *Canterbury Tales* stalk out in horrified incomprehension because they are unused to poets who "kan . . . geste 'rum, ram, ruf' " (*PP*, 43); and yet there would be no reason for this kind of warning if the audience were at ease with the rhetoric that follows. To return to my ongoing comparison, I would give odds that many a prospective buyer of Hollywood Bugattis has to be given a brief historical introduction before being persuaded to buy what must initially look like a very strange piece of machinery. Yet no one who ever followed international automobile races before the Second World War would require such an explanation. I should accordingly suggest that prospective interpreters of *Sir Gawain and the Green Knight* should take cognizance of the oral-formulaic elements therein but might nevertheless do well to approach it primarily as a written text composed for an intended audience perhaps even less attuned to oral-formulaic rhetoric than the audience which I have surmised for the *Nibelungenlied.*

The views I have advanced are obviously tentative and must perforce remain so until we have learned additional facts about the actual circumstances of composition of those poems which belong in the limbo between oral and written performance. My approach has likewise been much too mechanical to prove satisfactory, and I should not want to be suspected of having come by my views on the basis of the number of lines one can count between the various elements of a theme.

On the contrary, I have merely used line counts as practical means of illustrating what instinct had told me after many readings and rereadings of the texts discussed and others like them.

Since I have likewise taken up much too much space to say very little, I shall atone by stating with utmost brevity the conclusion toward which I have been fumbling. When interpreting a presumably written literary work with roots in oral tradition, we ought not to attempt forcing the text into the canons of a rhetorical tradition or another; we ought, instead, to take the text on its own terms and to base our interpretation on such rhetorical tradition or traditions as we find clearly represented there. In so doing, we shall spare ourselves the frustration of looking for things that are not there while overlooking those that are, and our reading will accordingly prove much more rewarding than it would otherwise be. Since I am naive enough to believe that the study of literature should be the most rewarding occupation in the world, I suggest that those who disagree with my premises might do well to consider the very real advantages of moving to Hollywood to manufacture enormous pseudo-Bugattis for the wealthy.

6
THE REMAKING OF *BEOWULF*
Robert P. Creed

I want to begin exploring the possibility that the poem *Beowulf* is not the work of a literate Christian antiquarian or even the performance of an illiterate but well-trained Christian poet simply reworking the old Germanic tradition. I want to explore the idea that the *Beowulf*-poet whose poem survives in British Library MS Cotton Vitellius A. xv. was, instead, a virtuoso traditional poet who may have radically reshaped the tradition in order to preserve it. I suppose every traditional poet reshapes the tradition in some ways. But there may have been a special sense in which the *Beowulf*-poet accomplished his transformation. In the scenario I am sketching, the *Beowulf*-poet preserved something important from the heathen past by making parts of that past acceptable to his own newly adopted Christianity. At the same time, he also—and very subtly—reshaped for himself and his people Christian ways of thinking.

The *Beowulf*-poet was in a position to accomplish such a transformation. His poem reveals his mastery of the traditional verse dialect. But there is a dimension to this statement that post-traditional people like ourselves are apt to miss. To be a traditional poet is to make one's *self* the record of the past. From the earliest days of the serious study of Old English we have been hearing that some of the Anglo-Saxon poets drew on their past. I am sure they did. But they did so in ways different from what that phrase is apt to suggest to us. Before I discuss those ways, let me quote from one of the great scholars of just a few generations before mine, Sir H. Munro Chadwick:

The conclusion to which I have been brought is that the resemblances in the [early heroic poetry of the Teutonic and Greek peoples] are due primarily to resemblances in the ages to which they relate and to which they ultimately owe their origin. The comparative study of heroic poetry therefore involves the comparative study of 'Heroic Ages'; and the problems which it presents are essentially problems of anthropology.[1]

Like Chadwick, I think the Anglo-Saxons knew something about their past, about the culture many generations of their ancestors had developed in what we now call southern Scandinavia, Germany, and parts of the low countries. But I differ from Chadwick and other historically oriented scholars in thinking that we know something about the *ways* these people kept track of their past.

Those ways are, I think, preserved in the text in the MS. But the "ways"—the *forms,* as it were—are also the *content.* If we ask where the knowledge of their Germanic past existed for the Anglo-Saxons of early England, we can say that that knowledge was the tradition stored in the memories of individuals and constantly renewed—and therefore constantly changed, whether subtly or radically.

I think it likely that the changes, insofar as we can think about them in any detail, were generally very subtle, something like the kinds of changes one makes while trying very hard to tell again the same story in the same way. There may have been fewer noticeable changes of this sort in the performances of poets of the tradition simply because they had the support of careful training in a tradition. They also had the enormous enhancement of working with and within a tradition that makes elaborate use of the human memory—more elaborate use, perhaps, than do syllable-count or foot-count traditions. Let me digress to explain.

The tradition of the *Beowulf*-poet pays attention to stress and may, perhaps, be characterized as stress-timed. But the verse line is solidly built on *sound-patterning.*

Sound-patterning always means some form of repetition, of the *sharing* of sound by syllables usually separated from each other by other syllables. Sound-sharing always depends upon the perception by speaker and hearer that the "same" sound is being pro-

---

1. H. Munro Chadwick, *The Heroic Age* (Cambridge: Cambridge University Press, 1912), p. viii.

duced, often within a carefully calculated interval of time. It is perhaps very human to discriminate large classes of sounds and to select certain sounds within a particular culture as "the same." It is probably even less difficult to discriminate the "same interval." Birds, after all, seem to make that discrimination. Yet, to listen to many prosodists of Old English poetry, one would think that humans have a special problem in detecting the same interval in utterances.

But that last remark is probably unfair. Prosodists of Old English poetry have so far simply not realized that at least two of the intervals of the verse line, the line designed by the poets of the Germanic tradition, are clearly marked by the kind of sound-patterning we call—unfortunately—alliteration.

I say unfortunately because it is not the *letters* that create the patterns but the *sounds.* We ought to have a better term than *alliteration* to talk about patterns created by the repetition within a short period of time of the same initial sound of certain syllables. I have thought of using a phrase like *initial sound-sharing,* but that, too, has its problems.

Let me give you some examples of the use of alliteration to mark certain intervals in the verse line of *Beowulf.* In the second verse line, alliteration simply marks the division of the verse line into two halflines: *þeodcýninȝa þrým ȝefrunoṇ.* In the eighth verse line, alliteration marks *three* divisions: *weox under wolcnum weorðmýndum þah.* Notice that alliteration marks the division of the first halfline into two parts. In the seventh verse line something even more interesting is happening: *feasceaft funden he þæs frofre ȝebad.* Alliteration first marks the beginning of the verse line, then marks a division within the first halfline, as it does in verse line 8. Then *something else* marks the division between the two halflines, the division between *funden* and *he.*

To determine what that something is, I must digress still further. For 150 years just about every scholar of *Beowulf* has accepted that there is an important division between *funden* and *he.* The scholar who first determined most such divisions within the text of *Beowulf,* John Mitchell Kemble, printed *feasceaft funden* on one line and *he þæs frofre ȝebad* on the next. Verse line 7 is not like either verse line 2 or 8, in which an alliterating syllable marks the division into two halflines. Yet no scholar is likely to dispute Kemble's division of verse line 7.

The reason lies partly in the fact that the second halfline of verse line 7, *he þæs frofre ʒebad,* begins a new *clause,* with the pronoun *he* marking the beginning of that clause. Clause boundaries have a tendency to occur at this point in the verse line more frequently than at the beginning of the verse line. The reason is not far to seek. Whereas a new *alliteration* that continues the previous *sentence* nevertheless marks the beginning of a new verse line, the poet can begin a new *sentence* before he has completed the alliteration of the verse line. The *Beowulf*-poet, interestingly enough, almost never includes the *second* of three alliterating syllables in a new clause but builds that clause around the *last* alliterating syllable.

What I have been trying to do is illustrate the way in which the *Beowulf*-poet constructs his verse line. Let me sum up: he does so around two or three alliterating syllables. For him, alliteration does far more than simply ornament his verse line: it defines it. It does so by marking the beginning of at least two intervals in every verse line. To put the matter another way, the alliterating syllables form the *core* of every verse line in the poem.

Let me conclude these illustrations of the building of the verse line of *Beowulf* by showing that alliteration sometimes marks in a verse line the beginning of two intervals, each of which is *inside* its halfline. I quote verse line 26: *him ða scyld ʒewat to ʒescæphwile.* Recall that this verse line, divided into its two halflines, has been acceptably extracted from the text in the MS. This verse line begins with a clause boundary, but the second halfline of this verse line does not. The second halfline begins instead with a preposition preposed to the *last* alliterating syllable of the verse line, *-scæp-.* The beginning of neither halfline of this verse line, then, is marked by an alliterating syllable. The first halfline—the beginning of the verse line—is marked by a clause boundary.

The point I want to make is that both the clause boundary and the preposition define the line *in relation to* two of the alliterating syllables of the verse line. In a lengthy, not yet published study titled *Reconstructing the Rhythm of Beowulf* I have shown that Kemble extracted from the MS the halflines (he called them "verses") by working *back* from each first alliterating syllable. Kemble thus not only set out the whole text of *Beowulf* in acceptable halflines, he also demonstrated the fundamental importance of alliteration.

The alliterating syllables may be more than the key to the structure of the verse line. They may also be the most important key to the Germanic tradition. Almost everything in *Beowulf* can be shown to depend on each successive series of alliterating syllables. If there are formulas in *Beowulf,* the formulas are built around alliterating syllables. And, if there are very old ways of thinking preserved in the poem, as I think there are, these ways are very likely preserved in syllables bound together by alliteration.

It may not be possible to take apart performances in other oral traditions so neatly as I think we can take apart *Beowulf.* In any case, we can speak of *Beowulf* as consisting of a repertory of sound-linked syllables, like *scyld, sceaf,* and *sceaþ[a]* in verse line 4, and strategies for incorporating these sound-patterned syllables into a verse narrative.

The mind of the traditionally trained Old English poet became, as I suggested earlier, the record of the tradition—indeed, the tradition *itself* as it existed at that moment in that place. It is very important, then, to examine *Beowulf* carefully to determine the state of the tradition at that moment and in that place—whatever the precise moment was and wherever the place. It was the *verse tradition* that carried the information about the past of the Germanic folk who migrated to and gradually set themselves up in Britannia. I do not think the *Beowulf*-poet went about asking the older members of his family and clan about their recollections of the past. He didn't need to. That was what the *tradition* kept track of, and he was trained in—had become part of—the tradition.

Centuries of history-writing have trained *us* to be wary of oral traditions as reliable sources of information about a people's past. If we have to choose between *Beowulf* and Tacitus, the Roman ethnographer, for information about the prehistoric Germanic peoples, we are likely to choose the latter. We have been schooled to think that an ethnographer will write about the past *objectively* while a poet will allow his imagination to dictate what he says. I firmly believe that an ideal of objectivity is a most desirable guide in any venture. But the thinking of certain scientists today leads me to focus on *both* the ideal and the individual who firmly believes that he or she is practicing that ideal. The universe, let alone the past of a particular folk, seems to look slightly different to each observer.

So the *Beowulf*-poet was both the careful preserver of the past of his people and the transformer of that past. In most of what he tells us about the Danes and the Geats, he is to be trusted more than Tacitus, I believe. Tacitus, after all, worked at some distance from the Germans he wrote about. He also seems to have based much of his *Germania* on accounts—probably traditional tales in some cases—filtered through the Roman-trained mind of his father-in-law. Nevertheless, we should try to make the best use of Tacitus's *Germania,* even though *Beowulf* may turn out to be the better ethnography—or ethno-*speaking.*

But before I take up the ways in which the *Beowulf*-poet *re*made the past, I want to take a closer look at the past as it seems to have existed in the tradition before the *Beowulf*-poet set about transforming it. To try to perform this interesting feat I turn to—of all things—the text of *Beowulf,* particularly to those parts of the tale that are not likely to have been affected by the *Beowulf*-poet's transformation.

I begin by trying to follow the *Beowulf*-poet through his poem back across the North Sea to the continental homeland of the Germanic folk. The folk who were to become first the proto-Germans and later the Germanic people arrived in their continental homeland from the southeast at least four thousand years ago. That is the consensus of archaeologists working in the countries of northern Europe today. These Indo-European speakers settled down around the North Sea and the Baltic and became farmers. A few of them became traders, exporting amber to peoples south of them in order to get scarce goods such as gold. In any case, they kept open some lines of communication with the peoples to the south, many of whom had sprung from the same roots as they had. But they were far enough away from most of their ancient kin to begin to go their own ways in developing various facets of their culture. Or, did they hold on more tenaciously or at least conservatively to the older ways than did their kin who encountered the civilizations of the Mediterranean or the Indus Valley? I think that possibility needs to be explored more thoroughly and thoughtfully in the light of recent archaeological findings. For example, if there is any value in the series of maps from the *Penguin Historical Atlas of Ancient History,*[2] then we must conclude that the ancient Germanic folk were very conservative indeed. From map to map,

2. Edited by Colin McEvedy (Harmondsworth, Eng.: Penguin, 1967), pp. 28–76.

while we see indications of much activity to the south, we see few such indications among the "Teutons," as the historical cartographer calls them.

These maps suggest to me a possibility based on the fact that the folk, once they had settled around the northern seas, seem to have moved very little for more than two millennia, that is, from about 2000 B.C. till the first millennium A.D. The possibility is this: these folk, even though for some of them, like the Anglo-Saxons, we have written records for only about the last fourteen hundred years, may nevertheless have held onto the old ways more than those whose traditions were recorded more than a thousand years earlier. I think it is easy to slide into the assumption that what happens to have been *recorded* earlier will reflect a more conservative holding onto of earlier Indo-European ways. But several indications suggest the opposite possibility to me, namely, that the *Iliad* and *Odyssey,* the *Gathas* of Zarathustra, and the Vedic Hymns just *might* represent *less* conservative, more altered versions of the common earlier Indo-European culture than does *Beowulf.* The most important indication is this: the branch of the Indo-European stock that produced *Beowulf* was not directly confronted with either the Phoenician cities or the great cities of the Harappan culture in the Indus Valley.

There is no doubt, on the other hand, that there was something special about the proto-Germans that caused them to develop the set of sound-changes that we know as "Grimm's Law." Grimm's Law sets this folk apart and probably represents a linguistic variation developed by the proto-Germans away from earlier Indo-European. But everything else that we know about the proto-Germans suggests conservatism. And until archaeologists unearth something like the cities of the Phoenicians and of the Indus Valley in northern Europe, I think we must regard these people more as conservers than as innovators.

These people were certainly farmers. At some point the making and guarding of *loaves* was so central to their lives that the maker, the *lady—hlafdiʒe* in Old English—and the guard or *ward* of the loaf, the *lord—hlaford* in Old English—came to signify high rank. How that came about may be an exciting story in its own right, taking us away from the northern shores and into the heart of what the archaeologist Marija Gimbutas calls "Old Europe."[3]

3. See especially "The Temples of Old Europe," *Archaeology* 33, no. 6 (November/December 1980): 41–50.

The prehistoric Germanic folk drank, and probably brewed, *mead* and *beer*. The former drink may link their ways to what I have elsewhere suggested might have been a harvest ritual, a "communion," first practiced by the Indo-Europeans before their diaspora. There are other possible indications in *Beowulf* of earlier ways carefully preserved. But these few will have to do as indicators of agricultural activity in the poem.

The prehistoric Germanic people were sailors, though I know of no clear evidence for when they began to sail the northern seas. It seems likely that they were less venturesome than the Greeks, who had, after all, the practices of the Phoenicians and other Mediterranean peoples to learn from. In any case, the tale of Scyld and Sceaf ends with the dead King Scyld placed on a magnificently laden funeral ship. But I should add that alliteration just might have led at some point to the association of *Sc*yld with a *sc*ip.

But the prehistoric Germans liked most of all to think of themselves—or at least the *men* did—as brave fighters generously offering service to and being duly rewarded by a generous war-leader. They chose *not* to celebrate themselves as farmers, plowing and harvesting and doing daily chores. They preferred to characterize as a *meadhall* the wooden building in which they ate, drank, talked, listened to tales, and slept. The chair of the most important man in the group became a throne, his wife became a *queen*.

This last development is particularly interesting. Our Modern English word *queen* is derived from an Indo-European word meaning *woman*. The Old English source of *queen* is *cwen*. The Indo-European root of *cwen* is something like *gwen-*, from which the more usual Greek word for woman, *gyne,* is also derived. The development in Old English seems to go from the woman in general to the particular woman of the folk. The Swedes appear to have been more conservative than the Anglo-Saxons, since the generic term for woman in Modern Swedish is derived from the Indo-European *gwen-, kvinna*. The men, in any case, liked to tell about gold-adorned women and gold-decked halls—and kings who distributed gold for services well done. Archaeologists have shown that, at times, the kings *did* have gold to distribute. They also had *exotic* treasures at their disposal, as the Old English word *maddum* informs us. This word is derived from the Indo-European root *mei-*, which means to exchange. But mostly the men liked hearing about useful and valuable *weapons*.

Talk about weapons raises some interesting questions. The

weapons described in *any* tale may be venerable, but they are not likely to be antiquated. André Leroi-Gourhan argues, "In the life of a society models of weapons change very often." He goes on to say that "models of tools" change "less often and social institutions very seldom, while religious institutions continue unchanged for millennia."[4] Although weapons are likely to be constantly updated by the tradition, tools and institutions are not. The fact, then, that a tradition tells about the most modern weapons and armor gives no ground for arguing that *everything* described in the traditional tale is recent. Let me end this digression by suggesting that no poet is going to get very far singing to men who use weapons about weapons no longer in use.

I think Leroi-Gourhan is right when he argues that social institutions and religion change very slowly. The primary institution of society, language, probably changes slowest of all in traditional societies. Thus, we cannot apply to such societies rates of linguistic change observed in or calculated for post-traditional societies. Traditional societies *live* by the *spoken* not the written word. That fact seems to me to point to their developing every means possible to conserve the forms of language by which they function. Only in severe crises, I believe, will the poets of the tradition find ways to accommodate new ideas.

That brings me to our *Beowulf*-poet and to the accommodation he may have accomplished largely alone. I think there can be no doubt that the *Beowulf*-poet celebrates the past. I think it likely that he celebrates what he knew was the *heathen* past. Yet he himself was clearly a Christian. He knew that Beowulf and Hrothgar were not. The *Beowulf*-poet even seems to have sensed, with disapproval, that Beowulf had been regarded as some sort of god.

Now the Christian poet was not about to violate the First Commandment. If earlier people had regarded Beowulf as a god, they had simply been mistaken. But the poet does not fall into the other trap: he does *not* denounce Beowulf as a devil. The tradition of the great hero who used to come to the aid of the sorely distressed contained much that was worth keeping. So the poet retold the old tale and rehabilitated the old god by turning him into a hero— an almost superhuman hero, of course. Beowulf came when men's need was upon King Hrothgar and remained to help the old king

4. *The Art of Prehistoric Man in Western Europe* (London, 1968), p. 48.

when Grendel's mother attacked. In telling the tale about the superhuman hero the poet preserved what was best in the old traditions and presented it as a model for living men.

Beowulf the god seems always to have come from afar, probably at the request of suppliants. He brought with him his band of warriors, much as the Vedic god Indra brought the band of Maruts. But all such trappings had to be abandoned. The companions had to become mere men. Beowulf had to be located somewhere on earth, but somewhere far away from poet and audience. The *Beowulf*-poet, composing his poem in Anglo-Saxon England, seems to have thought of southern Sweden as sufficiently far away from both his new land and Denmark. And once the poet had located Beowulf in a particular spot on earth, certain consequences followed.

If this is a reasonable reconstruction of what happened, the poet's accommodation worked very well indeed. Locating Beowulf in a particular kingdom made it possible to end the tale of the god with the death of the god become a human hero. So the tale of Beowulf could survive as that of a model hero if not as that of a beneficent god. The important things from the tradition could be kept: Beowulf's bravery, his generosity, his willingness to travel distances to help those in dire distress. Beowulf the hero preserved most of the functions of the divine, or semi-divine, figure he may have been earlier in the tradition. In turning him into a hero, the poet was able to preserve very important things from the deep past, things that spoke about the identity of the folk and reminded them of their old ways.

Some of what I have been saying is highly speculative. All of it is subject to correction. All of it should indicate that I take very seriously the first poem in British Library MS Cotton Vitellius A. xv. I think I take *Beowulf* far more seriously now than I did, many years ago, when I thought of it as a piece of *literature*. I think we are more likely to take *Beowulf* seriously when we stop trying to think of it as the work of a learned antiquarian *writer* and begin to think of it as a unique and important link to our deep past. When we begin to do so, we are likely to begin questioning it with a new excitement. What does it tell us about the prehistoric Germanic folk? What does it tell us that can be compared with the artifacts dug up by the archaeologists? And, most interesting of all to my mind, what does *Beowulf* tell us about the shaping of our *memories,* of the very ways we think today? I think *Beowulf* may have something to say about the ways we have built certain memory paths through sound-patterning. I don't think we're likely to question a *literary Beowulf* in this way.

Nearly thirty years ago, inspired by the work of Albert Lord, I began to try to think about *Beowulf* as a traditional tale. It has taken me much of those thirty years to realize just what that means. I am convinced that it does *not* mean that the *Beowulf*-poet is some sort of automaton. On the contrary, he now seems to me always poised delicately between innovation and recurrence. If he chooses recurrence, that is, if he chooses to say *beowulf maþelode bearn ecgþeowes* at a number of points in his tale, it is because he *wants* to do so. The *Beowulf*-poet seems to me to be the master of the verse dialect we call his tradition.

But he is more than master. He is a *virtuoso* performer who might have had much to do with the fact that his performance has somehow survived. It is his virtuosity first of all that can attract audiences today. It was his virtuosity that must have caught the ear of his contemporaries. But then it was his *re*making of the tale of the beneficent heathen god into the tale of the beneficent hero that attracted the attention of those who could command the resources of the scriptorium. Those men were, like the poet, Christians, but they were also the proud descendants of the folk of Angeln in Denmark and Saxony in Germany. They knew at once the value of the remade tale.

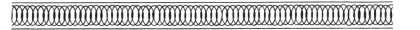

7
TEXT AS INTERPRETATION: MARK AND AFTER
Walter J. Ong, S.J.

To interpret, as I understand the term here, is to bring out what is concealed in a given manifestation, to make evident what in the manifestation is not evident to the milieu in which the interpreter's audience lives. Interpretation can be applied to anything that bears information: a human gesture, an eclipse, a chart, for example. To interpret verbal utterance is to bring out what the utterance does not of itself reveal to a given audience. What an utterance reveals calls for no interpretation. Interpretation deals with here-and-now nonevident, or not-so-evident, matter embedded in whatever is evident. Verbal discourse regularly calls for interpretation. All utterance both reveals and conceals. The quest for utterance that reveals all and never needs interpretation is a quest for a will-o'-the-wisp.

This simple definition of interpretation sidesteps the arabesqued intricacies of hermeneutic or interpretation theory as elaborated from the time of Schleiermacher, Dilthey, and Wittgenstein on through Edmund Husserl, Martin Heidegger, Rudolph Bultmann, Hans-Georg Gadamer, Paul Ricoeur, Jürgen Habermas, and others. The definition is, I believe, simply the most fundamental, general, and accessible meaning we can give to interpretation. Of course, it does not downplay theorizing but rather points to ground well traversed by those who undertake theorizing. For this understanding of the term *interpretation* itself both reveals and conceals. But in such a way that you can work with it. I often state to classes of mine, "Total explicitness is impossible." From time to time a student will raise a hand and ask, "What do you mean by,

'Total explicitness is impossible'?" I reply, "Your question makes my meaning about as clear as it is ever going to be." And we go on from there.

In interpreting verbal utterance, we can be called on to interpret oral performance or to interpret text. The two activities are different, but not entirely different. The world of oral utterance is typically one of discourse, in which one utterance gives rise to another, that to still another, and so on. Meaning is negotiated in the discursive processs. Negotiation begins even before utterance begins. What I say depends on my conjectures about your state of mind before I begin to speak and about the possible range of your responses. I need conjectural feedback even to formulate my utterance. Speaking of a given matter to a child, I am likely to say something quite different from what I say in speaking about the same matter to an adult. Your actual response to what I say may or may not fit my earlier conjecture. In either event, it enables me further to clarify my thought. Your actual response makes it possible for me to find out for myself and to make clear in my counter-response what my fuller meaning was or can be. Oral discourse thus commonly interprets itself as it proceeds. It negotiates meaning out of meaning.

It is easy to believe that texts are not at all part of such ongoing interpretive negotiation. One of the most widespread and fundamental errors of the past few generations of literary critics has been the assumption, most often not clearly articulated, that to put an utterance in writing is to remove it from this state of oral discourse and thus to "fix" it. "A poem [that is, a written or printed poem] should not mean / But be," Archibald MacLeish wrote in his "Ars Poetica." There it is, fixed. But there is no way to "fix" discourse, even by writing or printing it. A text does certainly separate an utterance from its author who, once he has written down his text, may as well be dead. In this sense, writing creates autonomous discourse. But removing an utterance from its author is not removing it from discourse. No utterance can exist outside discourse, outside a transactional setting. Putting an utterance into script can only interrupt discourse, string it out indefinitely in time and space. But not "fix" it.

When is a text an utterance? When does an inscribed work "say" something? Insofar as a text is static, fixed, "out there," it is not utterance but a visual design. It can be made into an utterance only by a code that is existing and functioning in a living person's mind. When a person knowing the appropriate code moves through the visual structure and converts it into a temporal sequence of sound, aloud or in the imagination, directly or indirectly—that is, when someone reads the text—only then does the text become an utterance and only then does the suspended discourse continue, and with it verbalized meaning. Texts have meaning only insofar as they are converted into the extratextual.

A distinctive feature of the textual utterance as against oral utterance is that its author cannot absolutely predict or often even discover who all will continue the discourse he or she has started. Anyone might pick up and read a text once it has been set down. This is one reason many persons discontinue writing diaries—or never start. But when the reader reads the text, the discourse resumes, perhaps after hundreds or thousands of years, and perhaps with great difficulty, implemented by laborious, self-conscious interpretive work, without which the inscription may say very little.

In this way, in their need to be uttered, all texts are part of discourse—and, as recent textualist studies have made us acutely aware, of discourse that not only engages oral discourse here and there, but also, and even more, engages other texts. Texts are essentially intertextual. A novelist can write a novel only because he or she has read other novels, or something approximating novels. A scientist can write scientific books because of immersion in scientific books written by others. Even a mathematical text is part of discourse. It represents an utterance of one mathematician at a given time and place to other mathematicians, wherever they are. All science is only arrested dialogue.

But even though texts are in this way part of discourse, the utterance making the discourse is not in the physical text but only in the reader or readers (or, originally, in the writer). There is no universal, time-free and space-free utterance or reader: every conceivable reader comes to the text out of a specific background, knowing certain things, not knowing other things, and so on. In this way, though not in many other ways, readers are like the listeners in spoken discourse. There is no universal listener. There are only individual listeners, real or fictional, but all time-bound, to whom you have to try to shape your discourse, with more or less success. Speculative theologians have liked to point out that even

God cannot be thought of as a time-free reader, for divine knowledge is not the kind of thing that could be generated from reading a text or listening to a human voice. Divine knowledge is eternal, totally alive. Human thought is contoured by time. This does not at all make human knowledge "relativistic" in the sense of indeterminate, floating, unverifiable. Quite the contrary, it makes human knowledge very determinate and eminently verifiable, but historically and complexly so. Human thought is marked not by relativism but by relatedness. It ties in with everything. No thought is ever free-floating abstraction or free-floating anything else. To interpret anything fully, you would have to know everything.

All this is, or should be, utterly commonplace in reader-oriented criticism and related criticism. But it is well to advert to it here because of the need to attend to what is alike and what is different when we contrast interpretation of oral work and interpretation of written work.

2

With these preliminaries behind us, I should like to turn directly to the question on which this collection of essays is based: "What difference does a work's oral traditional character make to its responsible, informed interpretation?" A recent book bears directly on this question with reference to material of the most urgent significance to millions of people today as well as to many more millions in the past and in the future. The book is *The Oral and the Written Gospel,* by Werner H. Kelber.[1] As no other work thus far has done, Professor Kelber's book brings to bear on biblical study all of the now vast and vigorously growing work on orality-literacy contrasts in a wide variety of fields: studies in oral tradition and performance, in linguistics, folklore, literary history and criticism, anthropology, sociology, intellectual history, cultural history, and much more. Armed with the new knowledge and sensitivities regarding orality-literacy contrasts and exhaustively familiar with earlier scholarship, Kelber undertakes to reconstruct what the kerygma, the preaching or proclamation

---

1. Werner H. Kelber, *The Oral and the Written Gospel: The Hermeneutics of Speaking and Writing in the Synoptic Tradition, Mark, Paul, and Q* (Philadelphia: Fortress Press, 1983). In the discussion that follows, further references to this work will be made parenthetically in the text.

of the Good News by Jesus, was like in the oral milieu in which he operated, then what it was like in the early Christian communities which preserved and circulated it after Jesus' death before any of the Gospels were put together, and, finally, what it was that Mark did with all this material when he undertook to compose his Gospel and how Mark's attitude toward textuality differs from Paul's.

In the wake of Kelber's work and within our present perspectives, we can say that, essentially, what Mark had to do was to interpret. The situation had become such that the old oral kerygma, which began with Jesus and was continued by Jesus' disciples, could no longer function effectively as it earlier had. Something had to be done to get the implications clear. The matter had to be reorganized. When Mark undertook to put the old oral heritage of stories and preaching about Jesus into writing, this was in effect what he undertook to do: to reorganize the oral kerygma so as to bring out its current relevancy. That is, he undertook to interpret the oral kerygma. His written Gospel was essentially interpretation. Early scholars, as Kelber carefully details, had some sense of the state of affairs here, before and after the written Gospel, but in the absence of today's fuller understanding of oral noetic processes they had not been able to describe adequately the oral base that Mark had to work from or the precise problems of interpretation in moving from such a base into textuality.

Mark's work of interpretation was of maximum urgency and significance because, for those who regarded the original oral kerygma by and about Jesus of Nazareth as true, Jesus was the way to fullness of life and to union with God for eternity. Any reconstitution of the kerygma, of Jesus' message, in writing—Jesus himself had left nothing in writing—would have to be one with the original oral preaching in the most profound way, or for the faithful all was lost. Mark's was not simply an aesthetic exercise. For the integrity of their faith, millions and billions of Christians who followed Jesus after New Testament times would be dependent upon the integrity of Mark's and others' written reconstruction of an oral tradition. The faithful could hold and have held into the present that God inspired the sacred text of the Bible, but what this means still calls for explanation when one becomes aware that what had been the kerygma for Christians before Mark's Gospel could not possibly have been simply the later, inspired textual kerygma, word-for-word.

Mark's Gospel, as the original major, extended interpretation of the oral kerygma that we have, would itself of course demand further interpretation. With such further interpretation, now bearing on the written Gospel as a text, the hermeneutic process entered into a new stage. The text was something temporally stabilized, context-free in the sense indicated above. It could be dealt with through the use of other texts as well as orally. But interpretation after the composition of the Markan text and the other New Testament texts that themselves also constitute interpretations of the original oral kerygma were all secondary to Mark's primary interpretive achievement, the first reconstitution of the oral kerygma in a new, written presentation, in words that floated context-free, visually fixed on a surface, retrievable now by anyone anywhere, as the utterances of the oral kerygma had never been.

3

Kelber's thesis is complex and its arguments carefully drawn. Scholars should be discussing it, pro and con, and further explicating it for years. Some of its general lines of development that are relevant here proceed as follows.

Earlier textual scholars had understandably thought of the oral kerygma, even when they were quite explicit about its orality, more or less in accordance with textual models: sayings were the sort of thing you found in texts, only they had not been written down. In this framework, scholars have looked, rather helplessly, for the "original" oral utterance, as one might look for an original or first text (p. xv). Oral utterances do not have originals quite as texts do. Texts provide what has been called autonomous discourse, context-free. Although textual utterance grows out of social settings and may refer to social settings, the text as text carries with it no real social setting such as always envelops oral utterance. Texts consist only of words inscribed on a surface. Written words can derive directly from other written words, as when a scribe makes a faithful copy of a text. But oral utterances cannot derive simply from other oral words.

Each oral utterance emerges from a situation that is more than verbal: a certain person or persons at this time situated in living relationship with a certain other person or persons. The repetition of oral utterance is itself not context-free. Certain persons may find themselves in a given situation that brings to mind a wise observation generated in an earlier, somewhat similar situation. The observation is repeated, most often not verbatim, but, even if verbatim, with a slightly different bearing, for its meaning includes its interaction with and adjustment to the real situation that now elicits it. The quest for an "original" utterance in this real, oral setting is quixotic, for each utterance emerges not simply from an earlier utterance but from a whole new existential context. In oral cultures even a fixed, formulaic saying is thus continuous with life more than it is continuous simply with other formulaic sayings.

Jesus' own words were subject to the rules of oral commerce: they were never context-free. The meaning of each oral utterance had to be gathered from the extraverbal as well as the verbal components. There was no way for Jesus to provide to the hundreds of different people he addressed orally in countless different situations a line of discourse such as one can find in an extended text. Doing so would have distorted his message or even have falsified it, and very likely have made it boring instead of dynamic, as it was. One has to discard the hermeneutic notion of "a tightly knit community of early Christians committed to the preservation and transmission of a single Gospel" (p. 31), that is, of a single set of fixed sayings of and about Jesus. Both Jesus' oral sayings and the oral memory of them were always contextual, though they of course could have universal relevance. He spoke in every case in a context of real concerns of real people in real social structures. Jesus' disciples, introducing his oral sayings orally into various contexts, lived in the same noetic economy, dipping into the store of his sayings and deeds for what was apropos in a given kerygmatic setting, for what would clarify and be clarified by a given state of affairs.

Giving some linearity to the mosaic configuration of such an oral kerygma meant decontextualizing the oral sayings by means of writing—of course only to a degree, since the Gospel text often states the setting of a given saying, but to a highly significant degree because a verbally stated setting itself is necessarily of a different order of existence from a real setting. A real setting is dense, never fully verbalized or verbalizable, involving all sorts of elusive but real imponderables. The real setting contours the saying designed for it, or elicited by it. Oral teaching must be "perceived as a speaking of living words in social contexts" (p. 33), and one must discard Rudolph Bultmann's model of an automatic evolutionary progression toward textual linearity which Mark's Gospel simply culminated as well as Birger Gerhardsson's model of passive transmission of a set of decontextualized oral sayings that people memorized verbatim and passed on (pp. 1–43). Mark's Gospel does not simply culminate orality but also runs counter to orality in being a "writing project" (p. 91). This Gospel

> is an act of daring and rife with consequences. . . . The voiceprints of once-spoken words have been muted. This is an extraordinary undertaking. . . . For the moment, language has fallen silent: the ground of Jesus' speech and that of his earliest followers is abandoned. . . . The text, while asserting itself out of dominant oral traditions and activities, has brought about a freezing of oral life into textual still life. . . .
>
> Mark's writing manifests a transmutation more than mere transmission, which results in a veritable upheaval of hermeneutical, cognitive realities.

What Mark undertook to do was to produce something that could never have existed as such before, though its elements existed. He undertook to produce and did produce a unified narrative, with some items thoughtfully and programmatically subordinated to others, with a focus or point of view shaped not by a particular audience such as a preacher or speaker was always faced with, but a point of view shaped by his sense of the way the kerygma had to be organized to make it most effective for the Christians who had been through the sacking of Jerusalem and the destruction of the Temple. Mark's organization was not so tight as a writer might produce today, but it clearly had a beginning, a middle, and an end. It opens, "Here begins the gospel of Jesus Christ, the Son of God" (Mark 1:1). Could any oral presentation of Jesus' teachings have begun, or even been conceived of, that way and carried through with the linearity that such a beginning presages? In Mark's chirographic organization of the kerygma, certain leading ideas develop, notably the well-known Markan idea of the Messianic secret: Jesus has a deeper meaning and message that the disciples at first had not at all fully understood and that all Christians must now understand if their faith is to survive. Mark's text, his gospel as a whole, was to present this deeper signification, centered ultimately in Jesus' person.

Of course, Mark's textuality, real though it is, never obliterates his oral sources. Not only do these provide his material, but also his writing style is residually oral. Discussing "heroic stories," "polarization stories," "didactic stories," and "parabolic stories" about Jesus in Mark, Kelber shows how these genres provided ways of digesting Jesus' work that were accommodated to oral noetic structures and oral memory. Underneath Mark's "intricate tapestry of linguistic patterns" in his chapters 1–13, there lies a "storied, oral heritage" where formulaic links, pleonasm, iteration, the paratactic *kai* ("and"), produce a narrative that lines up episodes "like beads on a string" (p. 65) and thereby creates a sense of spontaneity. Mark's textual world remains in many ways an orally styled textual world, where deeds and words are interchangeable (the exorcism in 1:27 is interpreted as though it itself "said" something, the exorcism itself is said to be "a new teaching! With authority").

In oral cultures words are more or less continuous with the rest of life, not so much part of a separate world as they appear to be in texts. "Mark shares the oral conviction that truth is not to be known nor redemption to be had by concepts estranged from life" (p. 70). In the oral world on which Mark's Gospel draws, "if Jesus is to be continued in the hearts and minds of people, then he must be filtered through the oral medium. What is summoned for transmission is fashioned for mnemonic purposes and selected for immediate relevance, not primarily for historical reasons" (p. 71). It has often been pointed out, by Albert B. Lord and others, that oral cultures do not generate even approximately complete biographies of their heroes or historically complete accounts of events. Or, to put it another way, oral transmission does not present anything like an academic "course" in "the life of Jesus," "the thought of Jesus," or "the theology of Jesus' parables." It favors individual, episodic stories about or sayings of Jesus, each of which can have an immediate, existential relevancy. In an oral world, narrative and other discourse must always be tailored to here-and-now communal expectations (it may of course attack these, but to do so it must touch them), just as social realities must in turn be validated, given meaning, in linguistic terms. The result is what Jack Goody and Ian Watt style the homeostatic balance of oral cultures, a continuous process of adjustment whereby linguistic expression and social actuality interact with and adjust to one another (p. 92).

Writing disrupts this homeostatic balance, for it "accords language a separate, bodily entity" in which "meaning may be suspended and hermeneutical ratification delayed." The author of a text "loses control over the process of interpretation." Yet text needs interpretation commonly far more than oral discourse, which tends to interpret itself in living exchange between speaker and hearer, as earlier noted. Thus Mark's conversion of the oral kerygma into a text disrupts the original living, oral synthesis. Oral or residually oral people are well aware of the problem here, and Lukas Vischer has pointed out the anxiety of early church Fathers regarding the way in which their own writing might compromise the living Christian gospel (Kelber, pp. 92–93). Katherine O'Brien O'Keefe has documented more recently similar misgivings in Aldhelm and other Old English writers about the newly introduced technology of writing, which they—as the early church Fathers before them—nevertheless used and developed, despite their uneasiness.[2]

There are marginal situations between orality and textuality, of course. In treating the world of oral commerce, Kelber does not preclude the disciples' use of notes and other textual aids to some degree, but he shows how, in the absence of any continuous text, the use of such aids was necessarily subject to "an oral ontology of language" (p. 91). To this one might add that the use of notes was always exceedingly cumbersome by modern standards in a culture where paper was unknown: wax-surfaced wooden tablets and stiff, bulky parchments are not so manageable as paper notebooks and, indeed, are not even very readily portable. The quite commonly postulated Q (*Quelle*) document, antecedent to Mark, would appear to lie on the margin between orality and full textuality. Q was apparently an agglomeration of disjunct sayings and incidents rather than an organized narrative.

In the transit from orality to textuality, Paul appears as a counterfoil to Mark in Kelber's account. "Faith comes through hearing" (Rom. 10:17). "The letter kills, the spirit gives life" (2 Cor. 3:6). Paul's hermeneutic is basically oral, though not entirely so, for he does appeal to written authority, as in 1 Cor. 1:19 and 3:19—"Scrip-

2. Katherine O'Brien O'Keefe, "Moths and Mouths: Some Anglo-Saxon Meditations on the Technology of Writing," a paper presented at the General Session on Old English at the Ninety-Eighth Convention of the Modern Language Association of America, 27–30 December 1983, New York, New York.

ture says . . . ." And he himself of course writes—but letters rather than a Gospel. Kelber notes that whereas the narrator Mark retreats behind his narrative text so as virtually to disappear, Paul himself very much emerges in the text of his letters, which are thus more closely linked with orality than written narrative is. Paul's favoring of the oral charism shows up also in what Kelber styles his "deep-seated anxiety" over the written Torah or Law (pp. 151–64).

Carefully nuanced to allow for convergent and divergent currents and countercurrents, Kelber's meticulous study shows, in sum, that the movement from the oral kerygma to the written Gospel is not simply a linear movement but in significant ways an antithetical one, involving a transformation of thought forms and of consciousness itself. Our recently acquired knowledge of the psychodynamics of oral noetic and cultural processes has brought out the antithetical relationship of textuality and orality in ways never before possible.

One of Mark's major themes, the one advertising the discontinuity of oral sayings and text, is the failure of the disciples to comprehend the full meaning of Jesus' sayings and of his life and death. The simple oral proclamation of Jesus' presence would no longer suffice. In the light of the disasters that had beset Christians by Mark's time—war and persecution, the sack of Jerusalem and dispersion of its inhabitants (Mark 13:3–20)—the simply oral proclamation of Jesus' presence among human beings no longer was effective enough. Crises generated unreal presences. In times of such disasters, oral proclamations of false Messiahs abound: "If anyone tells you, 'Look, the Messiah is here!' 'Look, he is there!'— do not believe it. False messiahs and false prophets will appear performing signs and wonders to mislead, if it were possible, even the chosen" (Mark 13:21–22). What was needed was not simple proximity to someone present, which orality gave, embedding each utterance in the here-and-now, but also distance—the distance for reflection that textual organization can provide, Derrida's *différence*—and which makes for a truly historical understanding. The kingdom Jesus preached has "a history mysterious in its entirety." Oral sayings are "too discrete, direct, and episodic to allow full revelation of the kingdom's mysterious history" (p. 101). Oral noetic processes bind the kerygma too much to the immediate social actuality for it to have its full effectiveness after a certain time. At this point, writing is necessary to present the fuller story of Jesus in some directional form, and the story cannot be a mere concatenation of earlier sayings by and about Jesus. It has to be recast for readers most of whom Mark could never hope to know. Once we understand the situation here, it is evident that the historical Jesus has to be discovered not by simply studying the text but by seeing the complex relationship of the Gospel text to the earlier oral noetic world in which Jesus lived. The relationship of this oral world to text is not one-to-one, although it is very real and not unrecoverable if we allow for its complexities. For what Mark wanted clearly to present was the real Jesus of Nazareth. Only now, textually.

4

The magnitude of Mark's task should not be underestimated. The textualization of the Christian kerygma was a special event in the history of textualization because the oral kerygma itself was so centered in the person of Jesus and in personal, loving identification with him. The focus on the person of Jesus comes clear in every book of the New Testament, including Pauline letters antecedent to Mark's gospel. It is unquestionable that Jesus was the personal center of the oral kerygma from the start. The relationship of the sacred texts of the world's larger religions to the founders of these religions differs in each case. For example, Buddhist texts postdate the life of the Buddha (Siddhartha Gautama, circa 563–circa 483 B.C.) by centuries and variant canons define individual Buddhist sects, whereas the Koran is coeval with Muhammad himself: John Burton's recent work has undertaken to show that the text is actually Muhammad's own.[3]

In Mark's presentation, Jesus' mission is the preaching or proclamation of the Good News: "that I may proclaim the good news. . . . That is what I have come to do" (Mark 1:1 compare Mark 1:14–15, 38–39). This heralding of the Good News was an activity that Jesus had his disciples also take up (3:14, 6:12). The disciples learned by attending on Jesus and listening to him, not by reading, and were trained to be activists, preachers, interacters with peo-

3. John Burton, *The Collection of the Qur'ān* (Cambridge: Cambridge University Press, 1977).

ple, not readers. Their obligation is remembering (Kelber, p. 96), not memorization, which is not the same as remembering.[4]

Ultimately, Jesus makes the kerygma, that is, the personally interactive proclamation of the Good News, the mission of the entire Church (13:10, 14:9).

The Good News that Jesus proclaims is fundamentally the mystery of the kingdom (Mark 4:11), at the heart of which is Jesus' own identity as a person sealed by his passion and death (8:32). Jesus preaches complete personal attachment to himself on the part of his disciples (8:20–25), leading to the sharing of his passion and death (8:34–35, 10:35–40). Jesus is the Son of God (1:1) and the kerygma he preaches is the way to the Father (13:32–37), whom Jesus calls on in his passion (14:36) and who is the disciples' Father also (11:25). The kerygma or proclamation which the written text works up out of oral tradition is thus not simply a series of more or less unified exhortations or observations about a state of affairs, human and/or divine, but is intimately involved with and hinges on the personal identity of Jesus, of his followers, and of the Father himself. The kerygma, the Good News, was not simply about Jesus. It was Jesus. "Your faith in me shall be shaken. . . . But after I am raised up, I will go to Galilee ahead of you" (14:27–28). And it involved not merely the thoughts and actions but the entire persons of those he came into contact with, directly or through his disciples. The kerygma was both public and intensely personal.

The textualization of such a message, taken from an oral, person-to-person context, is a formidable one, for the relationship of person to person in a text is essentially indirect, and particularly in a narrative (by comparison with an epistolary text). Not long after Mark, the Gospel according to John would proclaim Jesus as the Word of God—certainly not by analogy with the written word of human beings but with the spoken word, which thus in the last of the four gospels asserts its ascendancy over the written text. "In the beginning was the Word; the Word was in God's presence, and the Word was God" (John 1:1).

---

4. See my *The Presence of the Word: Some Prolegomena for Cultural and Religious History,* (New Haven and London: Yale University Press, 1967), pp. 23, 168–69.

5

It would be tempting to reduce the antithesis of textuality and orality to simple destructiveness. But the relationship of writing and orality is far more complex than such reductionism would allow. Putting a strain on a system does not necessarily mean destroying it: the strain might even improve the system, or force it to improve itself. For there are no totally closed systems.

The subversion of orality by writing was gradual, and of course has never been complete. Between biblical times and our own, orality throve in various degrees of integrity or disarray and interacted vigorously with textuality to a degree that literates have tended to forget. As Kelber takes pains to point out (p. 93), "it is not within the power of a text to stem the flow of spoken words." Mark's text did not at first change the oral climate much at all. Kelber calls attention to Helmut Koester's findings that the writings of the Apostolic Fathers (A.D. 95–150) rarely cite the sayings of Jesus verbatim from Markan or other texts. Their citations are not usually textual derivatives at all but normally variant continuations of the old oral transmission. Only at the time of Justin Martyr, in the mid-second century, did verbatim citations from the synoptic gospels, most notably Matthew and Luke, begin to supersede oral transmission. From this point on, the oral way of life was more seriously contested, for "speaking was no longer the dominant, life-giving force in Christianity" (pp. 93–94) that it earlier had been.

Yet orality remained a powerful force in culture. First, as we need constantly to remind ourselves, until the past three centuries or so, few Christians—and, indeed, few human beings of any religious affiliation or of none—have been able to read and write. Those who wrote left verbal records behind them, and we tend to take the mentality these records represent as typical of the entire culture, though it could hardly have been so. Studies of orality have lately awakened us to the limitations of earlier historiography which looked to the "high" culture of literates or of classes operating in close touch with literates—such as the noble or landed or military classes of Europe—as representative of most things in the culture worth attending to. Such literary exclusionism, however unwittingly practiced, can vitiate textual hermeneutic itself, giving rise to the futile quest for a historical Jesus to be reconstructed directly from the biblical text without allowance for the tensions between the text and the quite different, nontextual, oral psychodynamics of the world in which Jesus lived and thought and preached and did good works.

Second, we need to be aware how residual orality can envelop even a highly developed textuality.[5] For example, as István Hajnal has shown,[6] in and around the universities of the Middle Ages, despite the fact that universities were far more committed to literacy than antiquity had ever been, the vast amount of writing generated by the universities was actually at the service of orality—though, of course, an orality whose thought processes had been infiltrated by literacy to a degree. In medieval universities no one was ever tested academically by having to write anything. All assaying of intellectual prowess and accomplishment was oral, in disputations and the like, so that the intellectual world, while styled largely by writing, was in performance oral to a degree difficult for high-technology literates to conceive.

6

What was the hermeneutic situation in cultures that mingled an intensive textuality with a high residual orality, such as those of the European Middle Ages? Only recently have in-depth studies of such questions begun to appear. Let me here attend to one, the recent book by Brian Stock, *The Implications of Literacy.*[7]

Although medieval culture was marked by bewildering orality-literacy relationships, among literates literacy was ideologically triumphant. The "most injurious consequence of medieval literacy," Stock finds (p. 31), was "the notion that literacy is identical with rationality." This of course meant Latin literacy, since the vernaculars, even the very few that were written at all, were not yet developed to handle highly abstract, analytic thought. Diglossia, with a "high" language chirographically managed and a "low," or

5. See my *Ramus, Method, and the Decay of Dialogue* (Cambridge, Mass.: Harvard University Press, 1958).

6. István Hajnal, *L'enseignement de l'écriture aux universités médiévales* (Budapest: Academia Scientiarum Hungarica Budapestini, 1954), p. 64.

7. Brian Stock, *The Implications of Literacy: Written Language and Models of Interpretation in the Eleventh and Twelfth Centuries* (Princeton: Princeton University Press, 1983). In the discussion that follows, further references to this work will be made parenthetically in the text.

vernacular, language orally managed, created a special hermeneutic climate. Because the "high" language, Latin, had
become a foreign tongue for all its users, the native, oral tongue of
no one any longer, unknown to anyone who could not write it, it
evoked a textual world even when it was spoken, as it was by millions of persons (almost without exception males) over the centuries. Under such circumstances, culture was centered, so far as
literates were concerned, not simply on literacy—the ability to
read and write a basically spoken tongue—but upon textuality,
upon extant texts as objects in which all language and thought
worth attending to ultimately lodged.

Such textuality had widespread implications and effects. For
example, liturgical worship, which is normally and necessarily
connected with extraliterate life, declined and theological scholarship grew vigorous. The priest-king, integrated into an "oral,
pictorial, gestural, and liturgical culture," gave way to the
desacralized law-king, linked to "the literate, the administrative,
the instrumentally rational, and the constitutional" (p. 33).
Whereas at the beginning of the eleventh century illiteracy was no
disability for administrators, who could hire scribes to handle
what little documentation there was, two centuries later illiteracy
was disabling for administrators, though not in the same way
everywhere. Stock details scores of other widely diversified
effects of the growth in literacy, though the range of literacy was
always severely limited by modern high-technology-society standards.

Stock makes clear, however, that writing did not simply take
over the culture but created all sorts of complicated interdepen-
dencies between itself and the underlying oralities. Some of the
most complex developed in the "textual communities" to which
Stock devotes a great deal of his book and which are relevant to
our concerns here with biblical text and interpretation. Textual
communities are "groups of people," not necessarily all literate,
"whose social activities are centered around texts, or more precisely around a literate interpreter of them" (p. 522). Such communities are pivotal in the development of a vast array of
interpretive phenomena: for example, in the organization of
reform groups attacking nepotism, nicolaitism, and other widespread objectionable practices, in disputes about the eucharist
that virtually created eucharistic theology, in the making and

unmaking of heresies, in the revision of philosophical and theological concepts of "nature," in the rise of intellectualism, and in much else. Stock's perspectives reveal the universities, which began in the Middle Ages, as not unlike the textual communities he treats of. The universities were organized around a body of texts subjected to programmatic interpretation which could diversify and divide the university textual community into subcommunities or schools of interpretation. The paideia of Greek and Roman antiquity did not function by textual interpretation the way universities did—and to an extent still do. But textuality, to the modern mind the protosymbol of order, could in fact be highly disruptive, Stock points out (p. 9 and passim), in orally organized society: it undid longstanding and effective oral institutions to impose its own new organization.

The textual communities Stock studies generated not only many texts but also, and perhaps even more, vigorously charismatic oral performance, such as that of the illiterate French peasant Leutard (pp. 101–6). Orality and literacy contrasts often polarized issues. The popular oral account of Leutard describes the rapport between Leutard and his audience behaviorly (orality tends normally to coalesce words and deeds), whereas the analysis worked up by literates interprets Leutard's activity in terms of isolated, definable doctrines (pp. 101–6). But polarization could also be convoluted. The Pataria reform movement in Milan raised its following largely through oral preaching (p. 166), though at its core it was a confederation of literates. Yet, despite its literate core, it found itself fiercely attacked by the highly literate Arnulf of Milan, who attributed its success with the oral populace to the election of a country-born archbishop who was illiterate (*idiota,* an "idiot," a common term for one unskilled in Latin literacy). The milieus Stock studies preserve conspicuously, in their writing as well as in their oral performance, the agonistic lifestyle that is one of the hallmarks of primary oral cultures,[8] and that still marks the still highly oral Mediterranean region,[9] on which Stock's attention concentrates.

8. See my *Presence of the Word; Fighting for Life: Contest, Sexuality, and Consciousness* (Ithaca and London: Cornell University Press, 1981); and *Orality and Literacy: The Technologizing of the Word* (London and New York: Methuen, 1982).

9. See J. G. Peristiany, ed., *Honor and Shame: The Values of Mediterranean Society* (Chicago: University of Chicago Press, 1966).

Stock's work shows the interplay between oral and charismatic interpretation of texts and the more analytic textual interpretation of texts. All the texts back of Stock's interpretive communities were not biblical, but most of them appear to have been, and those that were not, including texts that were only putative (as Stock notes, some were; p. 105), were interpreted after the manner followed for biblical texts. That is, the textual communities organized themselves around interpretations of texts as impinging on the world of human action, particularly in its moral aspects. Thus texts did not stand on their own but were taken as meaningful in the context of nontextual life, including nonverbal life—that is, as involved in the total social setting. A text could be objectionable not only because of what it said but also because of the one who wrote it. Interpretation of verbalization in terms of total setting is characteristic of oral cultures. The written text was to this extent still being processed or interpreted orally.

7

The notion of a textual community is far from being entirely new. It is related to, but not quite the same as, the "interpretive communities" that Stanley Fish and others write about.[10] Interpretive communities are less tightly organized around specific texts, but are rather held together by a hermeneutic heritage applicable to any number of texts or any text. Textual communities are held together by a specific text or texts subject to competing interpretations from outside. Today's vast literature on intertextuality and on interpretive communities has made it quite clear that texts come into being through interaction with other texts and are interpreted in traditions worked out by specific groups engaged with other texts. But intertextual analysis has commonly paid relatively little attention to the interaction between texts and their circumambient orality. The orality of a milieu can deeply affect both the composition of texts and their interpretation. Orality-literacy contrasts and interactions, we must remind ourselves, involve not merely different "channels" for units of "information" but different noetic worlds and different psychodynamics.

10. Stanley Fish, *Is There a Text in This Class? The Authority of Interpretive Communities* (Cambridge, Mass.: Harvard University Press, 1980).

In the history of textual study the Bible occupies a unique place. The greatest unitary mass of textual commentary the world knows has grown up around it. This commentary has been a stimulus and often a model for all sorts of extrabiblical textual learning, theorizing, and exegesis from Origen through Dante and Milton on to James Joyce and beyond. The title of Northrop Frye's magisterial book, *The Great Code,* a title garnered from Blake, advertises the unique place of the Bible in the history of interpretation. A code both interprets and itself needs interpretation—as all utterance does, only more so.

Hermeneutics evolves, and as it evolves today, it grows more aware of orality-literacy contrasts in verbal expression and in noetic processes and of the implications of these contrasts for interpretive study. In it orality and literacy intersect in seemingly the most intensive fashion possible, in the Hebrew scriptures, the Law, the Prophets, and the Writings, and through the Christian books, and most crucially in the Gospels.

Paul Ricoeur notes that the Christian kerygma is itself "the rereading of an ancient Scripture."[11]   He is referring here, it appears, to the kerygma found in the gospel texts. The gospel text certainly does incorporate an interpretation of the pre-Christian books of the Christian Bible. Northrop Frye insists that in the Christian mind this becomes the chief business of the Old Testament, to illuminate and be illuminated by the New.[12]   But the new interpretation of the pre-Christian books, though it enters into the New Testament texts, was originally and fundamentally not a textual operation, not a text-to-text transaction. Jesus' kerygma, which included, but was not restricted to, an interpretation of the ancient books, was in itself a completely oral event or series of events. (Spoken words are events, not things: they are never present all at once but occur seriatim, syllable-after-syllable.) New Testament texts follow on the oral hermeneutic of Jesus, interpreting his interpretation for textual conveyance.

The involvement of orality in hermeneutic processes was intensive for centuries after Jesus' life on earth and has continued, somewhat abated, to our own time. Although the Bible lies at the

---

11. Paul Ricoeur, *Essays on Biblical Interpretation,* ed. with an introduction by Lewis S. Mudge (Philadelphia: Fortress Press, 1980), p. 51.

12. Northrop Frye, *The Great Code: The Bible and Literature* (New York and London: Harcourt, Brace, Jovanovich, 1982), pp. 78–101.

heart of Christianity, over the centuries by far most Christians have been illiterate. Until the Protestant Reformation, with its stress on private reading of the scriptures, Christianity had never regarded illiterates as salvifically disadvantaged. In relation to Jesus and before God, they were at least as well off as literates, and maybe better off, for God "singled out the weak of this world to shame the strong" (I Cor. 1:27), though obviously the Christian community needed at least some literates to deal directly with the sacred scriptures and to a degree with certain administrative matters.

Because of the free flow between orality and literacy in the Church, despite the centrality of the biblical text, the full spectrum of interpretive activity in the Church in terms of orality-literacy contrasts is as fascinating as it has been little understood. Once you are aware that oral noetics differ from chirographic noetics, what can you say about what went on, and had to go on, when through the Middle Ages and the Renaissance and later the gospels were interpreted for illiterates by literates—often literates themselves marked by a high residue of orality, not even known to be such? When we add to the hermeneutic perspectives here the further perspective that the gospel itself was a literate interpretation of oral-traditional materials, the questions become even more intriguing. Easygoing categories such as "superstition" or "lack of historical sense," often applied to the illiterate world, appear curiously out of touch with reality. All these new perspectives make the situation much more complex, but also, I believe, far more understandable.

Of course, the reciprocal movement from orality to literacy back to orality and thence to literacy again had, in a dizzying variety of ways, marked the development of the Old Testament, too. For the kind of phenomenon that Kelber discusses in describing Mark's textual reprocessing of oral-traditional performance can be observed in one way or another from Genesis on. Oral materials are textualized, the textual materials then freely circulated orally, with or without some textual control conjoined to oral control, and then are reprocessed from orality into text again. This process is not restricted to religious texts, Christian or Hebrew or other: something like it goes on in ordinary secular learning, particularly in antiquity. The relationship of Aristotle's works, for example, to oral discourse and to texts remains a permanent puzzle: Aristotle at times apparently wrote texts, or perhaps dictated texts or parts of texts, but at other times left behind him only other persons' textualization of his oral performance, perhaps worked over more or less by him.[13]

But in such oral-literate-oral-literate sequences the oral heritage is never so intensive, so professedly integral, or so crucial as in the oral kerygma of Jesus underlying New Testament writings. This kerygma was one person's proclamation in which he incorporated his hermeneutic for an oral-chirographic heritage of a thousand years. Jesus' oral kerygma did not constitute the oral-traditional background of an intellectual elite but rather provided the basic interpretation of existence for an entire community still extant and held together by this kerygma of one who they believed, and still believe, still lives in a transformed, resurrected state. This oral-textual-oral-textual-oral interpretive community is the Church. Other major world religions have an oral-traditional heritage, too, but nothing constituted like this.

In 1974 Avery Dulles completed a small, deliberately popularizing, but scholarly and highly informative book, *Models of the Church,* in which he notes that ecclesiologists, Catholic and Protestant, over the years have explained the Christian Church in accord with various models that they had consciously or unconsciously appropriated: the Church has been viewed, variously and in each case inadequately, as an institution, as a mystical communion, as sacrament, as herald, as servant. Dulles notes that other models have been used as well, and states that his selection of these five for study has been made "for simplicity's sake."[14] He suggests that a multiplicity of models is needed to compensate for the limitations sure to mark each and every individual model.

I would suggest that it is possible today to add as a further, very helpful model, a model not yet so fully developed as those Dulles considers but now ready for quite full development, that is, a model of the Church as an oral-chirographic interpretive community, founded in oral-traditional materials early interpreted in textual form and thereafter interpreted in a historically continuous

13. See Werner Jaeger, *Aristotle: Fundamentals of the History of His Development,* trans. with the author's corrections and additions by Richard Robinson, 2d ed. (Oxford: Clarendon Press, 1948), pp. 168 ff.
14. Avery Dulles, S.J., *Models of the Church* (Garden City, N.Y.: Doubleday, 1974), p. 9.

communal setting by continuous interaction of the oral and the textual.

A model of the Church as an oral-chirographic interpretive community of the sort suggested here would provide new insights into a great many of the vexing problems centering around the relationship of the Bible and tradition. This relationship has plagued historians and theologians as well as worshiping ecclesial communities over the centuries, but it came to a head with the deep interiorization of literacy and the resulting reorganization of thought processes brought about by print.[15] The Protestant-Catholic division that developed in the wake of typography was marked by a Protestant insistence that Scripture alone (*sola scriptura*) was the source of divine revelation in the Church and the Catholic insistence that, in addition to Scripture, tradition was also a source.

Of course, neither side in the Reformation dispute could be aware of the orality-literacy conflicts at work in the consciousness of the time. Scripture is obviously a literate phenomenon, at least in its terminal phase. Tradition, as Catholics and their opponents understood it and as it has to be understood, involves orality. The Council of Trent (sess. IV, 8 April 1546) contrasts divine revelation in "written books" (that is, the Bible) and "unwritten traditions" (*sine scripto traditionibus*) which were "received by the Apostles from the mouth of Christ himself" (*ab ipsius Christi ore ab Apostolis acceptae*). Rejecting a proposed draft that divine revelation is contained "partly in the Scriptures and partly in tradition," Trent defined simply that it is contained "in the Scriptures and in unwritten traditions." And yet the explications of Trent's decrees by Renaissance Catholic theologians show the confusions typically deriving from the unexamined bias of the literate mind. Twentieth-century studies have shown how these earlier theologians tended to conceptualize oral tradition itself by implied, and unnoticed, textual analogies, as though tradition itself were a kind of second volume of the Bible which Catholics kept and Protestants had abandoned.[16] Here the same preemptive chirographic mindset evident in Protestant attitudes toward *sola*

15. See my *Orality and Literacy,* pp. 117–38.

16. Charles Baumgartner, "Tradition et magistère," *Recherches de science religeuse* 41 (1953): 161–87; Walter J. Burghardt, "The Catholic Concept of Tradition," *Proceedings of the Catholic Theological Society of America* (1951): 42–76.

scriptura manifested itself in a more subtle way. On the other hand, Protestants showed evidence of orality-literacy tensions in counterbalancing their heavy textual investment in *sola scriptura* with a stress on oral preaching that was not foreign to the Catholic tradition but that had never before been quite so strong. These are only samples of the many orality-literacy polarities in the Protestant-Catholic division which call for study.

Our present perspectives for interpreting complex orality-literacy relationships were of course not yet available in Reformation times. The perspectives suggested here have not been available even to present-day scholarship very long. It is not merely that the biblical text is preceded by oral tradition, which the text simply sets down, but that—to take Mark as paradigmatic of all the Gospels and even of all the Bible, though not rigidly so—the biblical text itself comes into being as an interpretation of what went before, the definitive written ecclesial hermeneutic of an original oral kerygma. This does not, of course, at all do away with or compromise Catholic belief as defined by Trent and the First Vatican Council that the Bible is the inspired word of God, having God as its "principal author," but it sets the scene for understanding in greater depth what such belief in divine authorship entails. God works in history—which is what the Incarnation is about. But the work of understanding is just beginning.

Finally, given that biblical hermeneutics has always historically been a major groundbreaker for textual studies generally, secular as well as religious, one can hope that the new orality-literacy perspectives opening on biblical textuality, with the particularly intense focus that biblical textuality has demanded, will also open new insights into many other fields and provide an enlarged understanding of the human condition in its totality which lies at the center of the Bible's own concern.

SELECTED BIBLIOGRAPHY
John Miles Foley

Abrahams, Roger D. "License to Repeat and Be Predictable." *Folklore Preprint Series* (Indiana University) 6, (August 1978): 1–13.

Adams, Kenneth. "The Yugoslav Model and the Text of the 'Poema de Mio Cid.'" In *Medieval Hispanic Studies Presented to Rita Hamilton,* edited by Alan D. Deyermond, pp. 1–10. London: Tamesis, 1976.

Alexiou, Margaret. *The Ritual Lament in Greek Tradition.* Cambridge: Cambridge University Press, 1974.

Alster, Bendt. *Dumuzi's Dream: Aspects of Oral Poetry in a Sumerian Myth.* Copenhagen Studies in Assyriology, vol. 1. Copenhagen: Akademisk Forlag, 1972.

Alwaya, Semha. "Formulas and Themes in Contemporary Bedouin Oral Poetry." *Journal of Arabic Literature* 8 (1977): 48–76.

Amory Parry, Anne. *Blameless Aegisthus: A Study of* AMYMΩN *and Other Homeric Epithets.* Mnemosyne, Bibliotheca Classica Batava, Supplementum 26. Leiden: E. J. Brill, 1973.

Anders, Wolfhart H. *Balladensänger und mündliche Komposition: Untersuchungen zur englischen Traditionsballade.* Bochumer Arbeiten zur Sprach- und Literaturwissenschaft. Munich: Wilhelm Fink, 1974.

Arant, Patricia. "Formulaic Style and the Russian Bylina." *Indiana Slavic Studies* 4 (1967): 7–51.

Armistead, Samuel G. "The *Mocedades de Rodrigo* and Neo-Individualist Theory." *Hispanic Review* 46 (1978): 313–27.

Barnie, John. "Oral Formulas in the Country Blues." *Southern Folklore Quarterly* 42 (1978): 39–52.

Başgöz, Ilhan. "Epithet in a Prose Epic: The Book of My Grandfather Korkut." *Folklore Preprint Series* (Indiana University) 6, 1, a (1978): 1–23.

Baugh, Albert C. "Improvisation in the Middle English Romance." *Proceedings of the American Philosophical Society* 103 (1959): 418–54.

Bäuml, Franz H. "Varieties and Consequences of Medieval Literacy and Illiteracy." *Speculum* 55 (1980): 237–65.

Beatie, Bruce A. "Oral-Traditional Composition in the Spanish *Romancero* of the Sixteenth Century." *Journal of the Folklore Institute* 1 (1964–1965): 92–113.

Beaton, Roderick. *Folk Poetry of Modern Greece.* Cambridge: Cambridge University Press, 1980.

————. "The Oral Traditions of Modern Greece: A Survey." *Oral Tradition* 1 (1986): 110–33.

Ben-Amos, Dan. "Folklore in African Society." *Review of African Literatures* 6 (1975): 165–98.

Benson, Larry D. "The Literary Character of Anglo-Saxon Formulaic Poetry." *PMLA* 81 (1966): 334–41.

Bessinger, Jess B. "*Beowulf* and the Harp at Sutton Hoo." *University of Toronto Quarterly* 27 (1957): 148–68.

Biebuyck, Daniel P. "The African Heroic Epic." *Journal of the Folklore Institute* 13 (1976): 5–36.

Bixler, Phyllis. "The Oral-Formulaic Training of a Popular Fiction Writer: Frances Hodgson Burnett." *Journal of Popular Culture* 15, 4 (1982): 42–52.

Bonjour, Adrien. "*Beowulf* et l'épopée anglo-saxonne." In *L'Epopée vivante,* a special issue of *La Table ronde* 132 (December 1958): 140–51.

Bošković-Stulli, Maja. "Usmena književnost u sklopu povijesti hrvatske književnosti." *Umjetnost riječi* 11 (1967): 247–60.

Bowra, Cecil M. *Heroic Poetry.* 1952; rpt. London: St. Martin's Press, 1966.

Brown, Mary Ellen. " 'That Bards are Second-Sighted Is Nae Joke': The Orality of Burns's World and Work." *Studies in Scottish Literature* 16 (1981): 208–16.

Bynum, David E. *The Daemon in the Wood: A Study of Oral Narrative Patterns.* Cambridge, Mass.: Center for the Study of Oral Literature, 1978.

Calhoun, George M. "The Art of Formula in Homer—ΕΠΕΑ ΠΤΕΡΟΕΝΤΑ." *Classical Philology* 30 (1935): 215–27.

Capek, Michael J. "A Note on Formula Development in Old Saxon." *Modern Philology* 67 (1970): 357–63.

Caraveli, Anna. "The Song Beyond the Song: Aesthetics and Social Interaction in Greek Folksong." *Journal of American Folklore* 95 (1982): 129–58.

Chadwick, Hector M., and Nora K. Chadwick. *The Growth of Literature.* 3 vols. Cambridge: Cambridge University Press, 1932–1940; rpt. 1968.

Combellack, Frederick M. "Homer the Innovator." *Classical Philology* 71 (1976): 44–55.

Conroy, Patricia. "Oral Composition in Faroese Ballads." *Jahrbuch für Volksliedforschung* 25 (1980): 34–50.

Coote, Mary P. "Women's Songs in Serbo-Croatian." *Journal of American Folklore* 90 (1977): 331–38.

Creed, Robert P. "The Making of an Anglo-Saxon Poem." *English Literary History* 26 (1959): 445–54.

————. "On the Possibility of Criticizing Old English Poetry." *Texas Studies in Literature and Language* 3 (1961): 97–106.

Crowne, David K. "The Hero on the Beach: An Example of Composition by Theme in Anglo-Saxon Poetry." *Neuphilologische Mitteilungen* 61 (1960): 362–72.

Culley, Robert C. *Oral Formulaic Language in the Biblical Psalms*. Near and Middle East Series, vol. 4. Toronto: University of Toronto Press, 1967.

————. "Oral Tradition and Biblical Studies." *Oral Tradition* 1 (1986), 30–65.

Curschmann, Michael. "Oral Poetry in Mediaeval English, French, and German Literature: Some Notes on Recent Research." *Speculum* 42 (1967): 36–52.

de Chasca, Edmund V. *The Poem of the Cid*. Boston: G. K. Hall, 1976.

Deyermond, Alan D. "The Singer of Tales and Mediaeval Spanish Epic." *Bulletin of Hispanic Studies* 42 (1965), 1–8.

Duggan, Hoyt N. "The Role of Formulas in the Dissemination of a Middle English Alliterative Romance." *Studies in Bibliography* 29 (1976): 265–88.

Duggan, Joseph J. *The Song of Roland: Formulaic Style and Poetic Craft*. Publications of the Center for Medieval and Renaissance Studies, University of California Los Angeles, 6. Berkeley: University of California Press, 1973.

————. "Formulaic Diction in the *Cantar de Mio Cid* and the Old French Epic." In *Oral Literature: Seven Essays,* edited by Joseph J. Duggan, pp. 74–83. Edinburgh and New York: Scottish Academic Press and Barnes and Noble, 1975.

Dundes, Alan, Jerry W. Leach, and Bora Özkök. "The Strategy of Turkish Boys' Verbal Dueling Rhymes." In *Directions in Sociolinguistics: The Ethnography of Communication,* edited by John J. Gumperz and Dell Hymes, pp. 130–60. New York: Holt, Rinehart, and Winston, 1972.

Edwards, G. Patrick. *The Language of Hesiod in its Traditional Context*. Publications of the Philological Society 22. Oxford: Basil Blackwell, 1971.

Edwards, Mark W. "Some Features of Homeric Craftsmanship." *Transactions of the American Philological Association* 97 (1966): 115–79.

Else, Gerald F. *Homer and the Homeric Problem,* Lectures in Memory of Louise Taft Semple. Cincinnati: University of Cincinnati, 1965.

Emeneau, Murray B. "Oral Poets of South India—The Todas." *Journal of American Folklore* 71 (1958): 312–24.

Evarts, Peter G. "The Technique of the Medieval Minstrel as Revealed in the Sicilian *Contastoria.*" *Studies in Medieval Culture* 6–7 (1976): 117–27.

Fenik, Bernard C., ed. *Homer: Tradition and Invention. University of Cincinnati Classical Studies,* ns 2. Leiden: E. J. Brill, 1978.

Finnegan, Ruth H. *Oral Literature in Africa.* Oxford: Clarendon Press, 1970.

————. *Oral Poetry: Its Nature, Significance, and Social Context.* Cambridge: Cambridge University Press, 1977.

Foley, John Miles. "Formula and Theme in Old English Poetry." In *Oral Literature and the Formula,* edited by Benjamin A. Stolz and Richard S. Shannon, pp. 207–32. Ann Arbor: Center for Coordination of Ancient and Modern Studies, 1976.

————, ed. *Oral Traditional Literature: A Festschrift for Albert Bates Lord.* Columbus: Slavica Press, 1980; 2d printing 1983.

————. *Oral-Formulaic Theory and Research: An Introduction and Annotated Bibliography.* New York: Garland, 1985.

————. "Literary Art and Oral Tradition in Old English and Serbian Poetry." *Anglo-Saxon England* 12 (1983): 183–214.

Frank, Roberta. *Old Norse Court Poetry: The "Drottkvaett" Stanza. Islandica* 42. Ithaca: Cornell University Press, 1978.

Fry, Donald K., Jr. "Old English Formulas and Systems." *English Studies* 48 (1967): 193–204.

————. "Cædmon as a Formulaic Poet." In *Oral Literature: Seven Essays,* edited by Joseph J. Duggan, pp. 41–61. Edinburgh and New York: Scottish Academic Press and Barnes and Noble, 1975.

Gesemann, Gerhard. *Studien zur südslavischen Volksepik.* Veröffentlichungen der Slavistischen Arbeitsgemeinschaft (Prague), I. Reihe: Untersuchungen, Heft 3. Reichenberg: Verlag Gebrüder Stiepel, 1926.

Gitay, Yehoshua. "Deutero-Isaiah: Oral or Written?" *Journal of Biblical Literature* 99 (1980): 185–97.

Goody, John R., ed. *Literacy in Traditional Societies.* Cambridge: Cambridge University Press, 1968.

Görög, Veronika. *Littérature orale d'Afrique noire: Bibliographie analytique.* Avec la participation de Michèle Chiche. Paris: G.-P. Maisonneuve et Larose, 1981.

Greenfield, Stanley B. "The Formulaic Expression of the Theme of 'Exile' in Anglo-Saxon Poetry." *Speculum* 30 (1955): 200–6.

Grobman, Neil R. "Thomas Blackwell's Commentary on the Oral Nature of Epic." *Western Folklore* 38 (1979): 186–98.

Gunn, David M. "Thematic Composition and Homeric Authorship." *Harvard Studies in Classical Philology* 75 (1971): 1–31.

—————. "Narrative Patterns and Oral Tradition in Judges and Samuel." *Vetus Testamentum* 24 (1974): 286–317.

Guyonvarc'h, Christian J. and Françoise Le Roux. "L'Epopée irlandaise du cycle d'Ulster." In *L'Epopée vivante,* a special issue of *La Table ronde* 132 (Dec. 1958): pp. 128–39.

Hainsworth, J. B. *The Flexibility of the Homeric Formula.* Oxford: Clarendon Press, 1968.

Hanaway, William L., Jr. "The Iranian Epics." In *Heroic Epic and Saga,* edited by Felix J. Oinas, pp. 76–98. Bloomington: Indiana University Press, 1978.

Harris, Joseph. "Eddic Poetry as Oral Poetry: The Evidence of Parallel Passages in the Helgi Poems for Questions of Composition and Performance." In *Edda: A Collection of Essays,* edited by Robert J. Glendinning and Haraldur Bessason, pp. 210–42. Manitoba Icelandic Series. Manitoba: University of Manitoba Press, 1983.

Havelock, Eric A. *Preface to Plato.* Cambridge, Mass.: Harvard University Press, 1963; rpt. 1982.

—————. *The Literate Revolution in Greece and Its Cultural Consequences.* Princeton: Princeton University Press, 1982.

—————. "The Alphabetic Mind." *Oral Tradition* 1 (1986): 134–50.

Haymes, Edward R. "Oral Poetry and the Germanic *Heldenlied.*" *Rice University Studies* 62, 2 (1976): 47–54.

Hédelin, François (Abbé d'Aubignac et de Meimac). *Conjectures académiques, ou Dissertation sur l'Iliade* (1715). Edited with an introduction by V. Magnien. Paris: Librairie Hachette, 1925.

Henige, David P. *The Chronology of Oral Tradition: Quest for a Chimera.* Oxford Studies in African Affairs. Oxford: Clarendon Press, 1974.

Hoekstra, A. *Homeric Modifications of Formulaic Prototypes: Studies in the Development of Greek Epic Diction.* Verhandelingen der Koninklijke Nederlandse Akademie van Wetenschappen, afd. Letterkunde, n.r., Deel 71, no. 1. Amsterdam: Noord-Hollandsche Uitgevers Maatschappij, 1964; rpt. 1969.

Hymes, Dell. "Discovering Oral Performance and Measured Verse in American Indian Narrative." *New Literary History* 8 (1977): 431–57.

Jacobs, Melville. "A Look Ahead in Oral Literature Research." *Journal of American Folklore* 79 (1966): 413–27.

Jason, Heda. *Ethnopoetry: Form, Content, and Function.* Forum Theologiae Linguisticae (Interdisziplinäre Schriftenreihe für Theologie und Linguistik) 11. Bonn-Rottgen: Linguistica Biblica, 1977.

Jeffreys, Michael J. "The Literary Emergence of Vernacular Greek." *Mosaic* 8, 4 (1975): 171-93.

Jensen, Minna S. *The Homeric Question and the Oral-Formulaic Theory.* Opuscula Graeco-Latina (Supplementa Musei Tusculani) vol. 20. Copenhagen: Museum Tuscularum Press, 1980.

Johnson, John W. Collected, translated, and edited with the assistance of Cheick Omar Mara et al. *The Epic of Sun-Jata According to Magan Sisòkò,* 2 vols. FPC Monograph Series, no. 5. Bloomington: Indiana University Folklore Publications Group, 1979.

Jousse, Marcel. *Le Style oral rhythmique et mnémotechnique chez les Verbo-moteurs. Archives de philosophie* 2 (1924): cahier 4, 1-240; rpt. Paris: Gabriel Beauchesne, 1925.

Kailasapathy, K. *Tamil Heroic Poetry.* Oxford: Clarendon Press, 1968.

Kelber, Werner H. *The Oral and the Written Gospel: The Hermeneutics of Speaking and Writing in the Synoptic Tradition, Mark, Paul, and Q.* Philadelphia: Fortress Press, 1983.

Kellogg, Robert L. "The South Germanic Oral Tradition." In *Franciplegius: Medieval and Linguistics Studies in Honor of Francis P. Magoun, Jr.,* edited by Jess B. Bessinger, Jr., and Robert P. Creed, pp. 66-74. New York: New York University Press, 1965.

————. "Oral Literature." *New Literary History* 5 (1974): 55-66.

Kerewsky-Halpern, Barbara. "Genealogy as Genre in a Serbian Village." In *Oral Traditional Literature: A Festschrift for Albert Bates Lord,* edited by John Miles Foley, pp. 301-21. Columbus, OH: Slavica, 1980.

————, and John Miles Foley. "The Power of the Word: Healing Charms as an Oral Genre." *Journal of American Folklore* 91 (1978): 903-24.

Kilson, Marion. *Kpele Lala: Ga Religious Songs and Symbols.* Cambridge, Mass.: Harvard University Press, 1971.

Kirk, Geoffrey S. *The Songs of Homer.* Cambridge: Cambridge University Press, 1962.

Krischer, Tilman. *Formale Konventionen der homerischen Epik.* Munich: C. H. Beck, 1971.

Latacz, Joachim, ed. *Homer: Tradition und Neuerung.* Wege der Forschung, 463. Darmstadt: Wissenschaftliche Buchgesellschaft, 1979.

Lohr, Charles H. "Oral Techniques in the Gospel of Matthew." *Catholic Biblical Quarterly* 23 (1961): 403-35.

Lönnroth, Lars. "Iord fannz aeva né upphiminn. A Formula Analysis." In *Speculum Norroenum: Norse Studies in Memory of Gabriel Turville-Petre,* edited by Ursula Dronke et al., pp. 310-27. Odense: Odense University Press, 1981.

Long, Eleanor R. "Ballad Singers, Ballad Makers, and Ballad Etiology." *Western Folklore* 32 (1973): 225-36.

Lord, Albert B. "Homer and Huso I: The Singer's Rests in Greek and Southslavic Heroic Song." *Transactions of the American Philological Association* 67 (1936): 106-13.

————. "Homer's Originality: Oral Dictated Texts." *Transactions of the American Philological Association* 84 (1953): 124-34.

————. "The Role of Sound Patterns in Serbo-Croatian Epic." In *For Roman Jakobson,* pp. 301-5. The Hague: Mouton, 1956.

————. *The Singer of Tales.* Harvard Studies in Comparative Literature, 24. Cambridge, Mass.: Harvard University Press, 1960; rpt. New York: Atheneum, 1968 et seq.; rpt. Harvard University Press, 1981.

————. "Perspectives on Recent Work on Oral Literature." In *Oral Literature: Seven Essays,* edited by Joseph J. Duggan, pp. 1-24. Edinburgh and New York: Scottish Academic Press and Barnes and Noble, 1975.

————. "The Gospels as Oral Traditional Literature." In *The Relationships among the Gospels: An Interdisciplinary Dialogue,* edited by William O. Walker, Jr., pp. 33-91. San Antonio: Trinity University Press, 1978.

————. "The Opening Scenes of the *Dumy* on Holota and Andyber: A Study in the Technique of Oral Traditional Narrative." *Harvard Ukrainian Studies* 3/4 (1979-80): 569-94.

McDowell, John H. "The Mexican *Corrido:* Formula and Theme in a Ballad Tradition." *Journal of American Folklore* 85 (1972): 205-20.

Magoun, Francis P., Jr. "Recurring First Elements in Different Nominal Compounds in *Beowulf* and in the Elder Edda." In *Studies in English Philology: A Miscellany in Honor of Friedrich Klaeber,* edited by Kemp Malone and Martin B. Ruud, pp. 73-78. Minneapolis: University of Minnesota Press, 1929.

————. "The Oral-Formulaic Character of Anglo-Saxon Narrative Poetry." *Speculum* 28 (1953): 446-67.

————. "Bede's Story of Cædman: The Case History of an Anglo-Saxon Oral Singer." *Speculum* 30 (1955): 49-63.

————. "The Theme of the Beasts of Battle in Anglo-Saxon Poetry." *Neuphilologische Mitteilungen* 56 (1955): 81-90.

Maranda, Pierre and Elli Köngäs Maranda, eds. *Structural Analysis of Oral Tradition.* University of Pennsylvania Publications in Folklore and Folklife, no. 3. Philadelphia: University of Pennsylvania Press, 1971.

Melia, Daniel F. "Parallel Versions of 'The Boyhood Deeds of Cuchulainn'." In *Oral Literature: Seven Essays,* edited by Joseph J. Duggan, pp. 25-40. Edinburgh and New York: Scottish Academic Press and Barnes and Noble, 1975.

Menéndez Pidal, Ramón. *La Chanson de Roland y el neotradi-cionalismo (orígines de la épica románica)*. Madrid: Espasa-Calpe, 1959. 2d ed., *La Chanson de Roland et la tradition épique des Francs*, trans. I.-M. Cluzel and rev. with René Louis. Paris: A. and J. Picard, 1960.

Miletich, John S. "The Quest for the 'Formula': A Comparative Reappraisal." *Modern Philology* 74 (1976): 111–23.

————. "Hispanic and South Slavic Traditional Narrative Poetry and Related Forms: A Survey of Comparative Studies (1829–1977)." In *Oral Traditional Literature: A Festschrift for Albert Bates Lord*, edited by John Miles Foley, pp. 375–89. Columbus, OH: Slavica, 1980.

Miller, D. Gary. *Homer and the Ionian Epic Tradition: Some Phonic and Phonological Evidence Against an Aeolic "Phase."* Innsbrucker Beiträge zur Sprachwissenschaft, 38. Innsbruck: Universität Innsbruck, 1982.

Monroe, James T. "Oral Composition in Pre-Islamic Poetry." *Journal of Arabic Literature* 3 (1972): 1–53.

Moore, Willard B. *Molokan Oral Tradition: Legends and Memorates of an Ethnic Sect*. University of California Publications: Folklore Studies, 28. Berkeley: University of California Press, 1973.

Murko, Matija. *La Poésie populaire épique en Yougoslavie an début du XXe siècle*. Travaux publiés par l'Institut d'Etudes Slaves, 10. Paris: Librairie Ancienne Honoré Champion, 1929.

————. *Tragom srpsko-hrvatske narodne epike: Putovanja u god-inama 1930–32*, 2 vols. Djela Jugoslavenske Akademije Znanosti i Umjetnosti, knj. 41–42. Zagreb: Jugoslavenska Akademija Znanosti i Umjetnosti, 1951.

Mustanoja, Tauno F. "The Presentation of Ancient Germanic Poetry—Looking for Parallels." *Neuphilologische Mitteilungen* 60 (1959): 1–11.

Nagler, Michael N. *Spontaneity and Tradition: A Study in the Oral Art of Homer*. Berkeley: University of California Press, 1974.

Nagy, Gregory. *Comparative Studies in Greek and Indic Meter*. Harvard Studies in Comparative Literature, 33. Cambridge, Mass.: Harvard University Press, 1974.

Nichols, Stephen G. *Formulaic Diction and Thematic Composition in the Chanson de Roland*. Studies in the Romance Languages and Literatures, no. 36. Chapel Hill: University of North Carolina Press, 1961.

Nilsson, Martin P. *Homer and Mycenae*. 1933; rpt. New York: Cooper Square, 1968; Philadelphia: University of Pennsylvania Press, 1972.

Notopoulos, James A. "Parataxis in Homer." *Transactions of the American Philological Association* 80 (1949): 1–23.

————. "Homer and Cretan Heroic Poetry: A Study in Comparative Oral Poetry." *American Journal of Philology* 73 (1952): 225–50.

————. "Studies in Early Greek Oral Poetry." *Harvard Studies in Classical Philology* 68 (1964): 1–77.

Ó Danachair, Caoímhin. "Oral Tradition and the Printed Word." *Irish University Review* 9 (1979): 31–41.

Oinas, Felix J. *Heroic Epic and Saga: An Introduction to the World's Great Folk-Epics.* Bloomington: University of Indiana Press, 1978.

Okpewho, Isidore. *The Epic in Africa: Toward a Poetics of the Oral Performance.* New York: Columbia University Press, 1979.

Ong, Walter J. *The Presence of the Word: Some Prolegomena for Cultural and Religious History.* New Haven: Yale University Press, 1967; rpt. New York: Simon and Schuster, 1970, and Minneapolis: University of Minnesota Press, 1981.

————. *Interfaces of the Word: Studies in the Evolution of Consciousness and Culture.* Ithaca: Cornell University Press, 1977, rpt. 1982.

————. *Orality and Literacy: The Technologizing of the Word.* New Accents series. London and New York: Methuen, 1982.

Opland, Jeffrey. *Anglo-Saxon Oral Poetry: A Study of the Traditions.* New Haven: Yale University Press, 1980.

Parry, Adam. "Have We Homer's *Iliad?*" *Yale Classical Studies* 20 (1966): 177–216.

————, ed. *The Making of Homeric Verse: The Collected Papers of Milman Parry.* Oxford: Clarendon Press, 1971.

Parry, Milman. *L'Epithete traditionnelle dans Homère: Essai sur un problème de style homérique.* Paris: Société Editrice "Les Belles Lettres," 1928; trans. by Adam Parry as "The Traditional Epithet in Homer." In A. Parry 1971, pp. 1–190.

————. "Studies in the Epic Technique of Oral Verse-Making. I. Homer and Homeric Style." *Harvard Studies in Classical Philology* 41 (1930): 73–147; rpt. in A. Parry 1971, pp. 266–324.

————. "Studies in the Epic Technique of Oral Verse-Making. II. The Homeric Language as the Language of an Oral Poetry." *Harvard Studies in Classical Philology* 43 (1932): 1–50; rpt. in A. Parry 1971, pp. 325–64.

————. "Ćor Huso: A Study of Southslavic Song. Extracts." Complete but unpublished, 1933–35; printed in part in A. Parry 1971, pp. 437–64.

Peabody, Berkley. *The Winged Word: A Study in the Technique of Ancient Greek Oral Composition as Seen Principally through Hesiod's "Works and Days."* Albany: State University of New York Press, 1975.

Quinn, William A. and Audley S. Hall. *Jongleur: A Modified Theory of Oral Improvisation and Its Effects on the Performance and Trans-*

mission of Middle English Romance. Washington, DC: University Press of America, 1982.

Raffel, Burton, "The Manner of Boyan: Translating Oral Literature." *Oral Tradition* 1 (1986): 11–29.

Renger, Johannes M. "Mesopotamian Epic Literature." In *Heroic Epic and Saga,* edited by Felix J. Oinas, pp. 27–48. Bloomington: Indiana University Press, 1978.

Renoir, Alain. "Oral-Formulaic Theme Survival: A Possible Instance in the *Nibelungenlied.*" *Neuphilologische Mitteilungen* 65 (1964): 70–75.

——————. "Oral Theme and Written Texts." *Neuphilologische Mitteilungen* 77 (1976): 337–46.

——————"Oral-Formulaic Context: Implications for the Comparative Criticism of Mediaeval Texts." In *Oral Traditional Literature: A Festschrift for Albert Bates Lord,* edited by John Miles Foley, pp. 416–39. Columbus, OH: Slavica, 1980.

Robb, Kevin. "Greek Oral Memory and the Origins of Philosophy." *The Personalist* 51 (1970): 5–45.

Rosenberg, Bruce A. *The Art of the American Folk Preacher.* New York: Oxford University Press, 1970.

Ross, James. "Formulaic Composition in Gaelic Oral Literature." *Modern Philology* 57 (1959): 1–12.

Russo, Joseph A. "How, and What, Does Homer Communicate? The Medium and Message of Homeric Verse." *Classical Journal* 71 (1976): 289–99.

Rychner, Jean. *La Chanson de geste: Essai sur l'art épique des jongleurs.* Société de Publications Romanes et Françaises, 53. Geneva and Lille: E. Droz and Giard, 1955.

Schmaus, Alois. *Studije o krajinskoj epici.* Rad JAZU, knj. 297. Zagreb: Jugoslavenska Akademija Znanosti i Umjetnosti, 1953, pp. 89–247.

Scott, William C. *The Oral Nature of the Homeric Simile.* Mnemosyne, Bibliotheca Classica Batava, Suppl. 28. Leiden: E. J. Brill, 1974.

Segal, Charles P. "Tragédie, oralité, écriture." Translated by Vincent Giroud, in *Généalogies de l'écriture,* a special issue of *Poétique* 50 (1982): 131–54.

Sen, Nabaneeta D. "The *Vālmīkī-Rāmāyaṇa* and the *Raghuvaṃśam:* Stylistic Structure of Oral Poetry as Contrasted to Classical Poetry." *Jadaupur Journal of Comparative Literature* 8 (1968): 85–95.

Shoolbraid, G. M. H. *The Oral Epic of Siberia and Central Asia.* Indiana University Publications. Uralic and Altaic Series, vol. 111. Bloomington: Indiana University Press, 1975.

Simon, Bennett. *Mind and Madness in Ancient Greece: The Classical Roots of Modern Psychiatry.* Ithaca: Cornell University Press, 1978.

Sioud, Hèdi. "La Poésie orale tunisienne: Structure formulo-orale." *Revue tunisienne de sciences sociales* 46 (1976): 153–92.

Skendi, Stavro. *Albanian and South Slavic Oral Epic Poetry.* Memoirs of the American Folklore Society, vol. 44. Philadelphia: American Folklore Society, 1954; rpt. New York: Kraus, 1969.

Smith, Colin C. *The Making of the "Poema de mio Cid."* Cambridge: Cambridge University Press, 1983.

Stevick, Robert D. "The Oral-Formulaic Analyses of Old English Verse." *Speculum* 37 (1962): 382–89.

Stolz, Benjamin A. "Historicity in the Serbo-Croatian Heroic Epic: Salih Ugljanin's 'Grčki rat.'" *Slavic and East European Journal* 11 (1967): 423–32.

———— and Richard S. Shannon, eds. *Oral Literature and the Formula.* Ann Arbor: Center for Coordination of Ancient and Modern Studies, 1976.

Tatlock, John S. P. "Epic Formulas, Especially in Layamon." *PMLA* 38 (1923): 494–529.

Tedlock, Dennis, trans. *Finding the Center: Narrative Poetry of the Zuñi Indians.* 1972; rpt. Lincoln: University of Nebraska Press, 1978.

Treitler, Leo. "Homer and Gregory: The Transmission of Epic Poetry and Plainchant." *The Musical Quarterly* 60 (1974): 333–72.

Trousdale, Marion. "Shakespeare's Oral Text." *Renaissance Drama* 12 (1981): 95–115.

Turner, Frederick. "Performed Being: Word Art as a Human Inheritance." *Oral Tradition* 1 (1986): 66–109.

Van Seters, John. *Abraham in History and Tradition.* New Haven: Yale University Press, 1975.

Vansina, Jan. *Oral Tradition: A Study in Historical Methodology.* Translated by H. M. Wright. Chicago and London: Aldine and Routledge & Kegan Paul, 1965. First published as *De la Tradition orale: Essai de méthode historique.* Annales du Musée Royal de l'Afrique Centrale, Sciences humaines, no. 36. Tervuren: Musée Royal, 1961.

Waldron, Ronald A. "Oral-Formulaic Technique and Middle English Alliterative Poetry." *Speculum* 32 (1957): 792–804.

Wang, Ching-Hsien. *The Bell and the Drum: "Shih Ching" as Formulaic Poetry in an Oral Tradition.* Berkeley: University of California Press, 1974.

Watts, Ann C. *The Lyre and the Harp: A Comparative Reconsideration of Oral Tradition in Homer and Old English Epic Poetry.* New Haven: Yale University Press, 1969; rpt. Ann Arbor: University Microfilms, 1980.

Webber, Ruth H. "Formulistic Diction in the Spanish Ballad." *University of California Publications in Modern Philology* 34, no. 2 (1951): 175-277.

————. "Formulaic Language in the *Mocedades de Rodrigo*." *Hispanic Review* 48 (1980): 195-211.

Webster, John. "Oral Form and Written Craft in Spenser's *Faerie Queene*." *Studies in English Literature* 16 (1976): 75-93.

Wender, Dorothea. "Homer, Avdo Medjedović, and the Elephant's Child." *American Journal of Philology* 98 (1977): 327-47.

Whallon, William. *Formula, Character, and Context: Studies in Homeric, Old English, and Old Testament Poetry.* Publications of the Center for Hellenic Studies. Cambridge, Mass.: Harvard University Press, 1969.

Whitman, Cedric H. *Homer and the Heroic Tradition.* 1958; rpt. New York: Norton, 1965.

Zumthor, Paul. "Le Discours de la poésie orale." In *Le Discours de la poésie,* a special issue of *Poétique* 52 (1982): 387-401.

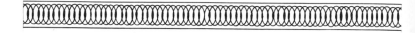

ABOUT THE CONTRIBUTORS

ROBERT P. CREED, Chair of the Department of Comparative Literature at the University of Massachusetts–Amherst, specializes in Old English literature and comparative oral traditions. His books include *Old English Poetry: Fifteen Essays* and *Franciplegius: Medieval and Linguistics Studies in Honor of Francis P. Magoun, Jr.,* the latter co-edited with Jess Bessinger, and he has contributed numerous articles on prosody, textual studies, and critical theory to a distinguished array of journals and collections. Professor Creed's re-creative performances of Old English verse have been recorded on a Folkways album and an award-winning PBS radio program.

ALBERT B. LORD, Arthur Kingsley Porter Professor of Slavic and Comparative Literature at Harvard University (Emeritus), is, with the now-deceased Milman Parry, the co-founder of the field of oral literature research. Professor Lord's *The Singer of Tales* treats the ancient Greek, Yugoslav, Old French, Old English, and Byzantine Greek oral traditions; since its original publication in 1960, more than one thousand books and articles deriving directly from its fundamental ideas and methods and touching on more than one hundred different language areas have appeared. Others of his chief publications include edition and translation volumes for the series *Serbo-Croatian Heroic Songs* and important articles on Homer, the Yugoslav *guslari,* and many other "singers of tales."

GREGORY NAGY has contributed significantly and innovatively to our understanding of Homer and other ancient poetry, most notably in his *Comparative Studies in Greek and Indic Meter* and *The Best of the Achaeans: Concepts of the Hero in Archaic Greek Poetry.* In the process he has developed a method of "linguistic mythology" that sheds light on the thematic content of Homeric narrative by examining key words in context. Nagy is Professor of Classics and Linguistics, as well as Head of the Program in Folklore and Mythology, at Harvard University.

WALTER J. ONG, S.J., is well known worldwide for his studies of Ramist theory and the hermeneutics of orality-literacy contrasts. In works like *The Presence of the Word* and *Interfaces of the Word,* he examines the cultural impact of shifts from an oral medium through the advent of writing and print and on to electronic media. Father Ong's latest book, *Orality and Literacy,* treats the implications of this kind of research for structuralism, deconstructionism, the teaching of reading and writing, and many other areas. He serves as University Professor of Humanities, William E. Haren Professor of English, and Professor of Humanities in Psychiatry at St. Louis University.

ALAIN RENOIR, Professor of English at the University of California/Berkeley, has long been a leader in comparative studies in oral literature. In addition to the standard *Wells Manual* section on John Lydgate, he has published nearly one hundred articles on subjects as diverse as Old English, Middle English, Old French, Latin, Old Norse, Old High German, and Middle High German literature, as well as classic essays on cinematographic structure in *Beowulf* and the crucial importance of oral traditional context for the aesthetic interpretation of numerous different works of art.

RUTH H. WEBBER, Professor of Spanish at the University of Chicago (Emerita), in her monograph *Formulistic Diction in the Spanish Ballad,* was the first scholar to apply Milman Parry's and Albert Lord's ideas about formulaic structure and oral tradition to the Romance literatures. Since that time she has compiled a distinguished list of publications on medieval French and Spanish narrative, as well as on the international ballad, and has contributed significantly to the revised "traditionalist" view of the origin of the *Song of Roland, Poem of the Cid,* and other medieval epic texts.

INDEX